HEALING
Mother-Daughter Relationships
WITH
ASTROLOGY

To Jackie,
A fun partner
generous friend
loving mother & great person.

Warmly,
Maritha Pottenger
5/24/2003

About the Authors

Maritha Pottenger (California) has taught astrology all over the world for twenty-five years. She is the recipient of the best lecturer award from the American Federation of Astrologers.

Zipporah Pottenger-Dobyns (California) also lectures around the world and writes for a variety of astrological publications. She has received numerous awards including two Regulus awards at UAC (United Astrology Conference). This daughter-mother team also wrote *Unveiling Your Future: Progressions Made Easy*.

To Write to the Authors

If you wish to contact the authors or would like more information about this book, please write to the authors in care of Llewellyn Worldwide and we will forward your request. Both the authors and publisher appreciate hearing from you and learning of your enjoyment of this book and how it has helped you. Llewellyn Worldwide cannot guarantee that every letter written to the authors can be answered, but all will be forwarded. Please write to:

Maritha Pottenger and Zipporah Pottenger-Dobyns
‰ Llewellyn Worldwide
P.O. Box 64383, Dept. 0-7387-0297-8
St. Paul, MN 55164-0383, U.S.A.

Please enclose a self-addressed stamped envelope for reply,
or $1.00 to cover costs. If outside U.S.A., enclose
international postal reply coupon.

Many of Llewellyn's authors have websites with additional
information and resources. For more information, please visit our website at
http://www.llewellyn.com

HEALING
Mother-Daughter Relationships
WITH
ASTROLOGY

Maritha Pottenger and Zipporah Pottenger-Dobyns

2003
Llewellyn Publications
St. Paul, Minnesota 55164-0383, U.S.A.

First Edition
First Printing, 2003

Cover art © 2002 by Digital Vision
Cover design by Lisa Novak
Editing by Andrea Neff

Chart wheels were produced by the Kepler program by permission of Cosmic Patterns Software, Inc. (www.AstroSoftware.com)

Library of Congress Cataloging-in-Publication Data

Pottenger, Maritha.
    Healing mother-daughter relationships with astrology / Maritha Pottenger and Zipporah Pottenger-Dobyns.— 1st ed.
        p. cm.
    ISBN 0-7387-0297-8
    1. Astrology. 2. Mothers and daughters—Miscellanea. I. Dobyns, Zipporah Pottenger. II. Title.

BF1711.P74 2003
133.5'83068743—dc21   2002044428

Llewellyn Worldwide does not participate in, endorse, or have any authority or responsibility concerning private business transactions between our authors and the public.
    All mail addressed to the author is forwarded but the publisher cannot, unless specifically instructed by the author, give out an address or phone number.
    Any Internet references contained in this work are current at publication time, but the publisher cannot guarantee that a specific location will continue to be maintained. Please refer to the publisher's website for links to authors' websites and other sources.

Llewellyn Publications
A Division of Llewellyn Worldwide, Ltd.
P.O. Box 64383, Dept. 0-7387-0297-8
St. Paul, MN 55164-0383, U.S.A.
www.llewellyn.com

Printed in the United States of America

Other Books by These Authors

Astrology, the Next Step by Maritha Pottenger

Easy Astrology Guide by Maritha Pottenger

Expanding Astrology's Universe by Zipporah Dobyns

Finding the Person in the Horoscope by Zipporah Dobyns**

Healing with the Horoscope by Maritha Pottenger

The Node Book by Zipporah Dobyns**

Past Lives, Future Choices: The Astrology of Reincarnation by Maritha Pottenger

Planets on the Move: The Astrology of Relocation by Maritha Pottenger & Zipporah Dobyns

Progressions, Directions and Rectification by Zipporah Dobyns**

Seven Paths to Understanding by Zipporah Dobyns with William Wrobel**

Unveiling Your Future: Progression Made Easy by Maritha Pottenger & Zipporah Dobyns

Your Starway to Love: The Astrology of Romance by Maritha Pottenger

**These books are only available through LACCRS, P.O. Box 1132, Jamul, CA 91935.

Forthcoming Books by These Authors

Chiron: Teacher, Healer, Idealist and Tragic Hero by Maritha Pottenger

Acknowledgments

We wish to acknowledge the help from all the participants in our case studies (in print, in classes, and in consultations) and dedicate this book to them.

Many thanks also for the great assistance we received from the staff at Llewellyn, especially from our editor, Andrea Neff.

Contents

PART ONE

Preliminaries

ONE

The Vital Importance of the Mother-Daughter Relationship

Every woman in this world had a mother. Even women who lost their mothers at birth had mother figures or people to play nurturing roles in their lives. The kind of care and support that we received (and did *not* receive!) as infants and children had a huge impact on our sense of emotional security, ability to look after others, sensitivity, feelings about home and family, issues of trust, loyalty, abandonment, and much more.

For both men and women, one of the developmental tasks of adulthood is to separate one's self physically, emotionally, and mentally from one's parents. In mother-daughter relationships, this is complicated because of the common gender. A daughter (ideally) looks to her mother as a positive role model for femininity, nurturing, the capacity to build strong emotional bonds, and the qualities needed to establish and maintain a home and family of one's own. At the same time, the daughter must differentiate her own character from her mother's. She (hopefully) learns to acknowledge and encourage her own special and unique qualities. She may view her mother as a negative role model in some areas—an example of what *not* to do or how *not* to be. It is not always easy to discriminate between what is constructive, where she wishes to emulate her mother, and what is not so constructive, where she needs to create her own path.

Some of the strongest "imprinting" that we get from the family crucible occurs in the preverbal stage of life. This is particularly true in terms of the experiences we had of our mothers. Such early conditioning is very emotional, unconscious, and difficult to access in the conscious realm—tough to put into words and understand objectively.

If we use the metaphor of people as plants, then the mothering we received (and did *not* receive) has much to do with our root system. It is deeply buried and hard to see directly, yet it is the foundation of everything that allows us to grow and develop. The more we can improve the health of our (emotional) roots, the better we will fare.

This book is written primarily for the daughter in each relationship. Certainly, mothers can find useful and helpful ideas within these pages, but our primary focus is on the experiences of the daughters. We offer tips, tools, techniques, insights, and ideas for how to heal and improve their feelings about and reactions to their relationships with their mothers. In many cases, the mother may no longer be living, or may be unavailable or unwilling to participate in changing the relationship. The daughter, however, carries an "inner mother" in her psyche—all the issues, fears, challenges, and strengths that are tied up with her experience of her mother. It is that "inner mother," and the choices and actions we have taken in reaction to what we feel, that can be healed and enhanced.

Astrology, with its unique perspective into the human psyche, is a primary tool for this journey. The more a daughter can understand her mother, the more clearly she can view the interactions she and her mother have had, and the more areas of her own psyche she can free up. This may entail getting past needless anxiety; facing and conquering fears of abandonment; seeing more clearly the constrained perspectives of her childhood and creating and sustaining a more supportive and hopeful worldview; forgiving old hurts; moving beyond self-doubts and excessive criticism; moderating overly idealistic yearnings; strengthening the capacity to identify her own needs and pursue them; achieving a healthier relationship with her own body; and much more. By bringing healing to the relationship with her inner mother, the daughter can also enhance and improve her relationships with partner(s), friends, children, colleagues, etc. The "psychic fingerprints" of Mom are likely to be found all over the way we relate to food, housekeeping, finding a mate, expressing love, seeking safety, and more.

Delving into these emotional roots allows us to break past old barriers and blockages. Rather than being restricted to "choices" that we made as infants, we can alter our habit patterns and move into more fulfilling, satisfying patterns of behavior. Although the journey may be uncomfortable at times—old "demons" could rear their heads—the results are well worth the effort! In the end, coming to terms with more of your experience of your own mother means coming to appreciate more aspects of your own being and potential, and freeing yourself to be more fully the special and unique person that you are. Join us!

TWO

Spotting Repeated Themes in the Horoscope

Although much of this book is designed as a traditional astrological "cookbook" (i.e., instant interpretations of planets in sign, house, and aspect), we must emphasize the importance of looking for repeated themes in a horoscope. What is most significant in a person's nature is said over and over again—in slightly different ways—within the horoscope. In order to get the most out of horoscopes, one needs to quickly and easily spot those highlighted, repeated motifs.

One of the best tools for spotting repeated themes in a horoscope is the *astrological alphabet*, also known as the *Zip Code*. This approach focuses on twelve basic drives and issues in astrology, with each of the twelve connected to a particular planet, sign, and house. This is *not* saying that planets, houses, and signs are the same. They assuredly are not! Each set of three (the planet that rules a sign, the sign ruled, and the house associated with that sign in the natural zodiac), however, has common motifs. It is helpful to be aware of those connections and the basic twelve drives and desires.

After learning the twelve "letters," one can also mix and match various combinations that have something in common. This chapter will first introduce the basic astrological alphabet and then list a number of themes that can be found by combining two, three, four, or more letters of the astrological alphabet. For example, we could note an intellectual stimulation theme, a power theme, a risk-taking theme, etc.

The most important chapter in this book—chapter 8, which discusses healing options in detail—will use the astrological alphabet as a basis to offer ideas, suggestions, and insights to help daughters heal their relationships with their mothers.

The Astrological Alphabet, or "Zip Code"

Although we use the analogy of an alphabet (because an "A" is an "a" is an "𝒜" regardless of whether it is uppercase, lowercase, bold, italic, etc.), each "letter" of the alphabet is given a number, so we have Letters 1 through 12 in our astrological alphabet. A set of parentheses indicates that the factor involved is mixed—not a pure form of the letter.

For those of you who work with the "big four" asteroids and Chiron, we assign Pallas primarily to Letter 7; Juno primarily to Letter 8; Ceres primarily to Letter 4 (with overtones of Letter 6); Vesta primarily to Letter 6; and Chiron to Letters 9 and 12.

Letter 1

Mars, Aries, 1st house—I should have the right and the power to do what I want right now. Now that I have done that, I want to do something new. I like being a pioneer, and I will resist any limits on my freedom.

Letter 2

Venus, Taurus, 2nd house—I want to enjoy the material world on my own terms. I can enjoy making money and spending it, collecting possessions, indulging my appetites, creating beauty, and anything else that gives me pleasure.

Letter 3

Mercury, Gemini, 3rd house—I want to know a little about everything around me, to learn, communicate, take short trips, share life with people who are peers, including siblings and neighbors, maintain a broad perspective, and take life lightly.

Letter 4

Moon, Cancer, 4th house, (Ceres), North Node, (South Node)—Regardless of my age, part of me is a baby looking for a mother and a mother looking for a baby. I want emotional security with a home and family and basic necessities. I want to nurture others and to be nurtured.

Letter 5

Sun, Leo, 5th house—I want to do more than I have done before. I want to put my creative power out into the world and to receive a response from the world. I want to love and be loved, applauded, and admired. I am a leader and life should be exciting.

Letter 6

Mercury, (Ceres), Vesta, Virgo, 6th house—I need to accomplish something that is worth doing and to do it well. I want to analyze my job and my health, to function as effectively as possible, to get tangible results, and to feel a sense of accomplishment.

Letter 7

Venus, Pallas, Libra, 7th house—I want to enjoy lasting, pleasurable, equalitarian relationships. These can include marriage, work associations, and counseling interactions. Fair play is important to me, in competition and in cooperation.

Letter 8

Pluto, Juno, Scorpio, 8th house—I want a deep, committed, passionate relationship with a mate. I will be truly fulfilled when I can give, receive, and share pleasures, possessions, and power with a mate. I analyze the inner depths of life, learning self-knowledge and self-mastery through the mirror of others and through respect for their rights.

Letter 9

Jupiter, Chiron, Sagittarius, 9th house—I am looking for Truth with a capital *T*, the meaning of life and the nature of reality. My beliefs determine my morals and my ultimate destiny. I want to have clear ethical guidelines to set priorities and make choices. I will go wherever I have to, searching for the Absolute. The word *Absolute* can be a substitute for the word *God*, which means so many different things in various religions. Another alternative phrase is "the Infinite Whole that is the Source of All."

Letter 10

Saturn, Capricorn, 10th house—I want to understand the laws of nature and human societies, which I learn through the consequences of my actions. I want to live according to the laws voluntarily to produce positive consequences in my life and in the world. I want to have constructive relationships with authority figures and with my own conscience. I want a productive career, and to handle with wisdom whatever power I have earned.

Letter 11

Uranus, Aquarius, 11th house—I understand and accept the limits of nature and human societies that are necessary to survive in this physical world, and I am willing to fight for the freedom to go beyond what are currently believed to be limits. I seek new knowledge that frees us from previously accepted limits, and I want everyone to have the knowledge and freedom that I seek for myself. Friends who share my interests are important in my quest.

Letter 12

Neptune, (Chiron), Pisces, 12th house—I seek infinite love and beauty, and experience the connectedness of all, oneness with the Whole. I may choose to be an artist or a savior in some area of service or healing. I seek a way to use my talents that will help make a more ideal world. If I have unmet needs, I will call on the Infinite Spirit to guide and help me.

Rulers

We use the concept of rulers throughout this book. A ruler is the planet that has the most in common with a particular sign, e.g., Mars rules Aries, Venus rules Taurus, etc. The astrological alphabet links each planet with the sign it rules. When we refer to rulers within the text, however, we are usually looking at houses. The primary ruler of a house is the planet ruling the sign that falls on the cusp of that house. Thus, if Capricorn is on the cusp of the 2nd house, then Saturn (the ruler of Capricorn) would be the ruler of the 2nd house in that horoscope. If a sign is intercepted in a house (totally contained within one house that has a different sign on the cusp), the ruler of the intercepted sign is also relevant. Thus, if Capricorn is on the cusp of the 2nd house, but Aquarius is intercepted in the 2nd house, we would consider both Saturn (the ruler of Capricorn) and Uranus (the ruler of Aquarius) for 2nd-house matters. Furthermore, if a planet in a house is in a sign that is *not* on the cusp of that house, the ruler of that sign can also be included. For example, if Cancer is rising, the Moon rules the 1st house. However, if Pluto is in Leo occupying the 1st house, we would also consider the Sun (the ruler of Leo) as one of the keys to that 1st house. If you like keeping your life simple, include only the ruler of the sign on each house cusp.

Themes

There are four basic principles to consider when identifying themes in a horoscope:

1. *The more times a theme is repeated in a horoscope, the more important it is.* Themes can be repeated between planets; by sign emphasis; by house emphasis; by house/sign combinations; by planet/sign combinations; or by planet/house combinations. One old "rule" in astrological interpretation is the *Rule of Three:* If you see something three times in a chart, it is important.

2. *Themes involving planets are the most significant.* Planets are the power points in the horoscope. Themes involving houses and signs are not as important as those involving planets. (The Rule of Three does not apply with planets. Once is enough with a close aspect.)

3. *When theme factors back each other up, they are more powerful.* For example, Letter 3 (Mercury, Gemini, 3rd house) and Letter 11 (Uranus, Aquarius, 11th house) both emphasize mental restlessness and the quest for knowledge. Mercury-Uranus aspects would be the strongest form, as described in principle 2. However, if Mercury is in Uranus' sign (Aquarius) or Uranus' house (11th house), or Uranus is in Mercury's sign (Gemini) or Mercury's house (3rd house), that adds to the strength of the theme.

4. *When themes are mixed, consider all possible variants of those themes in combination with one another.* For example, if the "work" letters (Letters 6 and 10) and the "partnership" letters (Letters 7 and 8) of the astrological alphabet are strongly mixed with one another in the horoscope, these individuals could:

   a. meet a romantic partner through work

   b. work in a profession that involves much face-to-face interaction, e.g., law, counseling, consulting, personnel, etc.

   c. choose a partner to whom work is very important

   d. choose a partner who is a workaholic

   e. view partnership as their "job" (and perhaps not work otherwise)

   f. view their partner as a "chore" or something/someone they need to fix

   g. put much effort into improving their partnership(s)

    h. be "married" to their career and neglect partnerships

    i. work with a partner (a practical as well as romantic association)

Remember that none of these potentials are mutually exclusive. The individual could do all (or most) of the above!

List of Themes

Themes are listed here in terms of the numbers associated with each "letter" of the astrological alphabet. Please remember that each number represents one or more planets or asteroids, plus one sign, and one house.

Aesthetic

2, 7, 12—All are tuned in to beauty, and drawn to artistic/aesthetic experiences whether the individual creates them herself or enjoys the grandeur of nature or human art. Not just fine arts. Can be grace in motion (especially if connected with fire planets, signs, or houses), such as dancing, synchronized swimming, landscape gardening, meals as works of art, etc.

Air

3, 7, 11—Emphasis on ideas and people; need to give and get information; orientation toward peer relationships; objective, detached; able to have "space between" and a light touch (though less so with Letter 7, which emphasizes shared pleasures, the Venus desire).

Air-Water

3, 7, or 11 mixed strongly and repeatedly with 4, 8, or 12—Like mist, fog, or vapor. The most internal of the element combinations. Inner world (of mind and emotions) is very strong. Can be a good psychic or psychotherapist by blending conscious and unconscious understanding. May think and feel constantly without doing or showing much in the outer world.

Anxiety, Fear, Phobia

4, 10, 12—When expressed negatively, can be subject to much fear, depression, victim feelings, helplessness/hopelessness. Positive variant is caretaker (see *Caretaker*).

Cardinal Dilemma

1, 4, 7, 10—Internal struggle between freedom (Letter 1), dependency/nurturing (Letter 4), equality/partnership (Letter 7), and control/power (Letter 10). External struggle to divide time and energy between personal desires and development; demands and needs of home and family; desires of a significant other; and requirements of a career or contribution to society.

Caretaker

4, 6, 10, 12—Mothers, fathers, and saviors of the world; people who are both compassionate and competent, doing something practical to aid and assist others. The negative form (particularly of 4, 10, and 12) is subject to unreasonable fears, anxiety, avoidance, etc.

Closeness

4, 5, 7, 8—All seek emotional connections; to share the life with a significant other (or others); to make bonds of attachment and commitment.

Critical/Flaw-Finding

6, 10—Both are skilled at identifying shortcomings or problems, hopefully in order to fix them. Can be too judgmental.

Earth

2, 6, 10—Oriented toward the physical world; wanting to enjoy the world of the senses or needing to produce tangible results. Worker bees. Focused on what one can see, hear, touch, feel, measure.

Earth-Air

2, 6, or 10 mixed strongly and repeatedly with 3, 7, or 11—Like dust. Dry, logical, analytical. The most rational (and least emotional) of the element combinations. Good at both theory and practice; can solve problems.

Earth-Water

2, 6, or 10 mixed strongly and repeatedly with 4, 8, or 12—Like mud. Can be strong, supportive, helpful, and a Rock of Gibraltar, or depressive, hard to move, and stuck in the mud.

Fire

1, 5, 9—Has élan. Energetic, vivacious, vital, and oriented toward pursuing personal desires; also spontaneous, impulsive, and tends toward immediate gratification.

Fire-Earth

1, 5, or 9 mixed strongly and repeatedly with 2, 6, or 10—Like molten lava; nothing gets in the way. The most externally oriented element combination. Movers, shakers, doers. May get what they want and then feel "Is that all there is?" Can steamroll themselves and others. Motto: "Be careful what you want, even at the subconscious level, because you are likely to get it." You may not appreciate actually getting the results of some of your desires.

Fire-Air

1, 5, or 9 mixed strongly and repeatedly with 3, 7, or 11—Like hot air. Fun-loving, extroverted, restless, mobile, easily bored, entertaining.

Fire-Water

1, 5, or 9 mixed strongly and repeatedly with 4, 8, or 12—Like steam. Intense, emotional. May have staccato quality or mood swings. Water holds in and holds back until fire blows up. Very warm. Learning to identify and express emotions naturally and often, so they don't get to the point of explosion.

Fixed Dilemma

2, 5, 8, 11—Learning to give, receive, and share with intimate others in regard to power, possessions, and pleasures. May be feast/famine extremes around food, sex, money, etc. Balancing act in relationships with regard to sexuality, shared resources, ownership: attempting to pursue mutual gratification without coercion, emotional manipulation, hermit withdrawal, etc. Tremendous loyalty, perseverance, and determination are possible.

Freedom

1, 9, 11—All seek independence. To go one's own way, to resist limits or the control of others, to seek adventure or the new.

Idealism

9, 12—Quest for the best; seeking the Infinite. Expectations may be beyond human reach, what we associate with a Higher Power or something greater than self. Inspiration or cosmic discontent.

Interpersonal

(4), 5, (6), 7, 8—Urge for closeness, sharing with other people; desire for one-on-one inter-actions. (Same as *Closeness* theme, but chart can be divided into major thirds: personal, interpersonal, and transpersonal.) Letter 6 can be interpersonal in the sense of colleagues and coworkers, but lacks the emotional focus of the other interpersonal letters. Letter 4 is personal when the individual is focused on personal safety and security (the "baby" side of Letter 4) and interpersonal when the individual is oriented toward nurturing and taking care of others.

Mental (Intellectual) Focus

3, 6, 9, 11—Need to know. Urge to collect, disseminate, analyze, and pursue knowledge. Can be restless and variety-oriented (less so with Letter 6).

Mutable Dilemma

3, 6, 9, 12—Challenge of being multitalented and easily scattered; can be a professional dilettante; issues of perfectionism; learning to balance the ideal versus the real; may pro-crastinate or keep standards too high: "I won't do it until I can do it perfectly." Learning to develop a healthy faith in one's self and in something greater; knowing when to "let go and let God." Needs clear priorities.

Organizational Skills

6, 8, 10—Capacity to keep track of details, bring order out of chaos, get everything together and get the job done well. If carried too far, can be obsessive-compulsive and have tunnel vision.

Parental

4, 10—Keys to unconditional and conditional love parent(s). Either parent may be more conditional, more unconditional, or relatively balanced. In an actual family, there may be no unconditional love parent, or no conditional love parent. Our experience of the people who raised us and our own ability (or lack thereof) to nurture, take responsibility, guard, protect, preserve, and support.

Partnership/Equality

7, 8—Both are oriented toward having one-on-one interactions, sharing life with a signifi-cant other, and seeking peer exchanges. May cooperate or compete.

Perfectionism (or Practical Idealism/Realistic Mysticism)

9 and/or 12 mixed strongly and repeatedly with 6 and/or 10—May never be satisfied. Can procrastinate: "I won't do it until I can do it perfectly." May seek the impossible dream and be critical of all flaws and shortcomings along the way. Nothing is ever good enough. The positive side is making dreams come true; bringing visions into manifestation. Letters 9 and 12 both seek the ideal, while 6 and 10 look for flaws—the two sides of perfectionism.

Personal

1, 2, 3, (4)—Concern with one's own desires and needs. Focus on one's self and personal possessions, interests, and security needs. Letter 4 is personal when focused on the "child" side that seeks to protect only itself, but becomes interpersonal when oriented toward caring for others.

Power

5, 8, 10—Dominance, control. Need to be in charge, to make things happen, to push the world (and sometimes other people) around. Note: Letters 1 and 2 want power over their own lives, but add to the drive to control the world if mixed with 5, 8, or 10.

Risk-Taking

1, 5, 9, 11—All are drawn toward thrill-seeking, taking chances, risking for greater gain, and pursuing the rush of adrenaline. Enjoy the excitement of a challenge.

Security

2, 4, 8, 10—All seek the familiar, the safe, the status quo, what is known and established and dependable.

Self-Identity

1—Personal drives, desires. What we do instinctively from the beginning of life; what we "meet and greet" when first entering this incarnation.

Transpersonal

9, 10, 11, 12—Concerned with the big picture, the greatest good for the greatest number, the large perspective, the long-range view.

Water

4, 8, 12—Sensitive, empathic. Tends to dissolve boundaries; wants first to avoid being hurt and (with evolution) to avoid hurting others. May intuitively sense or "know" something without having any physical evidence; subconscious.

Work

6, 10—Diligent, disciplined. Oriented toward fulfilling one's duty, taking responsibility, doing things well, taking care of business, getting the job done. Needs tangible results and a sense of accomplishment.

Theme Examples

Just to be sure that the astrological concepts are clear, let's look at a couple of examples.

1. A *fire-earth theme* might show up in a horoscope with:

    a. five planets occupying fire signs (Aries, Leo, or Sagittarius) and earth houses (2nd, 6th, or 10th houses)

    b. Mars (fire) conjunct Vesta (earth)

    c. Sun (fire) in Capricorn (earth)

    d. Jupiter (fire) in the 10th house (earth)

    e. Saturn (earth) in the 5th house (fire)

2. An *artistic theme* might show up with Venus conjunct Neptune in Libra in the 12th house. (Any Venus-Neptune conjunction is enough by itself. Putting it in Libra—or in Taurus or Pisces—or in the 12th house—or in the 2nd or 7th house—is just icing on the cake.)

Analyzing Mother in the Daughter's Chart

When looking at a horoscope for information about a parent, it is important to remember that each child in a family will have his or her own experience of each parent. Therefore, the natal horoscope shows us an image of that child's experience of the parent(s). Mom and Dad may not be "objectively" (or in the eyes of themselves, other family members, friends, etc.) much like the experience of that child.

In the case of a daughter, we would begin with the daughter's natal chart, examining everything that is a potential key to the mother (figure). The outline in the next section provides a list of those potential keys (ranked roughly in order of importance). That includes the placement of the Moon by house, sign, and aspects. We would also include Ceres (the Earth Mother asteroid) and its house, sign, and aspects. We would look to see what planets occupy the 4th and 10th houses. Traditionally, the 4th house is the "unconditional love" parent—the one who provides loving care, support, and protection, while the 10th house is the "conditional love" parent—the one who emphasizes rules, getting what you've earned, fitting into society, etc. Traditional roles would assign the 4th house to the mother and the 10th house to the father, but in actual families, all variants are possible. Sometimes the 4th house describes Mom and the 10th house describes Dad. Sometimes the reverse is true. Sometimes both parents are in both houses. Sometimes one parent takes over both roles and seems to take over both the 4th and 10th houses as well.

We would also consider any planets occupying the 4th house (and the 10th house if we feel that the mother rules any of the 10th house), the signs on the MC/IC axis, and the signs occupied by planets in the 4th house (and in the 10th house). Because of the "maybes" involved with the 4th and 10th houses, items in the outline involved with the 10th house appear in parentheses. Finally, we would consider the nature of any planets in the sign of Cancer (the sign of motherhood).

As mentioned earlier, planets are the most important and significant elements in astrology, so we would give the most weight to any planets that are closely conjunct the Moon or Ceres. The following outline shows the factors to be considered. They are in a rough rank ordering (in chunks), with what is most important appearing at the top of the list. Anything that appears even once in the first "chunk" is significant enough to include. Anything that appears once in the second "chunk" is significant if it is repeated at least once elsewhere. Thus, for most mothers, we will have several (sometimes many) of the letters of the astrological alphabet in the picture. "Mom" will be manifesting a mixture of those themes.

Items further down the list (after the first two "chunks") are less important, and themes connected to those placements should be repeated at least two or three times before we consider them significant. Again, if we use the astrological alphabet, we can quickly and easily spot repeated themes with different combinations of the astrological alphabet.

Outline for Analyzing Mother in Daughter's Natal Horoscope

Moon conjunct _____.

Ceres conjunct _____.

Ruler of 4th conjunct _____.

(Ruler of 10th conjunct _____.)

_____ in 4th house.

(_____ in 10th house.)

Ruler of 4th house in _____ house.

(Ruler of 10th house in _____ house.)

Moon in _____ house.

Ceres in _____ house.

Moon in _____ (sign).

Ceres in _____ (sign).

Ruler of 4th house in _____ (sign).

(Ruler of 10th house in _____ [sign]).

Signs on MC/IC axis: _____

Cancer on the cusp of _____ house(s).

Houses of Nodes: _____

Signs of Nodes: _____

Planets in _____ (sign) occupying the 4th house.

(Planets in _____ [sign] occupying the 10th house.)

_____ [planet(s)/Ascendant] in Cancer.

House(s) ruled by planet(s) conjunct Moon: _____

House(s) ruled by planet(s) conjunct Ceres: _____

House(s) ruled by planet(s) conjunct 4th-house ruler: _____

(House(s) ruled by planet(s) conjunct 10th-house ruler: _____)

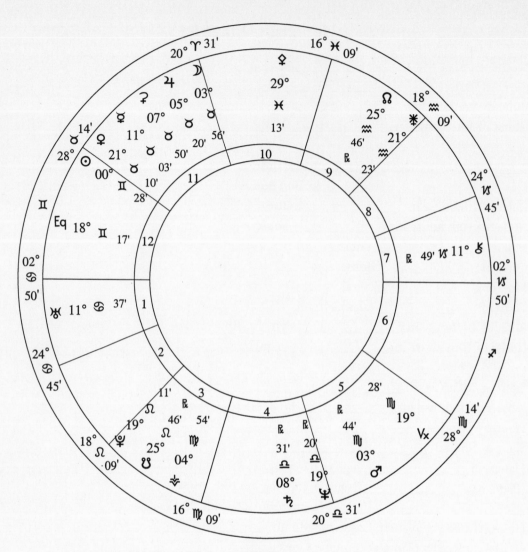

Ms. D
Natal Chart
May 21, 1952
7:36 A.M. MST
Tucson, Arizona
32N13 110W55
Placidus Houses

Case Study: Ms. D

To demonstrate the use of this outline and the astrological alphabet, we have filled out the outline for the following horoscope, and listed afterward significant themes denoted by the astrological alphabet.

	Letters of the Astrological Alphabet
Moon conjunct *Jupiter, Ceres, Mercury.*	9, 4/6, 3
Ceres conjunct *Mercury, Jupiter, Moon.*	3, 9, 4
Ruler of 4th conjunct *Ceres, Jupiter, Moon.*	4/6, 9, 4
(Ruler of 10th conjunct *nothing.*)	
Saturn and Neptune in 4th house.	10, 12
(*Pallas* in 10th house.)	7
Ruler of 4th house in *11th* house.	11
(Ruler of 10th house in *4th* house.)	4
Moon in *11th* house.	11
Ceres in *11th* house.	11
Moon in *Taurus* (sign).	2
Ceres in *Taurus* (sign).	2
Ruler of 4th house in *Taurus* (sign).	2
(Ruler of 10th house in *Libra* [sign]).	7
Signs on MC/IC axis: *Pisces/Virgo*	6, 12
Cancer on the cusp of *1st and 2nd* houses.	1, 2
Houses of Nodes: *3rd/9th*	3, 9
Signs of Nodes: *Leo/Aquarius*	5, 11
Planets in *Libra* (sign) occupying the 4th house.	7
(Planets in *Pisces* [sign] occupying the 10th house.)	12
Uranus [planet(s)/Ascendant] in Cancer.	11
Ascendant in Cancer.	1
House(s) ruled by planet(s) conjunct Moon:	
Mercury and Jupiter are conjunct the Moon	
and rule the 4th, 12th, and 6th houses.	6, 4, 12

House(s) ruled by planet(s) conjunct Ceres:

> *The Moon, Jupiter, and Mercury are conjunct Ceres*
> *and rule the 4th, 12th, 6th, 1st, and 2nd houses.*   4, 12 , 6, 1, 2

House(s) ruled by planet(s) conjunct 4th-house ruler:

> *Mercury, the 4th-house ruler, is conjunct the Moon*
> *(ruler of 1st and 2nd), Jupiter (ruler of 6th), and Ceres.*   6, 1, 2

(House(s) ruled by planet(s) conjunct 10th-house ruler):

> *None.*

Definitely important: 3, 4, 6, 9
Also Important: 2, 7, 11, 12
Most Often Repeated: 2, 4, 6, 11

Themes: mutable (3, 6, 9, 12), **mental focus** (3, 6, 9, 11), **idealism** (9, 12), **air** (3, 7, 11), **independence** (1, 9, 11).

Having covered the basic principles of the astrological alphabet and how to identify significant themes, we will now move on to the "cookbook" section of this book.

PART TWO

Analyzing Mother in the Horoscope

THREE

Moon in Signs, Houses, and More

Although this chapter can be read as a "cookbook" for the Moon in each of the signs and for the Moon in each of the houses (and conjunctions to the Moon), it is more than that. As indicated in chapter 2, most daughters will be dealing with issues from several different letters of the astrological alphabet. This chapter gives an overview of the issues for each of the twelve letters in the astrological alphabet, and also includes a list (rank ordered roughly from most significant to less significant) of the different ways in which each letter could be emphasized in the daughter's chart. Repetition of a motif indicates increased significance of that letter. For example, the Moon in the 1st house, Ceres (the Earth Mother asteroid) conjunct Mars, Aries occupying the 4th house, and the North (or South) Node conjunct the Ascendant would reiterate a Letter 1 motif. Because "Mom" is sometimes in the 4th, sometimes represented by the 10th, and sometimes visible in both houses, the 10th-house placements appear in parentheses.

Letter 1: ☽ ☌ ♂, ☽ *in 1st house,* ☽ ♈

Assertive, Ardent, Active, Adventurous

Moon conjunct Mars
Ceres conjunct Mars
Mars conjunct ruler of 4th house (or ruler of 10th house)
Moon in 1st house
Ceres in 1st house

Ruler of 4th house (or 10th house) in 1st house

Mars in 4th house

(If 10th house is designated as Mom, Mars in 10th house)

Ruler of 1st house in 4th house (or 10th house)

Moon in Aries

Ceres in Aries

Ruler of 4th house (or 10th house) in Aries

Aries/Libra (or vice versa) across MC/IC axis

Mars in Cancer

Ascendant in Cancer

Ruler of 1st house in Cancer

Planets in Cancer occupying the 1st house

Nodes conjunct Ascendant/Descendant (also Letter 7)

Nodes across 1st/7th houses

Nodes across Aries/Libra

Planet(s) conjunct Moon or Ceres ruling the Ascendant

Ruler(s) of 4th house (or 10th house) conjunct planets ruling the Ascendant

Planets in Aries occupying the 4th house (or 10th house)

The influence of the mother (figure) is particularly pervasive with these combinations. The daughter's personal identity and sense of power are tied to her experience of her mother. Mom is a role model—positive or negative. If a constructive role model, the daughter is likely to try to act similarly to the mother. If a negative role model, the daughter is apt to go in the exact opposite direction. Either way, Mother is the measure—of what to do, or of what *not* to do. The individual is likely to compare herself to her mother (figure) often.

The daughter's ability to be assertive, to handle anger, to go after what she wants in the world, and to act openly on her desires are all affected by the example of the mother. On the positive side, Mom could have been courageous, forthright, independent, active, and energetic. She might have encouraged her daughter to be direct, pioneering, and enterprising. Less constructively, the mother could have been self-centered, angry, aggressive, rash, or impulsive. In extreme cases, violence was a problem in the home. In a healthy home, the daughter was nurtured with action, excitement, and a strong emphasis on her as a person. The mother was lively, fervent, independent, active, and full of initiative. The emotional life in the home was vibrant and new experiences were sought eagerly. Emotional safety became tied to freedom and going one's own way. Taking care of one's self was probably a major theme.

There is an inherent conflict between the nature of the Moon and the nature of Mars (and Aries and the 1st house). The Moon wants to nurture, to protect, to be safe and secure, and to go within. Mars wants to act, to be independent, and to do. The mother probably felt a "freedom-closeness dilemma" around mothering. She might have felt trapped or resentful of being tied down by family, or she might have set a good example of being warm and loving while clearly having her own interests and activities separate from her family. Inner conflict exists between dependency and independence, between nurturing and doing one's own thing. Moods can shift rapidly. People with this combination can "fly off the handle" rather easily. Their temper tends to be close to the surface. Those interacting with a Moon-in-Aries (etc.) individual may feel that she reacts to emotional tension like a "brat." Being strong and self-sufficient may be given more weight than being warm and caring or leaning on others for sustenance and support.

The daughter is often identified with the nurturing role. Depending on her experience, that could be comfortable or uncomfortable. If the mother overdid the self-centered freedom needs that are present, the mother might have encouraged the daughter to be nurturing and maternal so that the mother could escape some of her own familial obligations. If the mother was angry and frustrated with the caretaking role, she may have passed that message on to her daughter. If the mother pursued independence at any cost, the daughter might have followed her example or gone to the opposite extreme. The daughter will have to put effort into finding a middle ground between her own desires and the need to look after (and sometimes lean on) other people. Generally, these individuals want to nurture, but do best when they have lots of freedom and breaks. They want to provide support on their own terms and may need to "get away" from family periodically, and to go off on their own. When the "my way" tendencies of Mars go overboard, the individual may (consciously or unconsciously) gravitate toward being a single parent. Then she gets to call all the shots in terms of family matters.

Mars (and Aries and the 1st house) represents our right and power to do what we want. If the mother crippled this in the daughter, the daughter may have struggled for years to clearly define her own desires, seeking to find a sense of entitlement, a feeling that she has the right to go after what she wants. Sometimes, the daughter was given the script of "You will have to fight to get anything you want." The mother affects the daughter's self-expression, her ability to identify what she wants, and may affect her physical appearance as well.

Sometimes the daughter literally looks like the mother. The fire in the daughter's nature (and how comfortable the daughter is letting it out) is influenced by the mother's actions. Three extremes are possible—the loner, the mother, and the baby. A moderate, healthy expression of all the drives involved allows the mother and daughter to be maternal as well as independent, and to pursue their own desires while also accepting support from others.

Healing Options

Doing their own thing is nurturing for these individuals. Solitary tasks can affirm their strength. Building muscles can build self-confidence, so exercise or physical movement will often help them feel more secure. Taking a walk while discussing very emotional matters can be helpful. Sports or working out can be used to dissipate excess emotions.

These people feed themselves with new experiences, with pioneering acts. Being first feels reassuring. By focusing on anything that she can do, the daughter can strengthen her self-confidence, initiative, courage, and self-reliance. By practicing taking care of pets or little projects that involve guardianship, she can improve and enhance her nurturing abilities. An individual can learn to accept vulnerability more easily by asking for minor favors and occasionally relying on others.

Although an inner conflict exists, the nature of these astrological combinations highlights the urge to find a balance between dependency and independence, between caring for family and looking after one's own interests, between separation and appropriate emotional ties.

Your Affirmation

I am strong, independent, and nurturing.

Letter 2: ☽ ☌ ♀, ☽ *in 2nd house,* ☽ ♉
Satisfaction, Sensuality, Stability, Stubbornness, Satiation

Moon conjunct Venus

Ceres conjunct Venus

Venus conjunct ruler of 4th house (or ruler of 10th house)

Moon in 2nd house

Ceres in 2nd house

Ruler of 4th house (or 10th house) in 2nd house

Venus in 4th house

(If 10th house is designated as Mom, Venus in 10th house)

Ruler of 2nd house in 4th house (or 10th house)

Moon in Taurus

Ceres in Taurus

Ruler of 4th house (or 10th house) in Taurus

Scorpio/Taurus (or vice versa) across MC/IC axis

Venus in Cancer

Ruler of 2nd house in Cancer

Planets in Cancer occupying the 2nd house

Planet(s) conjunct Moon or Ceres ruling 2nd house

Ruler(s) of 4th house (or 10th house) conjunct planets ruling 2nd house

Nodes across 2nd/8th houses

Nodes across Taurus/Scorpio

Node conjunct ruler of 2nd house

Planets in Taurus occupying the 4th house (or 10th house)

The daughter is learning through her mother's example (positive or negative) how to relate to the material, sensual world. The mother (figure) may be attractive, hedonistic, pleasant, easygoing, materialistic, complacent, stubborn, or focused on her own gratification. Mother's imprints about money, possessions, and pleasures will have a strong impact on the daughter's ability to earn a living, enjoy the material world, and put herself and other people at ease. Loyalty and dependability are usually important issues within the home. With a healthy, functional home, the infant (and child) was nurtured through being fed, caressed, and held. Touch was an important form of communication. Emotional relationships were relatively predictable. In such cases, the daughter is likely to develop a sense of inner security and may nurture others by helping them relax, get comfortable, feel good, or provide for themselves materially and/or financially.

On the positive side, there can be a strong bond of affection between the mother and daughter. They may enjoy one another and feel comfortable when together, whether or not they are doing or saying anything. They may share a love of good food, drink, or other sensually satisfying activities. A sweet tooth is common. They may pamper one another financially or just try to "spoil" and indulge each other. Mom might contribute to the daughter's income, and vice versa.

On the negative side, the mother may be totally focused on her own pleasures and possessions. Indeed, she may view her daughter as a possession, treating her like a "thing" who is supposed to contribute to the mother's comfort. The mother may have major issues around money or overdo hedonism with food, sex, spending, etc. The mother may be nice only when the daughter is contributing to the mother's financial base, material goods, comfort, or personal gratification. Having and getting things could be valued more than people. Sometimes the mother may be too indulgent toward the child (though more commonly, toward herself). Mother is likely to seek security through familiarity, a predictable routine, and sensual pleasures. She may resist change or get stuck in ruts. If the nurturing was particularly destructive, the daughter may have great trouble earning a living, appreciating sensual pleasures, or just being able to relax and enjoy life. An unconscious script of "I don't deserve to feel good or to have nice things" could develop.

With these placements, either the mother or daughter may "anesthetize" herself from pain by eating or by pursuing money or sensual satisfaction. The mother and/or daughter may resort to food (or other physical pleasures or financial shenanigans) when emotional stress strikes. She may stuff herself in an attempt to "stuff" (repress, push down) her feelings. So, eating disorders, weight problems, problems with alcohol, and challenges around money are all possible. When the Taurus (or 2nd-house) side of life is connected to the Moon, the needy, frightened child in the mother and/or daughter can be triggered by experiences involving food, possessions, money, and sensual gratification.

Healing Options

These Moon combinations are "fed" through pleasing physical experiences. Getting a regular massage can help the individual maintain balance and emotional equilibrium. Having a home that is physically comfortable is very helpful. Having it be visually attractive would also be a plus. The mother and daughter need a nest that appeals to the senses, e.g., soft, cushy furniture, comfort food, etc. Familiarity is very reassuring. When feeling threatened, if the mother or daughter can make a connection to something that has already happened, then she can feel able to handle it. ("This has come up before. I know what to do.")

Moon-in-Taurus individuals handle repetition well. They can excel at self-improvement programs that require them to establish a routine and follow it. Their stamina is excellent and they are likely to be reliable. (Of course, we must consider the whole horoscope.) If the Moon is conjunct Venus, in the 2nd house, or in Taurus, or if Venus is in a parental house, one of the best ways to establish a greater sense of security and protection is to set up a regular regimen and follow it, particularly when healing old hurts. It is also helpful to celebrate the success of each step with sensual rewards or nice, attractive things . Enjoying goodies and feeling good really matter!

Developing a "family of choice" (e.g., good friends) who are physically demonstrative and readily express affection can be very helpful. The daughter will blossom in an atmosphere that accents beauty, fond and devoted interactions, and physical comfort. A variety of physical pleasures can aid in avoiding excesses or overdoing a single one.

If the mother has been a particularly negative role model about money (e.g., compulsive gambler, spender, stingy, overly materialistic, etc.), the daughter may need to take some classes, read books, or otherwise train herself to be more realistic about financial matters. Fortunately, these placements also indicate that the daughter has the potential to develop good skills at handling the material world. Again, once the daughter has gained the information she needs, establishing a healthy routine in terms of monetary practices would be an excellent idea.

Your Affirmation
I nurture myself and others by creating comfort and pleasure.

Letter 3: ☽ ☌ ☿, ☽ *in 3rd house,* ☽ ♊

Flexible, Fluent, Flippant, Fickle, Funny

Moon conjunct Mercury

Ceres conjunct Mercury

Mercury conjunct ruler of 4th house (or ruler of 10th house)

Moon in 3rd house

Ceres in 3rd house

Ruler of 4th house (or 10th house) in 3rd house

Mercury in 4th house

(If 10th house is designated as Mom, Mercury in 10th house)

Ruler of 3rd house in 4th house (or 10th house)

Moon in Gemini

Ceres in Gemini

Ruler of 4th house (or 10th house) in Gemini

Gemini/Sagittarius (or vice versa) across MC/IC axis

Mercury in Cancer

Ruler of 3rd house in Cancer

Planets in Cancer occupying the 3rd house

Planet(s) conjunct Moon or Ceres ruling 3rd house

Ruler(s) of 4th house (or 10th house) conjunct planets ruling 3rd house

Planets in Gemini occupying the 4th house (or 10th house)

Nodes across 3rd/9th houses

Nodes across Gemini/Sagittarius

Node conjunct ruler of 3rd house

The mother (figure) is teaching (well or poorly) the daughter about mental development, curiosity, versatility, and the ability to take things lightly. Mother may be bright, have a wide range of interests, and be multitalented, superficial, talkative, or eager to get more information. Mother's example and behavior have a tremendous impact on the daughter's ability to think, talk, write, and relate to the world of the mind. Often, the child is raised in an atmosphere that emphasizes mental stimulation, variety, communication, and change. Sometimes there could be information overload! Activities in the neighborhood may be quite important, or the daughter may have lots of toys or a wide array of environmental stimuli, e.g., music lessons, youth group activities, community theater, etc. Games and mental puzzles may be highlighted. The home is likely to be lively. The daughter will respond well to explanations and any activities that add to her store of knowledge or collection of interesting facts and figures. Safety and security are connected to knowing.

Depending on the interactions, the mother may encourage the daughter to develop her intellectual skills, refuse to let her get a word in edgewise, label her stupid, or share the excitement of constantly seeking more knowledge. Mom's fingerprints are all over the daughter's intellectual development and how she feels about her mind, ability to speak, communication skills, and capacity to learn. If done positively, the mother will feed that. If done negatively, the mother will squelch those potentials.

On the positive side, Mother can be like a sister in some respects, encouraging open communication and being willing to discuss just about anything. Mother may relate more as a peer than as an authority figure. Mother may constantly indulge her own curiosity and encourage the daughter to pursue all sorts of mental byways and highways. A lighthearted sense of humor could be a bond between the mother and daughter. The mother could have cultivated a love of learning. Sometimes the mother is literally a teacher or in a communication field, or very wrapped up in sharing ideas and seeking out fresh information and experiences.

Less constructively, the daughter may experience her mother as skimming the surface in life, as being too chatty or intellectual and not warm enough. The "mother as sister" motif could be expressed by a mother who just wants to be a "pal," or tries too hard to hang on to her youth, or treats her daughter as a rival (romantically, intellectually, etc.). There could be competition in the mental realm, and the daughter, being younger, is obviously at a disadvantage. In some families, the unconscious script is "Thou shalt not know more than thy parent(s)." If the mother is too casual, carefree, and scattered, important household duties like fixing meals could be neglected. Domestic matters may be competing with too many other priorities. The underlying assumption that "Nothing really matters much" could pervade the home. In some cases, when rationalization and intellectual emphasis are carried too far, the unconscious script becomes "No feelings are really important."

When there are interchanges between the 3rd and 4th houses (e.g., Moon in 3rd, ruler of 4th in 3rd, or ruler of 3rd in 4th, etc.), the horoscope is indicating a sibling-parent interchange. As said, Mom may act somewhat like a sister (positively: open, communicative, equalitarian; negatively: flippant, opting out of parental responsibilities, being too casual about her role as a parent). It is also possible that the daughter might (1) have a sibling or other collateral relative such as an aunt, uncle, cousin, etc., who plays a parental role, (2) be parental toward her sibling(s), or (3) have caretaking duties toward other relatives.

Healing Options

These individuals can gain perspective by using their brains. They may get a better understanding of their emotions through reading about them, thinking, and discussing feelings. Feedback from others is often helpful. Traditional "talk therapy" can be helpful. With these placements, learning to "label" feelings is particularly important—to put accurate words and descriptions onto one's emotional states. Being able to verbalize feelings can help both the mother and daughter feel better, and understand more.

Word play, jokes, and humor are also valuable tools. This is the best path for these individuals to take to lighten up, particularly when things get too "hot and heavy." Keeping a diary or journal may be a good idea. (A tape journal would probably have more appeal as Mercury in its Gemini form prefers talking to writing.) By reviewing what they have said or written in the past, they can start to spot patterns.

Therapeutic work that helps Moon-in-Gemini (or 3rd-house, etc.) people give more weight to emotions could be helpful. They may develop more insight into themselves and others. They can get more comfortable at bringing together the world of the feeling heart and the world of the thinking head.

Your Affirmation

I nurture and heal with bright ideas and insightful words.

Letter 4: ☽ ☌ ⚳, ☊, ☋, ☽ *in 4th house,* ☽ ♋

Safety, Sensitivity, Sustenance, Security, Suffocation

Moon conjunct Ceres
Moon conjunct ruler of 4th house
Ceres conjunct ruler of 4th house
Moon in 4th house
(If 10th house is designated as Mom, Moon in 10th house)
Ruler of 4th house in 4th house
Ceres in 4th house
Moon in Cancer
Ceres in Cancer
Ruler of 4th house in Cancer
Cancer/Capricorn (or vice versa) across MC/IC axis
Planet(s) conjunct Moon or Ceres ruling 4th house
Ruler(s) of 4th house (or 10th house) conjunct planets ruling 4th house
Nodes across 4th/10th houses
Nodes across Cancer/Capricorn
Planets in Cancer occupying the 4th house
Node conjunct IC
Node conjunct ruler of 4th house

The idea of "unto the next generation" becomes very important with these placements. The mother's own nurturing experiences (good and bad) have a profound impact on her ability to function as a parent. The issue of unconditional love, and to what degree it can—and cannot—be expressed, is central within the family. The mother-baby interchange is in high focus. This can indicate that Mother was wonderfully maternal, supportive, warm, nurturing, protective, and emotionally connected. It can also point to a "smother mother," one who tried to keep her child(ren) dependent, who could only relate as the parent, whose "need to be needed" was overdone. Another option is a parent who was really more like a child—emotionally needy and seeking support, protection, and security from others (including, sometimes, from her own children). Of course, some mothers may vacillate between these roles.

The highest ideal of the Moon, Cancer, and the 4th house is unconditional love—to be there for your nearest and dearest, to provide for them, to look after them, to meet their needs. This includes food, shelter, clothing, hugs, caresses, and the emotional responsiveness that gives the infant the message "You can trust your family to take care of you." (Psychologist Erik Erikson labeled the first stage of childhood as "Basic Trust versus Mistrust," depending on how well the caretakers looked after the very young infant.) Nobody is perfect, but some mothers did manage to nurture an inner sense of security in their infants. Those children were kept warm, safe, fed, caressed, hugged, and loved. As adults, these individuals are likely to be comfortable giving and getting emotional support—being able to look after others and also able to be vulnerable and open enough to receive from others. Blood ties are often quite strong.

Other mothers were too crippled by their own insecurities and childhood wounds to provide the safe environment that their children needed. These lunar combinations are very watery, and water is the universal solvent. Where water is involved, we want to absorb or be absorbed. With the Moon, Cancer, and the 4th house, we can have the mother so caught up in nurturing that she may not maintain good boundaries between herself and her child(ren). Or, we can see the mother who is identified with the role of the needy child, looking to those around her for caretaking and protection. The overprotective mother tries (consciously or unconsciously) to keep her children helpless and dependent. She may do too much for them, crippling their own confidence and competence. The needy, dependent mother may abandon her children (literally or emotionally), leaving them to fend for themselves or expecting them to be like a parent, robbing them of their childhood. Children of alcoholics or children who are expected to cook, clean, and look after younger siblings, etc., from a very young age are typical examples of this. In these cases, the "mistrust" option that Erik Erikson mentioned is more likely. If you could not depend on your own parents to protect and look after you, why would you expect to rely on anyone else as an adult?

The issue of boundaries and separation is vital when the Moon is strongly involved with water. With a Cancerian (or 4th-house) Moon, the child may not know how to separate himself or herself from other family members. Since such individuals are extra intuitive and extra sensitive, they tend to pick up on the feelings of others. They may have trouble sorting out their emotions from the environment in which they are living. The family may also teach them to believe that they are responsible for someone's reactions ("You make me feel . . ."). When emotional pressures become overwhelming, withdrawal may seem like the only escape route. Some children will look to "things" for security. They may develop sentimental attachments (or simply view some objects as if they were "security blankets") and have trouble letting go. This can manifest, for example, as more than one bank account with one kept secret from other people, hiding money, clinging to possessions, etc. Protection is a central issue, whether the individual is trying to protect herself or loved ones (or both).

Food is also a major issue where lunar motifs are strong. Some children (and parents) will try to anesthetize themselves from feelings through overeating. "Stuffing" themselves can be a way to try to "stuff" emotions that feel too powerful. Food is often equated with love, or at least security, within the home. Knowing that "I can always eat" can become a habit of reassurance. Excess weight can also provide a bulwark against a (potentially) threatening world. Because these individuals are more sensitive than the average person, they are also inclined to somaticize, i.e., their body speaks. They develop physical symptoms when under emotional stress.

Healing Options

A rich inner life is vital with these watery combinations. Privacy is very important. Keeping some separate space and time everyday—just for one's self— is advisable. Activities that allow these Cancerian individuals to vent emotionally will help, e.g., keep a journal, do Primal Scream, pound pillows, watch or read cathartic entertainment, talk with friends, etc. A good support system is necessary. Pets may be part of that support system. Animals are much better than humans at demonstrating unconditional love.

If the role of caretaker has been ingrained in Moon-in-Cancer (or 4th-house, etc.) individuals, they must practice small steps to become comfortable with dependency. They can ask for little favors—from people who are almost certain to say "Yes." They need to get used to leaning a bit on other people, and choosing people who are likely to be supportive rather than people who will let them down and reinforce the "mistrust" reaction. People who have been "stuck" in the needy, dependent role can take baby steps toward nurturing others. Often, starting by taking care of a pet or someone who is very young or helpless will help develop protective instincts. To move toward emotional health, these individuals must establish a balance between giving and getting support, between taking care of others and allowing others to look after them.

Because water is important, a sense of safety and security can be built through literal contact with water. Taking a bath before tackling situations that are emotionally challenging is an option, or walking by water or a fountain. Water can operate as a soother and as a strengthener. Because food is important, a special meal can be used to build one's confidence, as long as food does not become the only source of security, since that can lead to a battle with being overweight. Anything these individuals do to create a warmer, cozier, familiar nest is likely to be helpful. If a difficult conversation must be held, doing it within their own territory (whatever is "home" for them) is probably best. That will feed their strength. Practice can also add to emotional resiliency and coping skills. The more often they create a "safe" environment within which to meet an emotional challenge, the better they tend to fare in each subsequent encounter.

Your Affirmation
I know that true security lies within.

Letter 5: ☽ ☌ ☉, ☽ *in 5th house,* ☽ ♌

Self-Esteem, Showmanship, Star (Power), Self-Expression

Moon conjunct Sun

Ceres conjunct Sun

Sun conjunct ruler of 4th house or ruler of 10th house

Moon in 5th house

Ceres in 5th house

Sun in 4th house

(If 10th house is designated as Mom, Sun in 10th house)

Ruler of 5th house in 4th house (or 10th house)

Ruler of 4th house (or 10th house) in 5th house

Moon in Leo

Ceres in Leo

Ruler of 4th house (or 10th house) in Leo

Leo/Aquarius (or vice versa) across MC/IC axis

Sun in Cancer

Ruler of 5th house in Cancer

Planets in Cancer occupying the 5th house

Planet(s) conjunct Moon or Ceres ruling 5th house

Ruler(s) of the 4th house (or 10th house) conjunct planets ruling 5th house

Nodes across 5th/11th houses

Nodes across Leo/Aquarius

Planets in Leo occupying the 4th house (or 10th house)

Node conjunct ruler of 5th house

The mother (figure) is very significant in the daughter's development of self-esteem and personal pride. On the positive side, Mother can be extremely warm, generous, exciting, encouraging, and vibrant. Mother may demonstrate a childlike enthusiasm, a love of life, and an excellent capacity for joy and play. She could operate as a great coach or cheerleader, praising and affirming the best in her children and encouraging them to do more. In a healthy home, the mother (figure) will feed the creativity, charisma, and confidence of her child(ren). In such homes, love is freely given and expressed, and the daughter—as an adult—is likely to be an excellent trainer and motivator herself, having mastered the art of giving compliments sincerely and readily. Such people are often spark plugs for those around them—their enthusiasm is contagious and gets other people involved. An instinctive stage presence and charisma are commonly present.

On the negative side, the mother could be very self-centered, arrogant, and childish. The mother may expect to always be the star and center of attention—a prima donna. She might demand constant applause from those around her and become angry if anyone seems to be competing for the limelight. Mother could be immature and believe she has the right to laugh, play, and to do whatever she enjoys (like a child) rather than take care of important duties and demonstrate the ability to delay gratification. The mother may expect to rule domestically by "divine right" and get upset if any of her "subjects" appear to question her royal authority. The daughter may feel eclipsed or overshadowed by the mother.

Another potential downside is when the child is made too much into the star. If a child is seen as the center of the parents' universe, she may be (unconsciously) encouraged to carry that sense of being special too far. She could become a spoiled brat, someone who has been treated royally by her parents and now expects the rest of the world to fulfill her every wish, to kowtow to all her desires. She could be too arrogant and self-centered as an adult. The daughter's generosity and attitudes toward loved ones will be strongly affected by the nurturing she received. Unfinished business with the parent is likely to be faced again in love relationships—with our lovers or our children. We may meet a romantic partner or have a child who pushes the same emotional buttons as our mother did.

With these placements, drama and sparkle are important. The parenting experience may feature excitement, thrills, enthusiasm, creativity, and lots of fun, or it may involve exaggeration, bombast, making mountains out of molehills, and egotistical excesses. The mother or child may be a drama queen, and extravagant displays of emotion could have been the norm within the home. Perhaps the child developed a sense that feelings had to be blown up and made more impressive. There may have been pressure to perform within the home. (Attention, admiration, and fame could be given too much weight: "You're nobody unless you are somebody.") Risk-taking may have been common—gambling, speculation, financial schemes, physical chances, etc. Although the Moon represents a quest for security, in these cases that sense of safety is tied to thrill-seeking. The child may grow up looking for security by chasing the rush of adrenaline! Emotional reactions are likely to be fiery and dramatic. These individuals are often more in tune with their inner child. They can be somewhat flamboyant, but also very generous, enthusiastic, and encouraging.

A degree of emotional volatility is possible because this is a fire-water combination. (The Sun, Leo, and 5th house are fiery, while the Moon, Cancer, and 4th house are watery.) When the extroverted fire side is dominant, the individual is expressive, seeks attention, and enjoys excitement. When the water side takes over, the individual may retreat, go inside, and even hide her light under a bushel basket. Learning to move comfortably between these inner and outer worlds is important.

Healing Options

Individuals with these Sun-Moon combinations need lots of positive excitement in their lives. This can be sought through a vocation (e.g., the salesperson, actor or actress, promoter, stockbroker, worker in the entertainment fields, etc.), through personal hobbies and interests (e.g., theater, artistic creativity), or through physical means (anything that gets the blood flowing and provides some thrills). Because praise and admiration are vital and help these people feel safe, they need to associate with very positive individuals—people who are generous with compliments and positive feedback. The support system for Moon-in-Leo (or 5th-house) people needs to include friends and colleagues who are very expressive and free with affirmations.

Feeling special and significant matters much to people with these lunar placements and combinations. When feeling threatened or "down," one of the best steps they can take is to pamper themselves. They can take the role of King or Queen for a Day. Treating themselves to extra indulgences or catering to their preferences will pick up their mood quickly. Also, exciting activities can be part of their support system. Any kind of creative self-expression (artistic and otherwise) is likely to build their personal vitality. Hobbies are an excellent outlet. Loving and being loved is also very important, so romantic gestures, courtship, or flirtation can be another way to lift their spirits. Anything that makes these individuals feel special or lets them be the star can bring in more positive feelings.

Your Affirmation

Love, excitement, and creativity nurture me.

Letter 6: ☽ ☌ ⚶, ☽ *in 6th house,* ☽ ♍
Careful, Competent, Conscientious, Critical

Moon conjunct Vesta
Ceres conjunct Vesta
Vesta conjunct ruler of 4th house or ruler of 10th house
(Moon conjunct Ceres)
Moon in 6th house
Ceres in 6th house
Ruler of 4th house (or 10th house) in 6th house
Vesta in 4th house
(If 10th house is designated as Mom, Vesta in 10th house)
Ruler of 6th house in 4th house (or 10th house)
Moon in Virgo
Ceres in Virgo
Ruler of 4th house (or 10th house) in Virgo
Virgo/Pisces (or vice versa) across MC/IC axis
Vesta in Cancer
Ruler of 6th house in Cancer
Planets in Cancer occupying the 6th house
Planet(s) conjunct Moon or Ceres ruling 6th house
Ruler(s) of 4th house (or 10th house) conjunct planets ruling 6th house
Nodes across 6th/12th houses
Nodes across Virgo/Pisces
Planets in Virgo occupying the 4th house (or 10th house)
Node conjunct ruler of 6th house

Issues of work and health are very important in the early nurturing environment. On the positive side, the mother may be hardworking, competent, dedicated, and practical. Mother may be very organized, capable, skilled in regard to nutrition, or just generally able to do whatever needs to be done. Mother may teach a good work ethic to her child(ren), largely by example. Sometimes, a family business exists, and all or some of the family members work together.

Less constructively, the mother may work too hard and the child may resent that, feeling that Mom's duties rob the child of some of the nurturing or attention that she wants. Or, the work attitude can interfere with emotional attachments. Mother may be critical, nitpicking, compulsive, or too focused on doing and not enough on being. Cleanliness or other Virgo fetishes may be taken to extremes. The home may be quite rigid, with firm, black-and-white views about right and wrong. Mother may constantly find "flaws" in the child (and the child may return the favor).

Another possibility is that everyone in the family had to work hard. Perhaps it was a farm situation, where everyone was doing some kind of labor from a young age. Perhaps poverty was an issue, so everyone had to chip in. Or maybe a parent was ill, and the child was expected to become a practical caretaker from a young age—perhaps even obligated to look after the ill parent. Perhaps the child was seen as a laborer and given only performance-based affection—approval when she did something practical and useful, but no real support for her as a person. Often, this child works from a younger age than his or her peers.

The attitudes within the early home will have a strong impact on the daughter's feelings about work and health. Her work ethic is strongly influenced by the kind of nurturing she did (and did not) get. If work is overvalued, then illness may be the "only" (unconscious) way to take a vacation. If the daughter is given the message that ill health is a way to escape from life's duties and labor, she may follow that pattern. If the daughter is trained to be a caretaker, looking after inadequate family members from an early age, she may continue in that role and unconsciously attract people who need "fixing" in one way or another. On the positive side, the mother (figure) may encourage the daughter to be effective and competent. The daughter may follow in the mother's footsteps professionally.

Typically, if the basic horoscope has some strength in it, Moon-in-Virgo (or 6th-house, etc.) individuals respond to emotional stress by working harder, trying to be more useful, trying to serve people better, and striving to increase their productivity and efficiency. Occasionally they respond by getting ill. The instinct toward repairs and improvement (of people, circumstances, situations, and projects) is strong. These individuals need to learn to delegate and to share the burdens. Just because they *can* do something does not mean that they *should* do it! They must learn to let other people make their own mistakes and gradually develop their own competence.

Healing Options

Pragmatism is one of the strengths of this placement. When emotional stress threatens, these individuals can stop and analyze the situation. Making lists is often helpful. Focusing on the bottom line can be useful. Taking any step—even a small one—toward improving things will lift the spirits of the Moon-in-Virgo (etc.) types. They can find security in being organized, sensible, healthy, and logical. Taking vitamins and other practices of good nutrition can be a security blanket and provide reassurance. Healthy habits of mind and body (e.g., Science of Mind) are likely to be appealing.

It is helpful for these individuals to learn to cherish making mistakes, because making mistakes indicates that a person is growing and learning. (If you did it right the first time, you haven't learned anything.) They can break the habit of coming down hard on themselves for committing errors, and instead appreciate any shortcomings as opportunities to further improve themselves.

Criticism is often an issue to be mastered. Developing and practicing tolerance—both of themselves and of others—is vital. If the daughter received a lot of negative messages as a child, she must practice positive messages and affirmations, such as internal self-talk, listening to tapes, getting good feedback from friends, etc. If she was trained to see life from a very literal perspective where there is only one right answer, she can do exercises in creativity and brainstorming, and learn to see multiple choices and options.

Your Affirmation

I am dedicated to maintaining good health, practical skills, and a service orientation.

Letter 7: ☽ ☌ ♀, ⚴, ☽ *in 7th house,* ☽ ♎

Attractive, Adaptable, Affiliative, Artistic

Moon conjunct Venus or Pallas

Ceres conjunct Venus or Pallas

Venus conjunct ruler of 4th house (or ruler of 10th house)

Pallas conjunct ruler of 4th house (or ruler of 10th house)

Moon in 7th house

Ceres in 7th house

Ruler of 4th house (or 10th house) in 7th house

Venus or Pallas in 4th house

(If 10th house is designated as Mom, Venus or Pallas in 10th house)

Ruler of 7th house in 4th house (or 10th house)

Moon in Libra

Ceres in Libra

Ruler of 4th house (or 10th house) in Libra

Libra/Aries (or vice versa) across MC/IC axis

Venus in Cancer

Pallas in Cancer

Ruler of 7th house in Cancer

Planets in Cancer occupying the 7th house

Cancer Descendant

Planet(s) conjunct Moon or Ceres ruling 7th house

Ruler(s) of 4th house (or 10th house) conjunct planets ruling 7th house

Nodes across 1st/7th houses

Nodes across Libra/Aries

Planets in Libra occupying the 4th house (or 10th house)

Node conjunct Descendant

Node conjunct ruler of 7th house

Mom is tied to partnership in a big way. Mom's attitudes about marriage, sharing, equality, appearances, and harmony have a strong impact on the daughter. On the positive side, the mother (figure) may operate like a partner, encouraging communication and openness and giving the daughter equal time. The mother and daughter may have an ongoing relationship—regular contact—even as adults. They may even form a business or other partnerships. The mother could be attractive, graceful, diplomatic, charming, artistic, and cooperative. The child may have been treated as a valuable and valued part of a team. Listening skills could be good on all sides. The child could be quite affectionate, charming, good-natured, and agreeable.

Less constructively, the mother may carry Libran qualities to an excess. She may be too concerned with appearances and "looking good." Worrying about "What will the neighbors think?" is possible. She could value style over substance. Or, the mother may be so wrapped up in her romantic relationship(s) or artistic interests that the daughter feels neglected. Also possible is a wishy-washy, other-directed mother who tries too hard to please and appease others and loses track of her own needs and desires.

Sometimes a partnership between the mother and daughter backfires. If the mother expects the daughter to be an "equal" when the age difference is great, it just becomes an excuse for the mother to be passive and lazy or to evade her responsibilities in the name of sharing with her child(ren). Another extreme is a mother-daughter connection that is so tight, the daughter has trouble breaking loose from it to form other adult partnerships. Too much of a good thing is possible! In some cases, the mother is very competitive with the daughter, treating her child like a rival. (Libra needs one-on-one interactions, but they can be competitive as well as cooperative.)

Nurturing may be tied to being sweet and nice. Although this can indicate homes with much affection and comfort, it can also point to families in which hypocrisy reigned supreme and the children were taught that the family always had to look good in the eyes of outsiders. "Keeping up with the Joneses" was important. In such homes, safety and security were tied to being obedient and "good," i.e., compliant. The child was trained to give in, be accommodating, and look nice. Being disliked felt like a threat. The child's basic safety was on the line. The daughter may inhibit her own emotional responses and try to mimic or even unconsciously adapt to the feelings of those around her. The desire to be popular could lead to insincerity or problems being decisive due to a desire to avoid any unpleasantness.

For the daughter, unfinished business with the mother (figure) is likely to be faced in adult love relationships. That is, the daughter is apt to attract potential partners who push the same emotional buttons that Mom did. So, partnerships bring up issues of security, safety, nurturing, and protection. On the positive side, the daughter will choose someone with whom she can take turns being the protector. Sometimes she is the caretaker, and sometimes her partner is. Family could be an important focus in one-on-one relationships. Family members could influence the partner the daughter chooses, or she may be attracted to someone due to her thoughts about what kind of parent he would be. On the negative side, what should be an equalitarian relationship becomes more like a mother-child interaction. One person is needy, whiny, and dependent, and the other person provides all or most of the emotional support and sustenance.

Healing Options

For these combinations, beauty can be an important source of comfort and security. A home environment that is attractive really is a source of strength. Messy or ugly settings can upset the emotional balance of these individuals. When under stress, taking any steps (even something small) to make the milieu more attractive is a good idea. Because Libra represents balance and justice, thinking about what is fair may keep Moon-in-Libra (or 7th-house, etc.) individuals from going too far in terms of pleasing others. Skills at comparing and contrasting are also present and can help these people find reasonable compromises and middle-ground answers to problems. One of their likely talents is a knack for finding win-win solutions.

For these individuals, music and other artistic outlets can soothe their psyche and provide support when they are under stress. Because partnership matters, sharing important goals will often help these people achieve them. For example, if they want to succeed with an exercise program, getting a "buddy" to do it with them is likely to help. Beautifying efforts can also be directed toward themselves (their own body) and provide another way to solidify a sense of safety.

Negotiating contracts can help keep these individuals on an even keel. If distressing issues must be discussed, they may get the other parties to agree beforehand to keep their tone kind and gentle, their wording polite, and their nonverbal cues friendly. These people operate best in a pleasant atmosphere.

Your Affirmation

I enjoy sharing with and caring for others.

Letter 8: ☽ ☌ ♇, ⚵, ☽ *in 8th house,* ☽ ♏

Powerful, Private, Passionate, Possessive, Probing, Persistent

Moon conjunct Pluto or Juno

Ceres conjunct Pluto or Juno

Pluto or Juno conjunct ruler of 4th house or ruler of 10th house

Moon in 8th house

Ceres in 8th house

Ruler of 4th house (or 10th house) in 8th house

Pluto or Juno in 4th house

(If 10th house is designated as Mom, Pluto or Juno in 10th house)

Ruler of 8th house in 4th house (or 10th house)

Moon in Scorpio

Ceres in Scorpio

Ruler of 4th house (or 10th house) in Scorpio

Scorpio/Taurus (or vice versa) across MC/IC axis

Pluto in Cancer

Juno in Cancer

Ruler of 8th house in Cancer

Planets in Cancer occupying the 8th house

Planet(s) conjunct Moon or Ceres ruling 8th house

Ruler(s) of 4th house (or 10th house) conjunct planets ruling 8th house

Nodes across 2nd/8th houses

Nodes across Taurus/Scorpio

Planets in Scorpio occupying the 4th house (or 10th house)

Node conjunct ruler of 8th house

This is another watery combination, so issues of boundaries are very important. The mother (figure) has a profound impact on the daughter's feelings about intimacy (emotional, physical), joint resources, and power. In a healthy family, the mother is likely to be psychologically aware, strong (emotionally, physically and/or mentally), and oriented toward transforming liabilities into assets. The family encourages the daughter to look beneath the surface in life, to become aware of her feelings, and to learn—through persistent focus and attention—to turn negative habit patterns into positive ones. Loyalty and perseverance are probably highlighted.

In a less healthy setting, the mother may be manipulative, vengeful, power-hungry, intrusive, and overwhelming. Or, the mother may be too dependent on a mate or other people, giving away all her potential power. Privacy issues often arise. The mother may invade the daughter's space physically and otherwise. In severe cases, there could be physical or sexual abuse. In more mild forms, the parent may read a child's diary or refuse to respect the child's differences. (When water goes too far in terms of dissolving boundaries, the mother may be "one" with the child, but that one gets defined in Mom's terms.) Suspiciousness and hidden agendas may abound within the home. Emotional exchanges could be quite convoluted. The child may be exposed to emotional blackmail (and learn to use it herself), passive-aggressive behavior, and double messages. The parent may withhold so much that the child becomes a little detective trying to get enough information to feel safe.

Shared resources are an important focus within the home. The mother's attitudes toward sensuality and sexuality strongly affect the daughter. How the mother shares (and does not share) her money and material possessions with a mate and with other people greatly influences the child(ren). With a constructive role model, the daughter learns to give, receive, and share power, possessions, and pleasures with other people. One option is the daughter literally inheriting from the mother. With a negative role model, the daughter is likely to have power struggles and experience manipulation, intimidation, or inequality in relationships in regard to money and sex. Cuddling, safety, and comfort needs may get mixed with sexual desires. Of course, even when the mother is very generous with her resources, it can be overdone. If it is carried to an extreme, the daughter may be disappointed when romantic partners are not as generous. Questions of vulnerability arise. Based on the experience in the early home, the daughter will decide how close (or not) to get to other people in emotional as well as sexual terms. She will consider how to open up, how much to share, and how vulnerable she is willing to be based on her early childhood.

Secrecy, scandals, and elimination can also be significant concerns. Mother may be somewhat reticent, or getting information may feel very difficult. Skeletons in the family closet are quite possible. In some cases, Mother (and perhaps the whole family) has to face issues of death or letting go at a relatively early age. Knowing when is enough—physically, mentally, and emotionally—is a challenge. Learning when to call it quits and move on is vital. Developing the capacity to forgive one's self and others can be a central lesson. Emotions tends to be extra-intense (and people may up the ante unconsciously), so catharsis and truly letting go matter much.

The child may come to feel that security comes through revealing as little as possible, and thus try to appear (and be) invulnerable. The daughter may be trained to seek revenge and to wait as long as it takes for "payback" of old wrongs. In severe cases, the Moon-Pluto (etc.) child becomes the family scapegoat. Blaming and shaming are directed primarily at that child, and other family members project their negativity and problems onto that one child.

Healing Options

Gaining a personal sense of control is very important. Any activities that allow the daughter to feel she is in charge may help. Therapy can be very valuable. Even if the daughter chooses not to see a counselor, she could benefit from keeping a journal and doing self-analysis. Groups that emphasize confrontation and facing the Dark Side of life could be appealing. Tools for making friends with the unconscious, including occult studies, are valuable. As with all watery Moons, some alone time is essential. That allows these individuals to sort through their feelings, to vent, and to gain more understanding of their inner world.

The daughter may choose the territory for threatening discussions, or she may limit the confrontation to certain issues. Agreements may be established about how long each person talks, how rebuttals are handled, etc. The more power the Moon-in-Scorpio (etc.) individual believes she has, the more secure she is likely to feel.

Rising to a challenge is very affirming. These individuals need to exercise their toughness and tenacity, so circumstances that activate the mantra "When the going gets tough, the tough get going" can promote growth. Sometimes these individuals will choose to consider worst-case scenarios, to "face the Dragon" of really difficult challenges, in order to test themselves. They have tremendous stamina and survival instincts and can surmount just about anything. They excel at facing circumstances, fears, and thoughts that would terrify and horrify others. These people can take destructive patterns and transform them into something useful (or at least harmless). They can be catalysts for major transformations within others as well.

Your Affirmation

I transform negative habit patterns into positive ones.

Letter 9: ☽ ☌ ♃, ⚷, ☽ *in 9th house,* ☽ ♐

Faith-Filled, Fervent, Philosophical, Far-Sighted, Freedom-Oriented

Moon conjunct Jupiter (or Chiron)
Ceres conjunct Jupiter (or Chiron)
Jupiter (or Chiron) conjunct ruler of 4th house or ruler of 10th house
Moon in 9th house
Ceres in 9th house
Ruler of 4th house (or 10th house) in 9th house
Jupiter (or Chiron) in 4th house
(If 10th house is designated as Mom, Jupiter [or Chiron] in 10th house)
Ruler of 9th house in 4th house (or 10th house)
Moon in Sagittarius
Ceres in Sagittarius
Ruler of 4th house (or 10th house) in Sagittarius
Gemini/Sagittarius (or vice versa) across MC/IC axis
Jupiter in Cancer
(Chiron in Cancer)
Ruler of 9th house in Cancer
Planets in Cancer occupying the 9th house
Planet(s) conjunct Moon or Ceres ruling 9th house
Ruler(s) of 4th house (or 10th house) conjunct planets ruling 9th house
Nodes across 3rd/9th houses
Nodes across Sagittarius/Gemini
Planets in Sagittarius occupying the 4th house (or 10th house)
Node conjunct ruler of 9th house

The daughter's faith in life, optimism, and quest for the best are strongly influenced by the mother (figure). In healthy homes, Mother is likely to be upbeat, confident, and eager to explore the world (mentally, physically, or both). She may be religious, philosophical, well educated, from a foreign country, or otherwise involved with the quest for meaning in life and the urge to expand horizons. The home may encourage learning or risking for greater gain, or it may foster an adventurous spirit or the desire to meet people from other cultures and to be exposed to a wide range of ideas, ideals, and perspectives. Mother can be a source of inspiration. Mother (and daughter) may be literary, witty, independent, and inclined to "go for the gusto" in life. The parent is a role model for enlightenment, the expansion of knowledge, the seeking of answers about why we are here and what it is all about, whether through travel, education, science, religion, or anything that stretches those intellectual boundaries.

Less constructively, Mother could carry a focus on religion or idealism too far. She might be perfectionistic and impossible to please. No matter what the daughter does, it is never enough. The mother may be committed to an impossible quest to be the perfect mother of perfect children. In some cases, the daughter is conditioned to a Don Quixote lifestyle—always trying, even when the cause is hopeless. Or, the mother may be too caught up in her own explorations and freedom needs to "be there" for the child. With a mother who is very independent, the child is likely to learn to look after herself and to seek emotional safety from intellectual means or the outside world rather than from family. Sometimes a parent travels a lot or is restless and easily bored; the child is trained to believe that emotional attachments only lead to loss (because people keep on leaving you literally or emotionally). In severe cases, the parent may be absent, and the child has only the ideal image that she created, of what she hopes her parent is like. The expectations can cut both ways: Mother may demand the impossible of the daughter, and the daughter may feel that Mother never lives up to her standards.

Issues of beliefs, moral and ethical principles, and values will be important within the home. Mother is a role model, positive or negative, for the daughter's worldview. The daughter may follow in Mom's philosophical footsteps, or go in the opposite direction. Either way, the mother is the role model—what to do or what *not* to do—in terms of what the daughter believes is true, real, and morally and ethically proper. Religious, spiritual, and ethical issues may be a significant focus, concern, strength, or source of conflict within the home. This mother (figure) affects the daughter's willingness to take risks, to go out on a limb, to be the explorer and adventurer in life.

Too much perfectionism can lead to procrastination by the mother, daughter, or both. ("I won't do it until I can do it perfectly.") It can also lead to much pressure—the individual keeps on doing more and more, trying to get it perfect, and gets frustrated because nothing is ever perfect. Disappointment and frustration are a danger. Overidealism can lead to intolerance and judgmental behavior. If we believe we know what perfection is, we are willing to criticize anyone or anything that is less than that. An unconscious hubris (an

"I am God" attitude) can develop. Feelings of entitlement can also be overdone if a mother is very, very generous and the daughter interprets that to mean that she is entitled to "only the best" from everyone else. There is a fine line between righteous (well-meaning, moral, ethical) behavior and self-righteous attitudes.

Healing Options

Learning the art of "good enough" is very important. The daughter can practice acceptance and tolerance toward herself and others. This means giving up the idea of "perfection," at least where people and projects are concerned. She can look for an Ultimate Ideal in religion, spiritual studies, or nature, but must get used to permitting mistakes and shortcomings in her own behavior and that of other people.

Space (literally, lots of room around you) can be very helpful. Holding emotionally difficult discussions outdoors may relieve some of the pressure. The Moon-in-Sag (etc.) individual needs to feel that the door is open, that she is not trapped.

Faith in an infinite beyond humans is the strongest resource. If these individuals have a spiritual or religious connection, they can deal with anything. Being true to their values keeps them centered and effective. Since one of their best talents is looking on the bright side and being optimistic, a good tack to take in tough times is to look for a silver lining—any small bit of brightness in the gloom. Then they can take that little sliver of positive focus and make it bigger and bigger.

Your Affirmation

I nurture faith and confidence in myself and others, and trust in a power beyond humans.

Letter 10: ☽ ☌ ♄, ☽ *in 10th house,* ☽ ♑
Practical, Productive, Puritanical, Presidential, Patient

Moon conjunct Saturn
Ceres conjunct Saturn
Saturn conjunct ruler of 4th house or ruler of 10th house
Moon in 10th house
Ceres in 10th house
Ruler of 4th house (or 10th house) in 10th house
Saturn in 4th house
(If 10th house is designated as Mom, Saturn in 10th house)
Ruler of 10th house in 4th house (or 10th house)
Moon in Capricorn
Ceres in Capricorn
Ruler of 4th house (or 10th house) in Capricorn
Capricorn/Cancer (or vice versa) across MC/IC axis
Saturn in Cancer
Ruler of 10th house in Cancer
Planets in Cancer occupying the 10th house
Planet(s) conjunct Moon or Ceres ruling 10th house
Ruler(s) of 4th house (or 10th house) conjunct planets ruling 10th house
Nodes across 4th/10th houses
Nodes across Capricorn/Cancer
Planets in Capricorn occupying the 4th house (or 10th house)
Node conjunct Midheaven
Node conjunct ruler of 10th house

These combinations show a mixture of the mother and father archetypes. So, the daughter received some sort of blend of conditional and unconditional love in terms of her home life. It might have been mostly positive, or mostly negative (or some of each). The possibilities for parents are varied.

One option is that one parent played both roles. Due to death, divorce, etc., Mother might have been both the nurturing and the authoritative parent, or Dad might have been both the supportive and responsible parent. Another option is that both parents played both roles. Mom could be warm and caring as well as a tough disciplinarian. Or Mom might have wielded more-than-average power within the home or been a professional as well as a nurturer. Dad could be gentle and helpful as well as hardworking and dutiful. Or, Dad was more physically present than most fathers. A third option is that the child was expected to parent her own parent(s). This is common in families where one or both parents are alcoholic or where the child is given responsibilities and duties at a much younger age than is appropriate (a parent may be gone, ill, inadequate, etc.). The fourth possibility is that both parents were struggling with the balancing act between conditional and unconditional love.

If the parents found a happy medium, the child was loved, held, protected, and cherished as an infant and youngster. She did not have to *do* anything—just be—to get the care and attention that she needed. As she got older, she was taught to deal with the consequences of her behavior. Limits were set and enforced. She learned about rules and the rights of other people. Her parents created a healthy blend of early support, sustenance, and security (which built trust) along with an emphasis on developing strength, competence, and responsibility as she got older. The parent(s) provided solid stability for the daughter, encouraging her to develop her strength, competence, and coping skills.

For many parents, due to their own backgrounds, this balance is out of whack. If the parents overdo the unconditional love side, they (consciously or unconsciously) try to keep the daughter young, helpless, and dependent on them. Her efforts toward independence may be undercut. Too much may be done for her. She may be encouraged to continue playing the role of the spoiled or favored child.

If the parents overdo the conditional love side, the child will face too much harshness when young. It may be that the parents are critical, judgmental, or restrictive. It may be that the whole family must deal with the constraints of poverty. Or, perhaps the child is expected to work from a young age. It may be that the daughter is given responsibilities that most people would consider to be beyond her age. (Again, she might have to parent her own parents.) The daughter may feel rejected, perhaps for her appearance, her gender, her behavior, etc. In extreme cases, she may literally be told that her parents did not want her or "had" to have her. If the constrictive tendencies of the parents are excessive, the daughter may end up feeling totally worthless and be afraid to try anything, convinced that she will just fail. The parent(s) fingerprints are all over the daughter's view of "reality"— what she feels is possible, the blinders and filters that she uses in life. Those can be very wide and encompassing, or very narrow and limiting.

Parental attitudes toward work and career are significant. The family will strongly influence the daughter's sense of competence and responsibility, and the jobs that she considers within her reach. Family businesses are also an option with these combinations—following in parental footsteps vocationally. On the positive level, the parent(s) encourage a good work ethic and the daughter develops strength, competence, and pragmatism. On the negative side, the parent(s) may treat the child like a drone or worker bee, try to control her vocational choices, damage her sense of competence, or criticize the way she handles responsibility and outer-world accomplishments. Or, the parents may embody the script "If you work really hard, perhaps you will not be hurt as much." The daughter's attitudes toward status and toward achieving notice, power, influence, and authority in the world will be strongly affected by her parent(s). Some parents teach the script "Thou shalt not do better professionally than thy parents did." (And, some adults are still living out that script at age fifty and beyond.)

When emotional stress arises, these individuals may react by giving up (if they have internalized the sense of worthlessness from a punitive, restrictive childhood) or by taking on more and more responsibility (if they have been trained to be the caretaker from an early age). The emotional tenor is serious, and people can incline toward depression if they have experienced much negativity when young or believe they have failed often. Self-control and discipline generally have strong appeal. These individuals tend to seek security by working hard, by being dedicated and responsible, and/or by seeking a position of status or power. Predictability and established routines often are reassuring.

As an adult, the daughter must find a happy medium between her conditional love and unconditional love needs. This includes making room in her life for both a private life (home, family, pets, something to nurture) and public accomplishments (career, community service, etc.). The daughter must balance her time and energy between loved ones and work in the world, between sympathy and "tough love." Some people may literally combine the two by working from their home, working with family members, working in a nurturing field (e.g., providing food, shelter, clothing, real estate, etc.), or creating a homey atmosphere on the job.

Healing Options

The daughter can benefit from a positive mentor. One way to overcome negative "tapes" about authority figures is to have new experiences that are affirming. By seeking out someone who is older, wiser, and more experienced, but also supportive and kind, the daughter can create more positive interactions with an authority figure. She can also learn that mistakes are not the end of the world—just a chance to do better in the future.

Because the element of earth is much involved here, taking sensible steps can be helpful. These individuals can put their problems down on paper. Breaking difficult tasks into smaller steps can make them seem less overwhelming. Use those natural skills of pragmatism and realism to get to the bottom line. Good resources of common sense and practicality are available to these people.

Exercises to build self-esteem are a good idea. These individuals can work on minimizing their inner critic, which is usually overdeveloped. They can practice taking inventory often of their assets, and reduce the importance of flaws. It is helpful for them to pay attention to compliments they get from other people and to hang out with people who value who they *are*, not just what they *do*.

Responsibility is a major issue—either too much (the caretaker) or too little (the person who feels useless and incompetent). It is a good idea for these individuals to ask themselves regularly, "Is this really my job?" If it is, then they can go ahead and do it, or get the training they need to do it better. If it is not, then they can let someone else take care of it—or allow it to *not* get done!

Your Affirmation

I carry out my appropriate responsibilities—and let others take care of theirs.

Letter 11: ☽ ☌ ♅, ☽ *in 11th house,* ☽ ♒

Independent, Individualistic, Innovative, Iconoclastic

Moon conjunct Uranus

Ceres conjunct Uranus

Uranus conjunct ruler of 4th house or ruler of 10th house

Moon in 11th house

Ceres in 11th house

Ruler of 4th house (or 10th house) in 11th house

Uranus in 4th house

(If 10th house is designated as Mom, Uranus in 10th house)

Ruler of 11th house in 4th house (or 10th house)

Moon in Aquarius

Ceres in Aquarius

Ruler of 4th house (or 10th house) in Aquarius

Aquarius/Leo (or vice versa) across MC/IC axis

Uranus in Cancer

Ruler of 11th house in Cancer

Planets in Cancer occupying the 11th house

Planet(s) conjunct Moon or Ceres ruling 11th house

Ruler(s) of 4th house (or 10th house) conjunct planets ruling 11th house

Nodes across 5th/11th houses

Nodes across Aquarius/Leo

Planets in Aquarius occupying the 4th house (or 10th house)

Node conjunct ruler of 11th house

Mother is a key figure for freedom, individuality, chaos, and our inventive spirit. With these combinations, Mother may be unusual in some way (or we experienced her as unusual—different from her peers). On the positive side, Mother was independent, innovative, bright, open-minded, interested in the wider world, and tolerant. She encouraged the daughter to be true to herself, to explore multiple options, and to find the future exciting. Sometimes the mother is her daughter's best friend.

On the negative side, Mother could have been erratic, weird, chaotic, unpredictable, and strange. Her freedom needs might have been so excessive that she wasn't around (gone completely), was a parent intermittently, or was absent (physically or emotionally) enough that the child felt neglected or pushed aside. Perhaps friends or the mother's own interests (e.g., recreation, country club, groups, social causes, etc.) seemed more important than the daughter. The mother's detachment might have been carried to the extreme of being aloof or uncaring. She could have seemed quite cold. Unpredictability could have been rampant. Perhaps the family moved often or certain elements of the home life kept changing. Perhaps emotions were chaotic and "crazy" or rationalized away as if they didn't exist. The child may have learned that dependency was dangerous, that safety lay in being free and not leaning on anyone else. Or, perhaps security became tied to the mind.

If the mother was emotionally (or otherwise) unavailable, the daughter may have compensated with other people. Friends might have provided some of the nurturing. In some cases, good friends can become substitutes for blood kin. The daughter may nurture humanity or be particularly supportive of her buddies' intellectual development, unusual ideas, or openness to possibilities.

Both the mother and daughter are apt to be ambivalent about nurturing and casual about domestic matters. They want emotional attachments, but not to be tied down by them in any way. They want a home, but also want to know that they can always leave. This can result in some hot/cold interactions and families in which mixed messages abound. The mother may seem very warm and loving, and then distant and cool. Loving without possessiveness can be an excellent skill, or the individuals may simply end up confusing the people around them. Both the mother and daughter may be pulled between dependency and independence, or between nurturing and freedom. Their task is to make room in their lives for activities that feature warm, caring connections as well as pursuits that accent independence, individuality, and innovation.

An Aquarian (or Uranian) type of home can have open communication, an interest in the new and different, lots of intellectual stimulation, a fascination with the future, and plenty of freedom for all the family members. The mother and family life affect the daughter's ability to see other perspectives, to look at alternatives, to break the rules. What is most supportive for the daughter is a family that encourages her unique qualities and feeds her individualistic instincts.

Healing Options

The conscious, reasoning mind is a valuable resource, so these individuals can cope with emotional stress by looking over their options. A healthy response is to seek out other possibilities. They can experiment with altering their perspective. Often, if they can change their frame of reference, they will come up with other solutions and fresh information. A degree of objectivity (but not too much) can be helpful.

One of the strengths of Uranus and Aquarius is tolerance. The ability of these individuals to withhold judgment is often their best first step toward solving disagreements. If they can truly listen to (and hear!) the other party's complaints and concerns, they will do well.

These people will probably continue to work on the balancing act between head and heart, logic and feelings. Recognizing that a healthy life includes both will help them consider both sides and find a healthy middle ground.

Your Affirmation

I feel safest when being myself and nurturing the individuality of others.

Letter 12: ☽ ☌ ♆, ⚷, ☽ *in 12th house,* ☽ ♓

Imaginative, Intuitive, Illusory, Illuminative, Idealistic, Inspired, Impressionable

Moon conjunct Neptune

Ceres conjunct Neptune

Neptune conjunct ruler of 4th house or ruler of 10th house

Moon in 12th house

Ceres in 12th house

Ruler of 4th house (or 10th house) in 12th house

Neptune in 4th house

(If 10th house is designated as Mom, Neptune in 10th house)

Ruler of 12th house in 4th house (or 10th house)

Moon in Pisces

Ceres in Pisces

Ruler of 4th house (or 10th house) in Pisces

Pisces/Virgo (or vice versa) across MC/IC axis

Neptune in Cancer

Ruler of 12th house in Cancer

Planets in Cancer occupying the 12th house

Planet(s) conjunct Moon or Ceres ruling 12th house

Ruler(s) of 4th house (or 10th house) conjunct planets ruling 12th house

Nodes across 6th/12th houses

Nodes across Pisces/Virgo

Planets in Pisces occupying the 4th house (or 10th house)

Node conjunct ruler of 12th house

The mother (figure) is involved with the daughter's search for infinite love and beauty. On the positive side, Mother may be artistic, idealistic, religious, spiritual, imaginative, or attractive. She may be a healer, helper, compassionate individual, or someone who inspires others. The mother influences the daughter's capacity for transcendence, to be uplifted from the mundane into other realms of consciousness. The family can enhance magical and mystical feelings.

On the negative side, the mother may be an escapist (into drugs, alcohol, chronic fantasy), a victim (ill, emotionally or mentally disturbed, helpless or hopeless), or someone who carries rescuing to an extreme (a would-be saint can rapidly become a martyr). The daughter may learn that running away from pain is the accepted course of action. Food, imagination, drugs, or just about anything can be used as an escape. Lies, deception, misdirection, confusion, and evasion can be employed by family members (and the daughter learns by example). In extreme cases, the Moon-in-Pisces (etc.) child is scripted to be the family victim. Everyone may pick on her, or encourage her to sacrifice herself. Sometimes the mother is too busy saving the whales or working in a prison, hospital, ashram, etc., to take proper care of the child. The child may feel invisible to the parent, or the parent may be literally invisible (gone) or emotionally absent.

The daughter's dreams and visions are affected by the mother. Her mother may help her develop a connection to her inner wisdom and intuition and a belief in a Higher Power. Or, her mother may contribute to the daughter's disappointment, disillusionment, and frustration with a world that is far from ideal. The mother's fingerprints are all over the daughter in terms of whether she experiences Oneness, how she tunes into the infinite (or does not), her feelings about a Higher Power, and how she seeks transcendence and cosmic consciousness.

A strong unconscious connection usually exists between the mother and daughter. Often, the daughter feels the mother's pain and suffering whether or not the mother intends it. Sometimes, the daughter is scripted (consciously or unconsciously) to pursue the mother's dashed dreams. Sensitivity is high. The mother and/or the daughter may be quite intuitive and open to the influences of those around her. Indeed, learning to "shut off" the input she receives from other people could be a challenge. She is likely to be a "psychic sponge" and take on other people's emotions without intending to.

If the mother (or family) carries religion or idealism too far, the pressure can be considerable. The daughter may be held to unrealistic expectations—expected to be perfect. That is a set-up for failure and frustration on everyone's part. It is also possible that the daughter will dream of the "perfect mother" that does not exist. In some cases, the mother is literally absent and the child creates a dream image for solace. The mother may fall into a martyr, rescuing role, which would unconsciously encourage the child to remain a victim, or Mom may expect the daughter to rescue her (the parent) from any possible unhappiness. In such cases, the daughter is scripted to be the all-compassionate rescuer. Motherhood and sacrifice—or pain—may be all too closely linked. Utopian, idealistic imagery may pervade the home.

Healing Options

Solitude is important. (Again, the Moon is watery.) Alone time allows the daughter to meditate, to "veg out" and relax. Then she can clear her psyche and feelings, getting rid of any emotions or problems she may have absorbed from other people.

The initial response to emotional stress generally is to hide or run away, so the daughter must train herself to know when to stand her ground. This means being objective about when the best move is to retreat, and when staying to confront unpleasantness is essential.

Tough emotional discussions are best held in serene, lovely settings. Beauty will soothe and refresh the Moon-in-Pisces (or 12th-house, etc.) individual. Having water nearby is often helpful as well. Training intimates to talk things over with gentle voices and a vocabulary that is empathic, rather than confrontational or aggressive, will also help. The daughter may want to establish the ground rule that she will leave if matters get too hot and heavy, returning when the other parties are prepared to be considerate.

Short "fantasy breaks" can also help. When used judiciously, getting away through imagination can provide a needed respite, as long as the daughter is willing and able to deal with reality thereafter (and these breaks are under conscious control—not done through substance abuse or an addiction to fantasy).

Empathy and understanding are valuable resources for these individuals and major assets when they are facing challenges. They can use their ability to tune in to other people to resolve many issues and find solutions to a number of problems.

Your Affirmation

I am part of the Infinite, and a Higher Power provides all the security that I need.

FOUR

Aspects to the Moon, Ceres, and More

The aspects to the Moon, Ceres (the Earth Mother asteroid), and the rulers of the 4th house (and often of the 10th house) give more details about the daughter's experience of her mother. It is important to remember that a horoscope reflects the understanding, reactions, and issues of the person to whom the horoscope belongs. Thus, we do not necessarily see parents as they were (or are) within a given horoscope. We see that child's experience of her parents. And, different children within the same family can have vastly different experiences of the same parents. Of course, they can also have strong similarities.

As usual in astrology, it is important to look for repeated themes. Thus, with aspects, we need to be alert for motifs that recur when considering all of the following:

1. Aspects to the Moon

2. Aspects to Ceres

3. Aspects to the ruler(s) of the 4th house (that is, rulers of any signs that appear in the 4th house—three signs if an interception occurs, otherwise usually two signs, and occasionally only one sign)

4. Aspects to the ruler(s) of the 10th house (bearing in mind that sometimes the 4th will pertain more to Mother, sometimes the 10th, and sometimes both)

5. Aspects to any planets in the 4th house

6. Aspects to any planets in the 10th house (remembering that they may reflect issues that are more paternal than maternal in some cases)

We already covered conjunctions in chapter 3, but we will revisit them here, along with other aspects. It is important to remember that "positive" aspects do not always manifest with good outcomes in a person's life. People can take sextiles and trines to excess and have problems. Similarly, challenging aspects—although they require work and effort to manifest constructively—can be expressed in helpful and healthy ways. Like resistance training in bodywork, paying attention and putting in the effort can lead to happy results and greater effectiveness with the "negative" aspects. What the person does with the basic potential is more important than the nature of the aspect.

Moon/Ceres/Planets in or Ruling 4th/10th Houses Conjunct the Sun

This combination often denotes a mother-father mixture. It could be that one parent played both roles (through death, divorce, etc.), that the parents were somewhat alike, and/or that the child felt she had to parent one of her own parents.

On the positive side, Mother is likely to be dynamic, charismatic, exciting, warm and loving. She may be a great cheerleader, motivator, and coach for her children. She may retain a childlike zest and enthusiasm for life, and may encourage joy and play.

On the negative side, the daughter may feel eclipsed by the mother. Perhaps Mom is a drama queen who never gets off the stage. Perhaps the mother seems very self-centered and expects (like a child) the world to revolve around her. Or, maybe familial pride is carried to extremes. Shaming and negative attention could be used to control loved ones. Sometimes the daughter feels that no one else in the family but Mom is allowed to shine or be significant.

Moon/Ceres/Planets in or Ruling 4th/10th Houses Sextile/Trine the Sun

These aspects carry the potential for a mother who feeds her daughter's self-esteem. Mother may be generous with praise, recognition, and compliments. She may encourage the daughter's creativity and playful side.

On the negative side, grandstanding could be overdone within the family. The mother and/or the daughter may get carried away with exaggeration, an addiction to adrenaline, or a childish, self-centered attitude. A "divine right" attitude could prevail.

If handled well, these aspects suggest much mutual warmth and joy. The mother and daughter can build each other up, and each finds the world a bit brighter because the other is part of it.

Moon/Ceres/Planets in or Ruling 4th/10th Houses in Conflict (Square, Opposition, Quincunx) with the Sun

Power issues are often present with this combination. Naturally, the mother holds the advantage in the beginning, being older and having more experience. However, over time, that balance of power can shift. Mother and/or the daughter may use dramatic emphasis (such as exaggeration), egotistical ploys, or an assumption of authority to try to get her way. Small issues can easily become magnified or blown out of proportion. Competition for the limelight could develop.

With awareness and effort, the mother and daughter can concentrate on sharing their excitement, enthusiasm, and leadership skills. They can each be directive in their own areas of talent, and be willing to follow when appropriate. They can feed each another's zest for love and life.

Moon/Ceres/Planets in or Ruling 4th/10th Houses Conjunct the Moon

Mother probably has a strong need to bond and is likely to be very maternal or quite dependent. In the former case, Mother needs to be needed and will want to nurture, protect, cherish, and look after her child(ren). This can, of course, be carried to an extreme, where the daughter is unconsciously encouraged to remain weak and dependent so that Mother can feel she is being a "good" mother. If the mom is identified more with the child role, the daughter may be expected to mother her own mother—to provide support and assistance even when very young. Mother could be clingy, needy, or overly emotional.

Familial ties are accented. The home is likely to be important to both the mother and daughter, and security needs are tied to domestic issues. (The familiar and familial may be given too much importance; change may be resisted.) Hanging on to things and feelings is quite likely. Pack-rat instincts or the urge to collect things is often present. The potential is here for a great deal of emotional warmth and caring between the mother and daughter and extended to anyone else seen as "family."

Moon/Ceres/Planets in or Ruling 4th/10th Houses Sextile/Trine the Moon

On the positive side, the mother and daughter are mutually supportive. They find sustenance and security with one another. They reassure each another. If the bonding and/or mutual dependency are too strong, the mother and daughter may be so connected that it is difficult for them to form other relationships. On the negative side, Mother could carry the dependent or the nurturing role too far. She could be emotionally immature and lean on her daughter even when the daughter is very young. Or, the mother may overdo the "need to be needed" and unconsciously cripple her daughter's skills and developing competence due to the mother's need to feel that she is a good, protective mother who helps her child(ren). The best manifestation of this combination is an interdependent family where everyone takes turns looking after and supporting one another.

Moon/Ceres/Planets in or Ruling 4th/10th Houses in Conflict (Square, Opposition, Quincunx) with the Moon

Mixed messages are usually present in regard to nurturing. The mother is probably unsure about what is the best way to be a mother. Depending on the signs and houses involved, she may be torn between committing herself to the family and pursuing her own hobbies, career, or other interests. She may be uncertain about how much to reveal and how much to hide. Her intellectual and emotional sides may be at odds with one another, etc. Sometimes, these patterns (especially if they recur) point to a situation with more than one nurturing figure—and those two individuals have differences of opinion to sort out.

Occasionally, when there are a number of separative aspects (particularly oppositions and quincunxes) to the astrological keys that represent nurturing, the mother (figure) may actually be gone. More commonly, the daughter is dealing with feelings of insecurity, abandonment, or a lack of the support that she wanted. The challenge here is for the mother and daughter to reach an agreement about which elements of family are the most important and what kinds of caretaking both feel are essential. Ideally, they find opportunities to strengthen their ties with one another.

Moon/Ceres/Planets in or Ruling 4th/10th Houses Conjunct Mercury

The daughter sees Mom as mercurial. On the positive side, this can be a mother who is bright, articulate, and multitalented. On the negative side, this can be a mother who seems too casual, flippant, gossipy, talkative, or scattered. The daughter may feel that her mother rationalizes and intellectualizes life too much. If the daughter has other sources of insecurity, even the bright, articulate mom can be challenging, because the child cannot keep up with her (particularly at a young age). More commonly, this is a home that emphasizes learning and communication. There is often an excellent exchange of information. Sometimes the home changes a lot—many moves and consequent school changes, lots of different activities, etc. The home may be full of simultaneous conversations, everyone talking, but no one listening.

Moon/Ceres/Planets in or Ruling 4th/10th Houses Sextile/Trine Mercury

There is an excellent potential here for a mother who encouraged her daughter to think, talk, and learn. The mother may have supported intellectual inquiry and curiosity. She could have fed her daughter's "need to know." The parent and child may find it easy to discuss things with one another. A friendly, open perspective is likely.

Sometimes the daughter perceives the mother as overdoing these mental qualities. Perhaps the daughter wants less analysis and discussion and more emotional warmth or action. Perhaps the daughter has trouble keeping up with Mom's varied interests. Ideally, both individuals sharpen their brains while sharing a caring connection.

Moon/Ceres/Planets in or Ruling 4th/10th Houses in Conflict (Square, Opposition, Quincunx) with Mercury

Challenges are likely in the realm of the mind and communication. It may be as simple as the mother and daughter having very different ideas (and learning to agree to disagree). Sometimes the daughter feels that the mother does not listen or will not "hear" what she has to say. Sometimes the daughter feels discounted—that her opinions are ignored or criticized. A multitalented daughter may feel that her family is trying to limit her options, constrain her viewpoints, or keep her from the myriad experiences she desires. The warm, fuzzy aspects of nurturing may clash with the intellectual understanding—the head and the heart are at odds. Ideally, all family members learn to combine thinking and feeling for satisfactory results.

Moon/Ceres/Planets in or Ruling 4th/10th Houses Conjunct Venus

This combination often shows a strong bond of love and affection between the mother and child. The mother may tend to pamper the child, particularly in terms of sensual or financial indulgence. Or, the mother may feed the daughter's interest in art, beauty, and aesthetic matters. Mutual comfort and pleasure are quite possible.

On the negative side, the daughter may experience the mother as being overly hedonistic, money-hungry, materialistic, and self-indulgent. The mother might overdo eating, drinking, making love, spending money, collecting possessions, etc. The mother may come across as stubborn, self-satisfied, and complacent.

The mother is an important role model (positive or negative) for the daughter to learn about sensuality, financial matters, grace, and beauty. Many times, the mother and home are associated with feeling good.

Moon/Ceres/Planets in or Ruling 4th/10th Houses Sextile/Trine Venus

A smooth flow may exist between the mother and daughter. It is quite likely that they feel at ease with one another and may encourage each other in the pursuit of beauty and pleasure. Indeed, either might even "spoil" or overindulge the other. If carried to an extreme, too much passivity, "making nice" (hypocrisy), or complacency could be a problem.

Often, the bonds of affection are strong. The mother may aid the daughter's accumulation of material goods, and/or the daughter may help out Mom financially. Support can be provided on emotional, aesthetic, and practical levels.

Moon/Ceres/Planets in or Ruling 4th/10th Houses in Conflict (Square, Opposition, Quincunx) with Venus

Clashing concerns about comfort are likely. What the mother enjoys may be quite different from what the daughter finds pleasurable. The parent and child may end up at odds over money or the handling of the material world. Sometimes the mother's style is so different from the daughter's that the daughter is "on edge" or even physically uncomfortable in Mom's presence. Or, the daughter may perceive her mother as too passive, concerned with appearances, or self-indulgent.

With age and self-awareness, both the mother and daughter can reach healthy compromises. They can build a pleasing connection by looking for areas of agreement and finding ways to come together, particularly in regard to sensual satisfaction, aesthetic experiences, and the financial world.

Moon/Ceres/Planets in or Ruling 4th/10th Houses Conjunct Mars

Mother is an important role model for the daughter—but that can be positive or negative. If constructive, the daughter is likely to try to follow the mother's footsteps in some fashion, to imitate what she admires. If the role model is negative, the daughter will strive to do the opposite of what her mother does. The mother's behavior and attitudes are particularly influential in terms of issues around anger, assertion, the ability (and right) to go after what you want, and general physicality (dealing with sexual and bodily needs). Mother's attitudes about men (conscious and unconscious) are also likely to strongly affect the daughter.

The daughter may perceive Mom as strong, forceful, courageous, and pioneering—or rash, self-centered, angry, and impulsive. Because the daughter is also identifying with the nurturing (and dependent) role, she is likely to feel helpless or less capable with a superenergetic, go-getter mother. If the mother is weak or inadequate in some fashion, the daughter is apt to take on the role of caretaker, even at an early, inappropriate age—and probably resent it.

This combination suggests a mom with a "freedom-closeness dilemma"—a mom who is torn between establishing a nest and warm, supportive interactions versus doing her own thing. If she reacts with anger and resentment or by feeling trapped, that will strongly impact the daughter's attitudes toward domesticity. If the mother presents a healthy balance between pursuing her own needs, providing appropriate care and attention to loved ones, and asking for help and leaning on others when necessary, the daughter is more likely to learn how to move easily between independence, dependency, and nurturing.

Moon/Ceres/Planets in or Ruling 4th/10th Houses Sextile/Trine Mars

The mother (and/or family) may have fed and encouraged the daughter's independence. She might have received support for her energy, involvement in physical activities, willingness to break new ground, or forthright integrity. If this was overdone, the child might have been expected to exhibit independence and self-reliance from an inappropriately young age. Or, the daughter might have come to believe that an extreme focus on herself was entirely appropriate, either because Mom was very self-centered and did exactly what she wanted or because the family egged on the daughter in terms of pursuing personal desires.

When affection and awareness are present on both sides, the relationship is likely to include an element of excitement. The mother and daughter may feed each other's energy. Each encourages the other to be fully herself. The home may contain a high level of activity.

Moon/Ceres/Planets in or Ruling 4th/10th Houses in Conflict (Square, Opposition, Quincunx) with Mars

The daughter is likely to compare and contrast her own behavior and desires with her mother's. Mother provides an important measuring stick, particularly in regard to personal desires, assertive instincts, power, and integrity. In the worst cases, there can be physical violence within the home. In more mild situations, the daughter may feel that Mom is selfish and intent on doing what she wants. Competition and conflict could reign within the nest. In some cases, the mother and daughter simply have very different approaches in regard to sexuality, independence, and personal expression. In some instances, where the parent is a "Supermom," the daughter may feel inadequate compared to her high-energy, active mother. Even if the mother does not promote that viewpoint, the daughter may feel that she can never "keep up with" (or measure up to) her mother. (Naturally, this is tougher when the daughter is younger, before she has developed some of her own strengths and talents.)

With warmth, caring, and awareness on both sides, the mother and daughter can egg each other on. Each may energize the other. They may be physically active and affirm one another's independence, and each may be a strong advocate for the other to go after what she wants in the world.

Moon/Ceres/Planets in or Ruling 4th/10th Houses Conjunct Jupiter

Mother's worldview has a profound impact on the daughter. Mother is a role model (positive or negative) for optimism, faith, and trust in a Higher Power. On a positive level, Mother's example encouraged the daughter to develop a firm sense of trust in the Universe—that everything will work out, that the Greater Good wins in the end. Mother could have been intellectual, philosophical, religious, involved with higher education, from another culture or country, exploratory, or an advocate for expanded consciousness and far horizons.

On the negative side, the daughter may have experienced her mother as bombastic, a True Believer, or a follower of "the grass is greener" philosophy (over there is always perceived as better than right here, right now). Since Jupiter is one of the "God" planets, Mother could have taught a strong faith and belief in a Higher Power, or could have demanded impossibly high standards of the daughter (or of herself). This combination can indicate a daughter who idealized her mother and thought she was (almost) perfect, or a daughter who was frustrated because she wanted her mother to be perfect and her mother was a human being (and fallible). The mother's expectations for the daughter may, likewise, have been impossible to achieve.

Where the bonds of love are strong, this aspect will show a vibrancy and buoyancy to the mother-daughter relationship. They help each another feel "up," look for the silver lining, and make the most of their potentials. They may share a love of books, adventure, enlightenment, or anything that adds to meaning and excitement in life.

Moon/Ceres/Planets in or Ruling 4th/10th Houses Sextile/Trine Jupiter

This combination can represent an encouraging note between the mother and daughter. The mother may feed the daughter's confidence, optimism, and eagerness to reach out and embrace life. The fire essence of Jupiter is ever ready to go exploring, whether mentally, physically, or spiritually. The mother may encourage the daughter's intellectual hunger, spiritual curiosity, openness to other cultures, or general optimism and faith in bigger and better things in the future. Naturally, if this motif is carried too far, the phenomenon of "Fools rush in where angels fear to tread" can occur. The nest may feature reckless behavior, extravagance, exaggeration, and overdoing of all sorts. The attitude of "God is on my side" can lead to all kinds of unpleasant excesses.

In moderation, with two caring people involved, this "go for the gusto" attitude can be very helpful—a great antidote to depression or insecurity. When the mother and daughter are attuned, this aspect shows the potential for two people who believe strongly in one another, who "keep the faith" and have a zest for living. An upbeat, exploratory attitude can lead them along many different highways and byways (mentally, physically, and/or spiritually).

Moon/Ceres/Planets in or Ruling 4th/10th Houses in Conflict (Square, Opposition, Quincunx) with Jupiter

A clash of values is quite possible. The implication is that the mother and daughter are coming from different places in regard to religion, philosophy, moral and ethical principles, or their sense of adventure and wanderlust. Depending on other factors, the problem may be unrealistic expectations. Where Jupiter is involved, either the mother or daughter (or both) may want more than is humanly possible from each other (and from themselves). When the Infinite is your standard of comparison, human beings will never measure up! Sometimes the mother is too involved with religion, education, travel, adventures, or her own quest for meaning, and the daughter feels neglected. Sometimes the mother is overly protective and tries to quash the daughter's need to explore, to push beyond the boundaries, to go where no one has gone before (physically, emotionally or spiritually). Self-righteousness can be an issue on either side—or with both individuals.

When the two people care about each other, they can usually work things out. They may agree to disagree about certain philosophical issues. They can learn to moderate their high expectations. They can focus on building each other's confidence, spirit of adventure, and zest for life and new possibilities.

Moon/Ceres/Planets in or Ruling 4th/10th Houses Conjunct Saturn

This combination is another "mother-father" blend. On the mundane level, we can have one parent playing both roles due to death, divorce, etc. Or, we can have parents who share the roles, who are both able to be strong and responsible as well as warm and nurturing. Or, we can have a daughter who felt like she had to parent one or both of her own parents. (More than one of these mundane variations is possible.) The home is intensely focused on the balancing act between conditional and unconditional love.

Many people assume that the parents will overdo the conditional love—with harshness, strict rules, criticism, or too much need to dominate. The daughter may feel squelched. Her own competence can be derailed because parental attitudes keep assuring her that she is inadequate, useless, a failure, etc.

Although this first scenario is possible, it can also be the case that the parents overdo the unconditional love. They do too much for the child, even when she is old enough to develop her own abilities and take on more responsibility. This can also cripple an individual. When we don't get a chance to exercise our skills, we are less likely to develop them— or even believe that we possess those skills.

Sometimes the daughter faced early burdens and responsibilities. For example, she may have been part of a poor family where everyone had to work, or a family where a parent was missing, ill, or inadequate, so the daughter "stepped up to the plate" and tried to be strong and capable from a young age. Such a scenario would have helped her become competent, but would also have tended to encourage feelings of abandonment and raise significant trust issues. If you could not depend on your parents to be supportive and protective when you were very young, how could you depend on loved ones to look after you later in life? Such individuals may have major issues with learning to allow themselves to be dependent and learning to get involved with other people who will be supportive. The usual pattern is to be attracted to people who need assistance because the "stiff upper lip, I can take care of things" attitude is so ingrained from childhood. In truly destructive homes, the daughter was expected to shoulder excessive responsibilities at an inappropriately young age, but her efforts were also sabotaged with criticism and harsh judgments.

When affectionate ties are strong and the mother is relatively aware, the home can provide a healthy balance of conditional and unconditional love. The daughter is given warmth, security, protection, and caring when she is very young, and is able to develop that basic sense of trust. As she grows older, she is taught about limits, rules, boundaries, and respect for the rights of other people. She learns to deal with the consequences of her actions. With such an environment, the daughter will find it easier to balance caring compassion with the bottom line in her own life.

Moon/Ceres/Planets in or Ruling 4th/10th Houses Sextile/Trine Saturn

This shows the potential for a home in which conditional and unconditional love were well-balanced. The daughter could have been held, fed, caressed, and protected at a young age—given security and a sense of safety. As she grew older, she may have been gently taught about consequences, responsibility, and respecting the rights of others. Sometimes a work ethic (or family business) is shared with other loved ones. The parents may reinforce each other's caring and strength. Anything, however, can be overdone. If the maternal side of this combination is carried to an extreme, the daughter may be (consciously or unconsciously) encouraged to remain dependent, to feed a parental "need to be needed." If the paternal side of this combination is carried to an extreme, work, restriction, authority, control or power may be overdone by a parent, or the child may be expected to be practical and capable at too early an age—a miniature "adult."

Where parents are self-aware and the bonds of caring are strong, this combination points to enduring connections. Saturn meets the tests of time. Both the mother and daughter may feel that they are involved with one another for the long haul. Each may encourage the other's professional efforts. As the daughter matures, both of them can become quite adept at taking turns taking care of one another, each giving to the other in her own areas of strength and competence.

Moon/Ceres/Planets in or Ruling 4th/10th Houses in Conflict (Square, Opposition, Quincunx) with Saturn

Reality was probably underappreciated in the home. This can manifest in many different ways. Sometimes the mother had to (or wanted to) work, and the daughter felt neglected. (Naturally, daughters with more emotional, dependent, family-oriented charts are more likely to have that reaction than daughters with independent, adventurous horoscopes.) Perhaps the daughter felt that the home had too many restrictions and excessive criticism, or that her parent(s) were determined to dominate and control everything. Perhaps the daughter felt her mother was at odds with the laws of the land, the expectations of society, or what is generally accepted as conventional and appropriate behavior. In some way, the daughter was more sensitive to a lack of balance in the nest between conditional and unconditional love in her family of origin.

With work and attention, the mother and daughter can handle this combination well. They may literally learn to work together, getting involved with a family business or supporting one another's professional aspirations. They may labor long and hard to achieve a comfortable give-and-take in terms of nurturing. They may get "hands-on" experience or take practical courses to enhance their family-building skills. They can become oriented toward solving problems within the nest and building a solid, enduring bond with one another.

Moon/Ceres/Planets in or Ruling 4th/10th Houses Conjunct Uranus

Mother is different in some way, because of her personality or because of the manner in which she operates as a mother—or both. Depending on the daughter's preferences and inclinations, this can be a source of joy, pride, and freedom—or a source of frustration, embarrassment, and insecurity.

Mother may be freewheeling, very independent, and unconventional. Depending on the daughter's horoscope and personality, that can encourage the daughter to find her own individuality, to break the rules, to march to a different drummer—or the daughter could feel her home lacked stability, her mother was erratic and unpredictable, or her mother was too into her own thing to provide important nurturing.

This combination implies a mother with an intense freedom-closeness issue around nurturing. When she is in a domestic setting, she may feel claustrophobic or trapped. Or, her focus within the family is on being independent, different, or getting away. Perhaps the mother is too involved with social activities, humanitarian causes, or other transpersonal issues to give sufficient attention to her family. When the mother is able to handle these drives positively, she encourages the daughter to find her own unique essence. The mother demonstrates, through example, that one can very much be one's own person and still a warm, loving, and supportive individual. When this combination is done well, the mother can be the daughter's best friend.

Moon/Ceres/Planets in or Ruling 4th/10th Houses Sextile/Trine Uranus

Seeming contradictions are possible with this combination: safe excitement, warm independence, unusual familiarity, and freedom-loving protection. The mother and daughter are learning together how to balance the quest for warm, loving, caring connections with the need to push the limits, be different, break the rules, and foster progress and change. If they don't quite manage this, they could feel torn between security and risk-taking, between a familiar (and familial) setting and the new and different, between the ties of blood and the ties of friendship and like interests, etc.

The best potential manifestation of this combination is a mother and daughter who cherish, support, and nurture one another's individualistic urges. They are warm and tender toward each other's need to do things a bit differently, to find a unique path in the world.

Moon/Ceres/Planets in or Ruling 4th/10th Houses in Conflict (Square, Opposition, Quincunx) with Uranus

The balancing act between having a secure nest and being independent is in focus. The challenge is to love with an open hand, without possessiveness. If the mother overdoes the maternal instincts, the daughter could feel confined, trapped, or smothered, or could feel that her individuality is dissed and dismissed. Rebellious urges may grow. The daughter might feel that she would have to run away in order to be herself. If the mother overdoes the accent on revolution and independence, she may be gone too much (saving the whales instead of looking after the family, at the club instead of at home, etc.), or she may come across as flaky, erratic, unpredictable, or even crazy. The daughter may have trouble figuring out her mother; the daughter just "doesn't get it," cannot find a pattern.

When the mother and daughter share a loving bond and commit to working things out, they find ways to move comfortably between an accent on warmth, sharing, and security and a love of freedom, risk-taking, excitement, and new experiences. They incorporate much open-mindedness and tolerance into their family relationships. They learn to prize their differences and enjoy the enlarged perspectives they gain by interacting when their viewpoints are quite dissimilar.

Moon/Ceres/Planets in or Ruling 4th/10th Houses Conjunct Neptune

Sensitivity reigns supreme. Both the mother and daughter are more psychically open than the average individual. They are more affected by the "vibes"—by the moods and ailments of those around them. Creating a sanctuary within the nest is extra-important: a serene, lovely environment where both of them can retreat, where they can escape from the hustle and (sometimes) negativity of the outer world and other people. They need more privacy than most people.

The daughter is very attuned to the mother's dreams. On the positive level, Mother could be artistic, compassionate, idealistic, and very involved with helping or healing activities. The mother's mystical, religious, or spiritual side could strongly impact the daughter. They may share an inspirational bent.

On the negative side, the mother may unconsciously expect (and script) her daughter to live out her unrealized dreams. The mother may be an escapist—someone with a problem with drugs, alcohol, fantasy, illness, etc.

Neptune is another "God" planet, so unrealistic expectations can be a problem on either (or both) sides. Mother may expect herself to be all-loving and all-giving, and to sacrifice for the sake of others—and may give the daughter strong messages about the appropriate feminine role being sacrificial. Mother may look to the daughter to make everything perfect for her, and be disappointed when she cannot. The daughter may expect the mother to be sweet, saintly, and perfect, and feel disillusioned and disappointed when she proves to be only human. Fantasy and illusion (or deception) may reign within the nest.

Having a spiritual connection can help. If both the mother and child look to a Higher Power (or nature or beauty) for experiences of perfection, they need not demand so much of themselves or of each other. They can use their visualization skills to envision possibilities and work toward manifesting them—but not expect "Heaven on Earth." They can soothe, succor, heal, and help themselves and other people, but know where to set the boundaries and how to protect themselves. They can use their sensitivity to empathize and tune in to others—but learn how to get rid of what they pick up from other people and how to cleanse their psyches and get the alone time that allows them to recoup and refresh their bodies and souls.

Moon/Ceres/Planets in or Ruling 4th/10th Houses Sextile/Trine Neptune

Seeking an ideal is connected to domesticity. The mother and daughter may work together to make the home more lovely or to assist the less fortunate in their community. Shared compassion could be a bond. Either may reinforce and aid the artistic or aesthetic inclinations of the other. A joint dream is likely to inspire them both. If these motifs are carried too far, family members may expect perfection from each other. They could feel disappointed and disillusioned that their loved ones are less than ideal. Or, unrealistic fantasies could be held about what being a family means or how families interact.

Often, these combinations point to a mother and daughter who can easily focus on the good points in the other. They concentrate on the highest potential for family members, and do their utmost to foster it. Forgiveness and empathy are very evident. Compassion and a willingness to assist others are highlighted.

Moon/Ceres/Planets in or Ruling 4th/10th Houses in Conflict (Square, Opposition, Quincunx) with Neptune

A good fantasy can have strong appeal. These combinations suggest that Mom has problems with her daughter's imagination, and/or that the daughter is uncomfortable with Mom's quest for "happily ever after." It might be that either the mother or daughter (or both) have challenges around drugs, alcohol, fantasy, or any kind of chronic, escapist behavior. Running away could have more appeal than facing the facts of life. It could be that either party is prone to lies, evasion, and avoidance behavior. "Playing pretend" may appeal to them. The true family history may be far from the story that is presented to the world. The mother or daughter may feel that the other is too available to help and heal "outsiders" and not available enough to family members. In extremes, either can feel "invisible" to the other.

With caring and commitment between the mother and daughter, these motifs can be directed constructively. The two people may share a dream—a spiritual or religious perspective, idealistic pursuits, healing activities, aesthetic interests, or anything with an element of inspiration or transcendence.

Moon/Ceres/Planets in or Ruling 4th/10th Houses Conjunct Pluto

Power issues are highlighted in this relationship. Mother's influence is extrasignificant in regard to the daughter's handling of issues of sexuality, shared resources, intimacy, intense emotions, control, and self-mastery. A mother who provides a positive Plutonian example is psychologically aware, able to use power constructively and wisely (including for self-control rather than trying to use or abuse others), and comfortable with merging body, soul, money, and possessions with a mate. She demonstrates concentration, focus, and determined perseverance to her daughter. As adults, the mother and daughter are likely to maintain a strong emotional bond and may share money and resources. Maternal inheritance is possible.

A mother who provides a negative Plutonian example can do so in several ways. She may be an agent provocateur, stirring up trouble between people, inciting riots and problems. She may be a master at manipulation, intimidation, or emotional blackmail (martyr syndrome, tears, suicide threats, etc.). She could be quite passive-aggressive or inclined to use back-door strategies and underhanded moves. She could have a penchant for secrets and scandals. She might do lots of blaming and shaming of her child(ren). In extremes, physical violence is possible. In more mild variations, the mother does not respect appropriate boundaries and often invades her daughter's space (from physical intrusions, to reading her child's diary, searching her room, etc.).

Sometimes the mother comes across as superpowerful, intimidating, and scary. Sometimes she comes across as dependent on others, especially on men or a mate, particularly in regard to sexuality or money. She may try to rule through strength (direct confrontations and power plays) or weakness (dependency and emotional manipulation).

The all-or-nothing motifs connected to Pluto mean that this relationship tends to be either very good or quite awful. Even if it starts on a negative note, however, the mother and daughter can achieve greater understanding and insight. This relationship can be a catalyst for going within, searching one's psyche, and learning about one's deepest motives. The mother and daughter can develop more self-control and learn the art of transforming negative emotions into positive ones and eliminating bad habits. This can be a bond that helps both family members discover and enhance hidden strengths, rise to challenges, and persevere even through the toughest of times.

Moon/Ceres/Planets in or Ruling 4th/10th Houses Sextile/Trine Pluto

Mom and daughter may be allies. These combinations can indicate a mother-daughter team, two people who depend on one another for emotional (and sometimes financial) support. Each may view the other as a strong bulwark against stress. The mother may have encouraged the daughter to look within and understand herself. Mom could have demonstrated guts, focus, determination, self-mastery, and the ability to share the emotional and physical world with an intimate partner. The mother might have encouraged the daughter to become stronger and more forceful, and to develop her capacity to transform lemons into lemonade (negatives into positives).

Sometimes the Pluto motifs are overdone and there can be problems with power struggles, manipulation, hidden agendas, or too much dependency on a mate. Obsessions or compulsive behavior involving appetites are possible, particularly in regard to sex and money. Often, however, both individuals are oriented toward understanding themselves and others on the deepest level, controlling their appetites (without extremes of asceticism), and creating and maintaining a healthy, intimate partnership with another person.

Moon/Ceres/Planets in or Ruling 4th/10th Houses in Conflict (Square, Opposition, Quincunx) with Pluto

Questions of control could arise. When the "power planets" (Sun, Mars, Saturn, and Pluto) are involved with parental keys, the wise and appropriate use of power is often a challenge. Parents have more than ordinary power over their children and must be judicious in their wielding of it, and sensible in the ways in which they train their children to develop inner strength and to begin to own their own power.

Where the mother falls short in these combinations, she may be abusing power. In extremes, sexual or physical abuse in the home is possible. In more mild variations, the mother ignores the daughter's rights to privacy and is "in her face"—physically, psychologically, and in terms of boundaries in the home. The mother may read the daughter's private correspondence, for example. The mother may attempt to control the daughter's sexuality, or use money as a weapon. (The daughter may "flaunt" her sexuality as a way to get revenge on the mother and hoard or keep secrets about possessions in order to thwart the mother.) Convoluted interchanges are quite possible. Both the mother and daughter may use indirect (passive-aggressive) approaches rather than come out in the open about what they want. Seemingly minor issues can become major battlegrounds. A "take no prisoners" style can be overdone by either the mother or daughter, or both.

With psychological awareness (a potential of positive Pluto motifs), the mother will encourage insight and self-examination within the daughter as well as herself. Both can learn to look beneath the surface of life, to analyze motives and emotions, and to practice becoming comfortable with giving, receiving, and sharing in regard to the sensual, sexual, and financial worlds. When this level of commitment and caring is present, the mother and daughter build a deep, soul-satisfying connection.

Moon/Ceres/Planets in or Ruling 4th/10th Houses Conjunct Ceres

This can be a strong maternal focus in the horoscope—a sort of "double mother" emphasis. It may add to the matriarchal feeling within a chart. The mother could be quite warm and supportive as well as practical and hardworking. The daughter may also have a maternal streak, an urge to look after others with both emotional assistance and practical aid. A family business is possible. The mother may work outside the home as well as inside, or be a role model for productivity, problem-solving, and efficiency instincts. Often, the mother has a strong interest in nutrition, alternative health practices, or other areas that contribute to maintaining a healthy body.

If these motifs are carried too far, the daughter may feel overwhelmed by a "Super-mom" who seems to do everything well. She might admire her mother, but feel she can never measure up to that standard. Or, the practical aspects of these combinations may overwhelm the emotional aspects and the daughter experiences the mother as too busy at work, taking care of others, solving problems, or being critical. If the daughter is very strong, the mother may express the dependency potentials of the Moon (or 4th house) and expect the daughter to take care of her (parenting one's own parent).

A family focus is likely. This reinforces nesting motifs within the horoscope, so having a home and domestic life is usually important to the daughter. When the bond is strong and positive, the daughter—like the mother—will demonstrate a good balance between warmth and efficiency.

Moon/Ceres/Planets in or Ruling 4th/10th Houses Sextile/Trine Ceres

A multifaceted mom is possible. These combinations can point to a mother who is able to combine emotional warmth, compassion, and support with practical problem-solving and efficiency. She is probably good at managing the everyday details of maintaining a home (nutritious meals, logistics for chores, coordinating family functions) as well as demonstrating much love and caring.

If either side of this combination is overdone, there could be an imbalance in the home. The mother figure might succumb to emotional neediness, too caught up in feelings and the seeking of safety. Or, the mother figure might rely excessively on logic, common sense, and flaw-finding (in order to fix things and make them better).

On the positive side, this can indicate a family that pulls together, is mutually supportive, and may even work together (e.g., family business). Support is provided on both the practical and emotional levels. The mother and daughter may take turns taking care of one another in age-appropriate ways.

Moon/Ceres/Planets in or Ruling 4th/10th Houses in Conflict (Square, Opposition, Quincunx) with Ceres

These combinations suggest conflicting urges in regard to nurturing. Sometimes other people (e.g., grandmother, sibling, aunt, father, etc.) are involved with the caretaking and providing emotional support, and there may be differences of opinion between two mother figures. Sometimes Mother is internally torn. She may be unsure how to balance the practical demands of child raising with the emotional needs of her child(ren). She might overdo the focus on matters such as nutrition, care of the body, problem-solving, etc., or she might be too caught up with issues of protection, security, and emotional connections. Sometimes there is a weak or inadequate parent, and the child is expected (or feels that she must) provide protection and caretaking for the parent.

With caring and awareness on both sides, this can point to a strong maternal figure. The mother can be both warm and practical, helping the daughter develop a sense of trust and reassurance ("I will be taken care of") as well as teaching her to cope with the material world effectively. Mother may have a strong work ethic and demonstrate pragmatism as well as strong family feelings.

Moon/Ceres/Planets in or Ruling 4th/10th Houses Conjunct Pallas

Mother is tied to balance, harmony, beauty, and equality. This can indicate a mother (figure) who is literally an artist or involved with aesthetic activities. It can point to a mother who is concerned with issues of social justice, humanitarian causes, or equal opportunity. The mother may be very involved with relationships (marriage quite important or working in a field such as law, counseling, personnel, etc.). The mother may treat her daughter like a partner, encouraging communication, openness, and sharing. When positive interactions predominate, the mother and daughter may be partners into adulthood, staying in touch and regularly interacting with one another.

Less constructively, the mother could compete with the daughter. Obviously, the younger the daughter is when this occurs, the less chance that the playing field is equal. The mother may be too wrapped up in relationships (or a single relationship, such as her marriage) so that the daughter feels shortchanged. The mother could be too caught up with outside social or political activities and the daughter feels neglected. The weighing and balancing function could be carried too far. The daughter may perceive her mother as vacillating, hypocritical, fence-sitting, too inclined to compromise, or overly concerned with appearances and "looking good" in the eyes of others.

With caring on both sides, the odds are high for a good partnership. The mother and daughter may enjoy doing things together and spend time with one another even after the daughter has become an adult. They are likely to spark each other's ideas and enjoy talking things over. They may be advocates for one another, each encouraging the other to pursue fairness within her life. They may share a love of beauty or passion for justice.

Moon/Ceres/Planets in or Ruling 4th/10th Houses Sextile/Trine Pallas

Comfortable interactions are quite possible. The mother may have encouraged her daughter to learn, discuss ideas, and reach agreement with those around her. The mother may have enhanced the daughter's negotiating skills or artistic/aesthetic ability. The daughter's passion for justice and desire for equality could have been reinforced by her mom. The family may have emphasized communication, awareness, understanding, and sharing.

On the negative side, any of these qualities could be carried to an extreme. The weighing and balancing of ideas and facts can turn into fence-sitting or the avoidance of taking decisive action. A logical emphasis can transform into overly intellectual exchanges or rationalizing away feelings. Artistic inclinations could be allowed to dominate and interfere with other important activities. A concern with justice and fair play could turn into competition and confrontations.

More commonly, these combinations suggest that the mother and daughter could find a meeting of the minds. They can usually find common ground in regard to beauty, balance, harmony, or the urge to learn and understand.

Moon/Ceres/Planets in or Ruling 4th/10th Houses in Conflict (Square, Opposition, Quincunx) with Pallas

The degree of closeness in this relationship is in question. The mother (figure) may feel torn between a very absorbing, emotionally bonding connection and a more detached, airy association. She might vacillate between being very protective and maternal versus expecting her daughter to operate somewhat as an equal and manage on her own. Or, the mother's ideas about relationships and equality could clash with the daughter's. If this is unresolved, the mother may end up at odds with the romantic partner the daughter chooses as an adult. The perspectives of the mother and daughter could be quite far apart.

If both individuals can remain open-minded and objective, the possibilities for learning and growth are excellent. Each can broaden her own understanding of justice, fair play, equality, communication, and comfortable relationships by listening to the feedback of the other person. Each can learn to move comfortably between the roles of dependent, equal partner, and nurturer, taking turns with loved ones as appropriate.

Moon/Ceres/Planets in or Ruling 4th/10th Houses Conjunct Juno

The potential of Mom as an emotionally close partner is present. On the positive side, the mother and daughter have a strong, enduring bond. They are likely to be psychologically open to one another. They may sometimes seem to read each other's hearts, understanding one another's motivations without words. They may have a partnership, even as adults, where they maintain regular contact. (Even this can go too far. If the intimate bond with the mother is too powerful, it may discourage the daughter from entering romantic partnerships.)

On the negative side, there can be issues of privacy and control. Mother may be overly intrusive (physically, emotionally, mentally). She may unconsciously see the two of them as "one" person—and, of course, that "one" is her! She may discount and undercut the daughter's quest for individuality and separate interests. Mother may use (and daughter may learn) power plays, manipulation, emotional blackmail, and covert strategies to get her way. Blaming and shaming could be prevalent within the home.

The mother's example regarding partnership, emotional and physical intimacy, and shared resources has a profound impact on the daughter's functioning in these areas. Sometimes the mother is too dependent—overly invested in her marriage or a partnership. Sometimes the mother has major issues around addiction—to money, sex, alcohol, etc. It is easiest for the daughter to learn from a positive example: giving, receiving, and sharing equally of the sensual, sexual, and financial worlds with a beloved mate. However, the daughter can also learn from a negative example: power struggles, passive-aggressive moves, etc.

The best potential manifestation of these combinations is an intense, committed connection between the mother and daughter that fulfills some of their needs for a deep, emotional bond and encourages them to share the physical world with others.

Moon/Ceres/Planets in or Ruling 4th/10th Houses Sextile/Trine Juno

The importance of loyalty and emotional bonds is highlighted. All these factors emphasize merging—a sense of connection or union with another person. The major issue to resolve is when that merging should be between a more dependent individual and a nurturer/protector, and when it should be between two equal partners. Obviously, in regard to mother-daughter exchanges, the former prevails when the child is young, and the two move toward equality as the daughter grows older.

If this balance is out of whack, the mother may expect equality from the daughter at too young an age, or try to keep the daughter dependent past the appropriate time. Loyalty to family can be overemphasized. Revealing "secrets" or letting outsiders in on certain information may be viewed as a "betrayal." Bonds could be made overly sticky with emotional blackmail or other manipulations.

With mutual caring, this can be a lovely connection with the mother and daughter finding it easy to share with one another. The mother may get along well with the daughter's choice of a life partner. The mother reinforces and supports the daughter's urge to be an equal and find a significant other. Both the mother and daughter appreciate the importance of emotional ties and spend time and effort in understanding each other and deepening their connections with loved ones.

Moon/Ceres/Planets in or Ruling 4th/10th Houses in Conflict (Square, Opposition, Quincunx) with Juno

Clashing ideas about intimacy may exist within the home. The mother and daughter may disagree about sexual issues, financial matters, or appropriate behavior in bonded relationships. Where these clashes are unresolved, the mother may end up at odds with the intimate partner (marriage, living together, etc.) of the daughter's choice. Power issues are likely to exist, and either party may use direct confrontation or manipulation and covert strategies to try to get her way. Hidden agendas are likely to abound. Both the mother and daughter may not be fully conscious of some of the issues they are trying to resolve. An urge to merge is present, but there can be tension between the loyalty one is supposed to feel toward one's family of origin versus the loyalty one owes a beloved partner.

When both people are willing to look beneath the surface and strive for deeper understanding, the capacity for an excellent relationship exists. Each can learn—through interactions with the other—to see her own motives and drives more clearly. They can master the art of compromise and practice giving and receiving from one other with comfort and ease (and eschewing power struggles and manipulation). In such cases, loyalty is heartfelt and the mother-daughter relationship is lasting and significant.

Moon/Ceres/Planets in or Ruling 4th/10th Houses Conjunct Vesta

Mom is linked to work in the daughter's eyes. This can be constructive in terms of a mother who works outside the home as well as within. (If overdone, the daughter may resent the time that job requires, feeling neglected because of vocational demands.) This combination can indicate a mother who has a strong work ethic and sets an example of practicality, dedication, and problem-solving for the daughter. Sometimes the mother is quite interested in nutrition, vitamins, and health and healing, and also encourages the daughter to focus on maintaining a healthy body. A family business is possible.

On the negative side, the work attitude can be a problem. Flaw-finding and criticism may be overdone—from the mother toward the daughter, from the daughter toward the mother, or both. Nitpicking could also be overdone in the relationship. In extreme cases, the daughter feels emotionally alienated from the mother ("I could never please her, no matter what I did"). Sometimes the mother is ill (or inadequate), and the daughter has to work hard within the home to make up for that. What should be a childhood with some support becomes a home filled with harsh judgments or excessive labor. Children may be viewed mostly as worker bees.

With sensitivity and a willingness to work things out, both parties can create a constructive focus. They may labor together on projects, directing the flaw-finding tendency toward the physical world rather than toward one another. They may put much time and energy into improving their relationship. An ability to face facts can help them fix what needs to be enhanced or downplayed.

Moon/Ceres/Planets in or Ruling 4th/10th Houses Sextile/Trine Vesta

This can be a home in which everyone worked together. Shared labors are possible (including a family business). Mother probably encouraged the daughter to develop a good work ethic, practical skills, and/or an interest in health and healing. Everyone may have chipped in to get things done within the domestic environment.

If the maternal motifs were overdone, the mother may have done too much for the daughter, crippling the daughter's competence because Mom always did things for her. Or, the mother may have overdone the critical judgment and flaw-finding, again negatively impacting the daughter's confidence and self-esteem. Work had to be done Mother's way. Work might have been given too much importance and the daughter felt she had value in the eyes of her family only for what she could do, not for who she was. Sometimes the mother is too invested in her outside accomplishments, and the daughter feels emotionally deprived.

When well integrated, these combinations point to mother-daughter relationships in which warmth and productivity are well-balanced. Both people feel a sense of safety and security (and are willing to ask for help if needed), and both people have the discipline and dedication to carry their fair share of the load. They find satisfaction in doing a good job and in strengthening their emotional bonds.

Moon/Ceres/Planets in or Ruling 4th/10th Houses in Conflict (Square, Opposition, Quincunx) with Vesta

There is a potential clash between home and work. This can indicate that the mother feels torn between her job (whether out in the world, community service, etc.) and her role as a nurturer. Or, perhaps the daughter resents the time that Mother devotes to work, practical projects, healthy interests, or her urge to be productive. If this remains unresolved, the daughter may feel she has to "choose" (when older) between family/children and work. Or, the daughter may constantly feel pressure (or guilt) about dividing her time and energy between loved ones who depend on her and her contribution to society. Sometimes the work attitude is the problem. The mother may be difficult to please and prone to finding fault with the daughter. The daughter may also tend to see what is wrong with Mom, rather than what is right. If these issues remain a problem, either individual may unconsciously succumb to illness as a way to escape frustrating work, or to avoid feeling guilty, or as a path to getting the nurturing that she feels she needs.

The key to positive expression is a comfortable "marriage" between the warm, nurturing motifs and the practical, efficient motifs. Both the mother and daughter can learn to be caring and supportive as well as pragmatic and effective. They can make room in their lives for both a family and a job (or career)—and not feel guilty about the fact that they cannot do it all (there are only twenty-four hours in each day). They can learn to ask for help and to share the load with others.

Moon/Ceres/Planets in or Ruling 4th/10th Houses Conjunct Chiron

The questing motif is mixed with maternal urges in these cases. On the positive side, Mother could be bright, a visionary, and motivated to seek higher meaning from life. She might be idealistic, spiritual, or caught up with inspirational activities. She is likely to have high standards for herself as a mother (and perhaps for her daughter as well). She may embody a restless, seeking, searching urge—helping her daughter see life as an adventure, and that the quest for Truth is paramount. The daughter may idealize her mom, seeing her as someone who expresses her best and her brightest in many ways.

On the negative side, either individual may expect more than is humanly possible from the other and feel disappointed (and wounded) when let down. The daughter may feel that her mother is too caught up with educational, spiritual, humanitarian, cultural, or other pursuits and does not pay enough attention to family matters.

When the mother and daughter seek the best together, the results can be quite positive. They may join forces in regard to spiritual, educational, or idealistic pursuits. A shared faith and confidence in a Higher Power can provide energy and motivation to make their lives and the world a bit better.

Moon/Ceres/Planets in or Ruling 4th/10th Houses Sextile/Trine Chiron

The mother may have strengthened and encouraged the daughter's faith, idealism, interest in education or other cultures, intellectual aspirations, or restless seeking and searching for the meaning of life. The mother and daughter might share an interest in healing, or an emphasis on moral and ethical behavior, or an adventurous curiosity about what lies "out there" beyond the beaten track. They may feed one another's spiritual hunger and urge to understand life's meaning. They may find it easy to see—and reinforce—the best in each other.

If these motifs are overdone, either the mother or daughter (or both) may be too restless, perfectionistic, or caught up in the search for something "more" (and fail to appreciate the "now"). They could feel torn between security and risk-taking, between roots and exploration. Expectations for family members may be too high.

These combinations can manifest as noticing and strengthening the highest potentials in one another. Each can be a source of confidence and inspiration for the other. Shared values and ideals can provide strength and motivation.

Moon/Ceres/Planets in or Ruling 4th/10th Houses in Conflict (Square, Opposition, Quincunx) with Chiron

High hopes can sometimes be a problem. The search for an ideal may get out of hand in this family. The mother may expect too much from herself (know all the right answers, always do the best thing) or from her daughter. The daughter may look for perfection in her mother and be disappointed with human fallibility. The two may clash in regard to moral or ethical issues, religious or spiritual principles, or long-range goals in life. Differing versions of "The Truth" could lead to conflicts. Health problems in either individual may require patience and extra support from the other.

If the mother and daughter can combine their visionary instincts, a happy ending is possible. They can look for ways to make a more perfect world, rather than either expecting the other to make "Heaven on Earth" for her. They can seek out and create common ground in terms of educational interests, travel, inspirational activities, or anything that adds to their sense of life's meaning and purpose. They can train themselves to focus on the best in each other (and themselves) without demanding perfection, and to strengthen their highest potentials.

Moon/Ceres/Planets in or Ruling 4th/10th Houses Conjunct the South Node

The emotional roots are deep with this combination. (Some would say the mother and daughter have strong links from past lives.) Issues of dependency and nurturing are highlighted. Sometimes it appears that the mother's style of caretaking does not seem to fit the daughter's style of receiving. The nurturing does not "get through" or really seem to sink in for the daughter. Feelings of insecurity may exist on both sides. The daughter has trouble developing that basic trust and the mother feels insecure about her nurturing role, unsure if she is doing things right. (Some past-life theories suggest that the daughter is triggering old pains within the mom—perhaps loss of children in past lives, death in childbirth or other difficult circumstances. Sometimes it seems that the mother and daughter have switched roles in this lifetime and neither is comfortable in the new roles.)

Mother may be overprotective or too dependent. The mother and daughter are likely to be unconsciously linked, so sometimes they may respond to each other's feelings without being fully aware of what is in the mix. This is another instance of a doubling-up of the mother-child motifs. If the mother is too nurturing and maternal, she may (perhaps unconsciously) cripple the child's confidence and competence (because Mom is doing too much). The caretaking from the mother to the daughter may last into the adulthood of the daughter. If the mother is too dependent and needy, the child is expected to mother her own mother and has to deal with issues of emotional abandonment and trouble trusting in future relationships. Dependency becomes a threat (because she was let down when very young). It is also possible that Mom might swing from one extreme to the other and daughter has to deal with the seesaw.

Because the tendrils of connection run deeply beneath the surface, the mother and daughter have the potential to build a strong, enduring, positive bond. Using their sensitivity, they can work toward greater understanding and establish a relationship of mutuality and interdependence. They can be supportive and take turns looking after one another as adults.

Moon/Ceres/Planets in or Ruling 4th/10th Houses Conjunct the North Node

These combinations double up the maternal emphasis, so the "baby-mother" interchange is extra-important. When positively expressed, the mother-daughter bond is extra strong. They are likely to be intuitively attuned to each other. They may feel each other's feelings. The need for family is probably strong. In a healthy relationship, the mother provides warmth, security, protection, and emotional reassurance when the daughter is young. As she gets older, the daughter is encouraged to develop her own skills at caretaking, to learn to provide comfort and caring for loved ones.

If any of the motifs are overdone, they can become uncomfortable. Mother may be too invested in the role of guardian and protector and unconsciously maneuver her daughter to remain dependent on her. The mother may feel insecure, inadequate, or helpless and expect her daughter to look after her (parent her own parent). Lack of good emotional boundaries can result in confusion around who is feeling what, and what each person's rights are in this relationship. The mother and daughter may swing between too much dependency and too much nurturing.

When the warmth and caring are put to good use, the mother and daughter have a lasting, strong connection. They are empathic and tender toward one another and the rest of the world. They have learned to move smoothly between the dependent role (able to ask for help when needed) and the role of protector. They cherish family feelings and emotional bonds.

Moon/Ceres/Planets in or Ruling 4th/10th Houses Sextile/Trine the Nodes

Emotional connections have more weight within the home. Issues of protection, security, and assistance are highlighted. It is quite possible that Mother is skilled at both looking after loved ones (with warmth and support) and at being dependent and vulnerable when appropriate (able to receive as well as to give). The mother may encourage her daughter to develop strong bonds of trust and caring—within the family and eventually within a committed partnership as well.

If these motifs are carried to an extreme, family feelings may go too far. Loyalty to the family may be expected to outweigh anything else, even later love relationships. Dependency may be fostered in the daughter (crippling her competence) or overdone by the mother (leading to a daughter who has to "grow up too soon" and look after her own mom). Maternal inclinations can be smothering.

Because much warmth and caring are possible, these combinations can be quite positive and mutually supportive. The daughter and mother both cherish family connections and continue to strengthen them. Both develop good maternal skills, but also know when to ask for assistance or allow others to help out. The ties of blood are a security blanket.

Moon/Ceres/Planets in or Ruling 4th/10th Houses in Conflict (Square, Quincunx) with the Nodes

Conflicts around intimacy and dependency are likely. Sometimes, the mother is torn about the best way to nurture, unsure of her mothering role. Sometimes there is more than one nurturing figure and they have clashes. Or, maybe the mother is very identified with a "need to be needed" and encourages dependency in her daughter. The mother may even (unconsciously) try to sabotage the daughter's romantic partnerships in order to keep the mother-daughter bond paramount. Where the mother is too insecure or inadequate, the daughter may be expected to provide the nurturing and reassurance to an emotionally needy and immature parent. In some cases, the mother is constantly seesawing between too much dependency and too much maternal protection. Feelings tend to be strong and gaining clarity and objectivity may be a challenge.

For positive outcomes, the mother and daughter need to use the empathy and caring inherent in these combinations. They can focus on understanding their emotional reactions and learning to balance the polarities. They learn appropriate times and places to lean on others and when to be the supportive partner in a relationship. They appreciate the importance of family and the security available in having loyal, dependable loved ones.

Moon/Ceres/Planets Ruling 4th/10th Houses Conjunct the Ascendant

Mother is an important role model. The daughter's sense of personal power, assertion, and entitlement is strongly affected by the example of her mother. With affection and admiration, the daughter will imitate the mother's behavior. If the two clash, the daughter is likely to take Mom as a negative role model and do the opposite of what Mom does.

The mother may be strong, forceful, and intent on getting what she wants. She could be quite physical, self-centered, or full of initiative. Mother's example is important in how the daughter learns to cope with anger, personal desires, and courage. The daughter is identified with a nurturing role. She is likely to try to take care of things, pets, or people, even from a young age. If the mother is inadequate or too focused on her own needs, she may aid and abet the daughter's caretaking instincts, and the daughter could end up parenting her own parent.

The daughter will be dealing with freedom-closeness issues around the home. She is apt to feel torn between doing her own thing and looking after others. Some people take the role of nurturing only on their own terms, e.g., the single parent or the individual who chooses to limit her family in order to preserve her own independence, etc. Some individuals feel strongest and most assertive within a domestic environment.

The daughter's behavior and sense of identity are strongly linked to her experience of her mother (figure). The more constructive and positive that is, the better the daughter feels about herself, the more easily she pursues her desires, and the more comfortable she is in moving between dependency, nurturing, and independence.

Moon/Ceres/Planets Ruling 4th/10th Houses Conjunct the Descendant

Mother is an important role model in relationships. Many times, strong bonds of affection exist and the mother and daughter cooperate with one another and continue as partners into the daughter's adulthood. The daughter may have regular, ongoing contact with her mom. The mother's attitudes about equality, sharing, teamwork, beauty, and appearances will have a strong impact on the daughter's actions in those areas. A lot of comparing and contrasting with each other is likely. In negative cases, the mother and daughter may compete with one another, or they may learn when to compete and when to cooperate through games or sports.

When the mother-daughter bonds are too strong, that can unconsciously handicap the potential of other (e.g., romantic) relationships. The daughter may get so much of her sharing and caring needs met through her mother that she is less motivated to seek other relationships. Or, the mother may unconsciously sabotage the daughter's forays into marriage and committed partnership, or set a script that family needs outweigh love relationships.

The daughter is likely to "marry Mom"—to unconsciously be attracted to partners who push the same emotional buttons as her mother did. So, she and her romantic partner will get to face again (and try to master and resolve) issues around emotional support, who nurtures whom, what family means, security, protection, and abandonment. If the daughter was expected to look after the mother, she is likely to continue a habit pattern of choosing potential partners who need assistance. If the mother was critical, later partners are likely to find fault with the daughter. And so on, until we learn better.

Once these motifs are integrated, the daughter can take turns with partners—caring and being cared for—with a healthy balance between being the nurturer and being vulnerable and open to support from other people. She can see her mother as an equal and seek out ways to operate as a team. The mother and daughter may find common ground through family activities, aesthetic interests, or an agreement about the importance of fair play and sharing.

Moon/Ceres/Planets in or Ruling 4th/10th Houses Sextile/Trine the Ascendant/Descendant

The potential is excellent for harmony between the mother and daughter. This can manifest as the daughter feeling that Mom was supportive of who the daughter is—her identity is affirmed by Mother's actions. Mom may have encouraged her daughter to be strong, assertive, independent, and able to define and pursue her personal desires. Family members may easily move between leaning on one another and doing their own thing.

If these motifs are overdone, the mother might have fostered a self-centered focus within the daughter. She might have done so much for the child, that her daughter felt a "divine right" or sense of entitlement—that life owed her satisfaction. Or, the mother may have encouraged the daughter to go overboard in terms of nurturing activities. Perhaps the daughter was expected to look after domestic duties that really were the mother's bailiwick.

With these combinations the odds are good for affection between the mother and daughter. They can focus on what they like about each other and affirm one another's individual needs. A good balance can be reached between warm, supportive activities and being independent and assertive.

Moon/Ceres/Planets in or Ruling 4th/10th Houses in Conflict (Square, Quincunx) with the Ascendant/Descendant

Disagreements between the mother and daughter are possible. With the separative aspects (opposition and quincunx), if these motifs are repeated in other ways in the horoscope, the daughter may be separated from the mother—sometimes literally losing her mom, or just feeling emotionally that she cannot connect or that Mother is unavailable or off doing something else. The daughter may feel that her mother did not (or could not) meet her basic needs, particularly in terms of issues of independence, assertion, and the right to go after what you want in the world. Sometimes the daughter feels that her mother cannot accept who she really is. When the estrangement is severe, the daughter may reject the notion of a family or domestic life along with her rejection of her mother (or her perception that her mother rejected or abandoned her).

Family demands may compete with the daughter's desires. This could indicate that the mother opposed the daughter's preferences, or that the daughter was expected to take on too many domestic duties rather than pursue her own interests. The daughter is likely to get more understanding of herself by contrasting her identity and behavior with her mother's; that is, by focusing on how she and her mother differ, the daughter gets a better sense of who she is and what she wants. Where other supportive factors are involved, this may not be negative at all. The daughter just gains self-awareness by focusing on the differences between herself and her mother.

Moon/Ceres/Planets Ruling 4th/10th Houses Conjunct the Midheaven

This is another "mother-father" blend in the horoscope. On the mundane level, several possibilities exist. Mother may have wielded more than average power within the home. Mother could have been a professional, worked hard outside the home, or been ambitious. Mother might have been more the "power" parent or the disciplinarian. The parents may have switched traditional roles, or shared roles so that both parents could be nurturing and set the rules. One parent may have played both roles with the other parent gone (divorce, death, etc.), ineffectual, or emotionally absent. The daughter may have felt that she had to parent one (or both) of her own parents—that she had to be strong and responsible and look after others from an inappropriately young age.

The central issue is the balancing act between conditional and unconditional love within the home. If the family overdid the unconditional love, the daughter was (perhaps unconsciously) encouraged to remain immature, helpless, and dependent. If the family overdid the conditional love, the daughter probably felt abandoned, unsafe, rejected, or treated harshly. A family business is also possible, or a home in which everyone was expected to work and be productive.

When a comfortable blend is achieved, the daughter receives the caring and protection that she needs when very young to develop inner security and trust. She also is trained to be realistic, practical, and aware of the rights of others and rules of society, so that she can work in the wider world and relate effectively with power people. She is given opportunities to take on appropriate responsibility and develop her own strength and expertise.

Moon/Ceres/Planets Ruling 4th/10th Houses Conjunct the IC

Here is another combination where the nurturing motifs are reinforcing and "doubling up" with one another. (Where the 10th-house ruler is involved, a bit of a mother-father blend also exists.) Mother could be extremely maternal—nurturing, warm, very present in the home, very involved with seeking security and emotional connections. Or, Mother could be very dependent, childish, insecure, and needy. (The daughter may have had to parent her own parent.) Food issues are possible with both the mother and daughter. Family usually matters much.

Where warmth and caring predominate, the mother and daughter are very aware of each other's needs, and naturally seek to protect one another. They may enjoy sharing domestic tasks or most activities that involve family members. A strong nurturing streak is likely, whether directed toward loved ones, pets, a garden, or any projects that one can nurture to maturity.

Moon/Ceres/Planets in or Ruling 4th/10th Houses Sextile/Trine the Midheaven/IC

Mother could have had skills in dealing with the "real world" or authority figures. Mother may have known how to work "the System," how to please the powers-that-be. Mother may have enjoyed work in the outer world as well as in the domestic sphere. Mother might have contributed materially to her daughter's career or success. Mother's example could have aided the daughter in finding a happy medium between time and energy for family members and time and energy for outer-world accomplishments.

If either end of this polarity is overdone, discomfort is likely. With too much focus on practical, pragmatic concerns, the mother and/or daughter could feel criticized, judged, expected to work too much, or too subject to authority figures. With too much focus on the gentle, compassionate, protective side, either individual could succumb to weakness, insecurity, avoidance, or retreating inside.

There is an excellent potential for the mother and daughter to move smoothly and adeptly between the internal, private world of family and loved ones and the public world of material success and accomplishments.

Moon/Ceres/Planets in or Ruling 4th/10th Houses in Conflict (Square, Quincunx) with the Midheaven/IC

Conflicts (inner and outer) about parental principles are possible. The mother may be unsure how much to be the authority figure and disciplinarian, and how much to operate out of warmth, compassion, and gentle protection. The mother may feel torn between devoting time to her family and pursuing a career or making community contributions. Conflicts between parents—or parental roles—are possible. Mom may be at odds with power people or the Establishment. Issues could arise around status, conventional expectations, and the demands of the outer world. The daughter may perceive Mom as harsh, punitive, too concerned with results, or dictatorial. Or, the mother may totally opt out of her parental responsibilities and expect the daughter to fill in.

When the mother and daughter work to integrate these combinations, they can achieve an excellent medley of caring and competence, being able to combine emotional warmth with efficiency and achievement. Responsibilities can be shared in an equitable manner. Both the mother and daughter can develop their skills and find their own arena in which to be the authority figure and expert.

PART THREE

Synastry

FIVE

Aspects Between Mother's and Daughter's Horoscopes

Synastry examines the aspects between planets and other factors in the horoscopes of two or more individuals. This book will concentrate on mother-daughter relationships, but the general astrological principles can be applied to any interaction between individuals. One of my interesting cases involved a mother dog and her four puppies. The puppy that the mother dog especially favored, saved tidbits for, and in general "spoiled," had its Ascendant on the mother dog's Venus, and its IC on the mother's Ceres, the "mothering" asteroid. The IC, the 4th-house cusp, carries a parallel meaning to the Moon, our primary key to mothering. Though the other three puppies were born just minutes apart, the chart angles of this puppy marked it as special to the mother dog.

Astrological factors can include chart angles, especially the Midheaven/IC axis and the Ascendant/Descendant axis, lunar and planetary Nodes where the body crosses the plane of the earth's path around the Sun, asteroids (which are small planets), midpoints, Arabic parts, etc. Astrology has many ways to say the same thing, many forms of our twelve primary principles that we call the "alphabet of astrology." In this section of our book, we will list the basic meanings of the aspects between each pair of traditional planets, and will include the Midheaven and Ascendant, the lunar Nodes, the first four asteroids that were discovered early in the nineteenth century, and Chiron.

We will not include separate sections on the different aspects. Many astrology books with "cookbook" sections separate aspects into three or four categories. Conjunctions often are presented separately. *Harmony* aspects include sextiles and trines, and sometimes semi-sextiles. *Conflict* aspects include squares, octiles (also called semisquares), and tri-octiles (also called sesquisquares or sesquiquads). Quincunxes and oppositions may be listed separately as symbolizing *separative* tendencies in the relationship, or they may be included with the conflict aspects. Many astrology books assume that harmony aspects will always be experienced as harmony between the individuals, while conflict aspects will always produce tension and problems, but actual life details are not so pat. Self-aware individuals who understand the nature of the potential conflicts can find compromises that build positive relationships. Individuals lacking understanding and flexibility may produce strife-ridden relationships. On the other hand, the potentially positive aspects may lead to trouble if they encourage destructive excesses in either or both individuals.

Conjunctions are the most important aspects, showing an intense interaction involving the principles symbolized by the factors. Traditionally, conjunctions between planets ruling signs that are square, such as Mars and Saturn which rule Aries and Capricorn, have been assumed to be negative. Conjunctions between the so-called "benefics," Venus and Jupiter, have been assumed to be positive. We think it is possible to integrate pairs of planets such as Mars and Saturn *if* the two individuals are aware and willing to compromise. It is also possible for conjunctions involving Venus and Jupiter to lead to excesses that produce challenges in the life.

Nothing in astrology is inherently and automatically "good" or "bad." Every chart and every pair of charts have both harmony and conflict aspects. The following paragraphs will explore the psychological drives/desires represented by each pair of factors, and will include both positive and painful potentials. The details in the lives of the two individuals cannot be predicted. They will depend on how well the individuals handle their own desires.

As already mentioned, there are many tools in astrology that symbolize the same twelve principles. For advanced students who work with some of these less familiar tools, you can include the geocentric Nodes of the planets as alternative forms of the planets. For example, the Nodes of Mars are like two more Mars in the chart. You can use midpoints as equivalent in meaning to a conjunction of the two planets that produce the midpoint, the center degree and minute between them. Obviously, the midpoint is not as intense as having the two planets actually in that center point, but it carries the same meaning and can be quite informative. In fact, a common technique in synastry uses a horoscope made of midpoints between each pair of the same factors in the two charts, e.g., Sun/Sun (midpoint of mother's Sun and daughter's Sun), Moon/Moon, etc. The shorthand symbol for a midpoint puts a forward slash between the symbols for the two factors. This "composite" chart of midpoints can offer insight, but should not be used alone. The aspects between all factors being used by the astrologer should be compared.

Time-sensitive information can also be gained by comparing the progressed positions of one person's planets to the natal and progressed positions of the other person. Students who use other techniques for current and future information can use their preferred system, including solar arc directions and returns. The preceding tools will be unique in the charts of the two individuals, while the current transits provide a universal set of positions that can be applied to both persons. Often, these temporary positions will help the two individuals increase their understanding of themselves, of each other, and of the relationship.

In the astrological alphabet, the planets carry the same meaning as the signs they "rule" and the equivalent houses. For example, the Sun, Leo, and the 5th house are different forms of "Letter 5." However, the planet is always the most important! The planet is like the verb in a sentence, and the signs and houses modifying it are like adverbs. In this section of our book, the nature of the planet will be emphasized, so the Sun, Mars, and Jupiter will be described as fire planets; the Moon, Neptune, and Pluto will be described as water planets, etc. Obviously, this system is complicated by the fact that Mercury and Venus rule two signs apiece. Each of these planets has a core meaning with different possible emphases. Venus seeks pleasure but can focus more on physical pleasure (Taurus) or on mental pleasure (Libra). Mercury learns and communicates, but can focus on a broad perspective (Gemini) or more on practical details and a desire to produce in tangible form (Virgo).

Though the nature of the planet is always paramount, the desires that it signifies will be modified by its sign and house positions. For example, fire planets in earth or water signs or houses will be more subdued, more concerned with security issues, and less impulsive. All of our major tools, planets, houses, signs, and aspects are important. Astrology is incredibly complex, with its many ways to symbolize the same twelve principles, so there will be basic, repeated "themes" in every chart, and in every relationship. Students who are familiar with the basic life "dilemmas" will be able to see which one or more are emphasized in the chart of each individual, and will almost always find the same "dilemma" in the chart of the other person. Often, one individual will be overdoing one of the primary desires while the other person is overdoing a different desire in the same dilemma. One may fight for freedom while the other seeks dependency or tries to nurture. One may hunger for equality while the other only feels safe in a power position. One may be intensely idealistic while the other is highly practical. It is also common for the players in the drama to switch roles, especially in a parent-child relationship when the child grows up.

Our goal is understanding. When we realize that all of the twelve desires can be positive or painful, depending on how they are handled, we can seek to work out compromises to make every relationship more satisfying. In cases where one of the individuals is unwilling or unable to compromise, we can wish him or her well, and spend more of our time with more satisfying associates.

Mother-Daughter Sun Contacts

Sun to Sun

The Sun is the center of the solar system, the source of our physical light and life. The sign and house positions of our Sun, and its aspects, show where we want to do more than we have done before, to give something to the world out of our own center, and to get a positive response from the world. Aspects between Suns in the charts of two individuals can range from deep, intense love to major power struggles. Negative potentials include arrogance, and prima donna and Queen Bee attitudes. In a positive relationship, the mother and daughter may be each other's biggest fans and cheerleaders of one another. Between self-aware individuals, the relationship can be truly joyous, as they encourage each other's creativity and emotional expressiveness. If either individual feels insecure, she may (probably subconsciously) put the other down to build up her own ego. Until the daughter reaches adulthood, the mother obviously holds most of the power. Often, the roles will be reversed as an adult daughter cares for an older mother. If both individuals can accept and give love, both can grow in their self-esteem, and can offer increasing light to the world.

Sun to Moon

The Sun shows our ability to procreate, among many forms of creativity, while the Moon shows our capacity to nurture the product of our creativity, or to be nurtured by it. With a healthy power balance between two individuals, there can be mutual love, compassion, and respect. Valuable emotional exchanges can be warm, supportive, and generous. One of the hazards in fire-water mixtures is a tendency to intensify feelings, and with the Sun involved, overdramatization is possible. One individual might play "star queen" while the other plays "needy-dependent." A fad in pop psychology focuses on "codependence" as a negative expression in a variety of love relationships, but a healthy interdependence is present when both individuals can give and receive support while still maintaining self-esteem. Caring may be demonstrated on any or all levels, whether physical, emotional, cognitive, or spiritual. Even when there is a sizable power difference (when the daughter is still a child or the mother is elderly), there can be a supportive give and take. The mother may give more physical care while the child is young, but receive it later while still offering the wisdom of later years.

If either the daughter or the mother can only feel safe in the power position, or if either is too insecure to give or to receive, the relationship will suffer. Feelings of helplessness and vulnerability lead to holding on or holding in. Letting go of anything may be threatening, so the individual may be unable to give. Alternately, to receive, we have to give up the power position, accept our own humanness, and perhaps even accept that a child or a parent can be superior in some way. A healthy self-esteem permits both giving and receiving. Mutual protection and support become very possible.

Sun to Mercury

Normally, aspects to Mercury are helpful since they encourage understanding and communication. The air element in astrology facilitates the ability to see a broad perspective and to relate to other individuals as equals. The Sun shows our passion, while Mercury is a key to the conscious intellect, with its ability to be detached and objective. If both the mother and daughter can express their feelings honestly and do not feel ego-threatened by mutual openness, the relationship can thrive and facilitate mutual growth. A positive handling of the Mercury principle can include the exchange of exciting ideas, producing lively and vibrant conversation. On the negative side, verbal grandstanding is possible if one ego hogs the floor, insisting on intellectual dominance. The urge of the Sun is always to do more than we have done before. If honesty is too focused on what are judged to be flaws in the other individual, with inadequate acknowledgement of assets, the target will obviously feel attacked. She may react by fighting back, or by retreating, or by outwardly giving in and using manipulation for self-preservation.

Mercury rules both Gemini and Virgo. Its Gemini potential with the talent for equality is appropriate for human interactions. Its Virgo potential should be directed into one's job where we need to look for flaws and correct them. In a healthy relationship, the shared information provided by Mercury can deepen mutual love and enhance mutual growth, the Sun's goal.

Sun to Venus

Venus symbolizes our capacity for whatever we define as pleasure. Obviously, with an aspect to the Sun, we want more. This mutual reinforcement of passion and pleasure can be very exciting to the two individuals, though it can also lead to excesses in almost any area of indulgence, especially physical and emotional. But it is also possible to overdo cognitive and spiritual desires, depending on the signs and houses involved and the general emphases in the two charts. A healthy balance of shared love and pleasure can include mutual pampering, generosity, and rewards for each other that increase mutual creativity and joy.

Conflict aspects may show a feeling that the power of either person is blocking a desired pleasure of the other. Alternately, there may be tension over different pleasure goals desired by the two individuals, or one may feel that the other makes her own gratification paramount. Feelings of inadequate love and self-esteem may be experienced by either or both individuals. Finding activities where pleasure can be shared and where neither feels ego-threatened can heal the tensions and lead to mutual growth.

Sun to Mars

Aspects between two fire planets can be intense and energizing. Mars wants to do what comes naturally, and the Sun wants to do more. If two individuals have similar goals, they are likely to reinforce the fire feeling that they have the right and the power to do what they want. If the individuals have conflicting desires, there can be a battle royal. The mother will have the power edge while the daughter is still a child, and the roles may be reversed as the mother ages, though obviously life circumstances can alter this, such as one or the other controlling more financial power. A link between the Sun and Mars shows a passionate relationship that may be deeply loving or incredibly competitive. On the positive side, the mother and daughter may build each other's confidence, courage, initiative, and willingness to take risks to prove themselves. On the negative side, they might egg each other on into really rash behavior, or one might assert her will at the other's expense, even to the point of violence.

Mars is always a major key to one's sense of personal identity, so conjunctions with Mars are a special aspect. A conjunction of Mars with the Sun in another person's chart intensifies the fire in both, and may increase the spontaneity and creativity of both. Mars is normally more focused on immediate personal desires, while the Sun looks farther ahead and wants others to be involved. With the sense of identity shown by a conjunction, either individual may be pulled in the direction of the other, subconsciously taking the other as a role model. Role models may be positive or negative. We may want to be like or the opposite of the other. With mutual self-esteem, both individuals can grow in self-confidence while sharing love bonds and exciting creativity.

Sun to Jupiter

This is an aspect between two fire planets that is usually experienced as stimulating and vitalizing. Both the Sun and Jupiter show the desire for more, so aspects between them encourage excesses on some level, whether physical, emotional, cognitive, or spiritual. If the two individuals hold similar values and goals, they will tend to feed each other's fire and spread like a forest fire in dry vegetation. If the two individuals have clashing values and goals, there is likely to be mutual condemnation and each may "dig in" to personal commitments. This is seen graphically in conflicts between individuals with different religious beliefs. We define fanatics as individuals so convinced of their own version of "truth" that they reject any compromise with contrary beliefs. Common sense suggests that no one has a monopoly on final "truth," that ultimate knowledge is a goal we never reach, but life is an exciting journey seeking it.

Fire in astrology represents the life urge in action. It can create new life or burn old bridges and walls. It needs to look at what will be the consequences of the action without damping its wonderful spontaneity too much. Life is a balancing act. Aspects between the Sun and Jupiter in the charts of two individuals can enhance mutual creativity in any area of life, but can be especially valuable in the quest for wisdom. In a positive interaction, the mother and daughter may feed each other's wisdom, confidence, and adventurous quest for more, better, faster, and higher. Too much fire can lead to acting without sufficient forethought, or to assuming that "God is on my side, so I can do anything I want." Fire is always followed by earth in the "natural" sequence of the alphabet of astrology. Action produces consequences that test our wisdom.

Sun to Saturn

Where the Sun symbolizes the height of personal power, Saturn signifies the impersonal power of the law. Its principles include natural law, cultural regulations, authority figures who enforce the law, and one's internal enforcers, the conscience and guilt. Where the Moon is ideally a parent who gives unconditional love, Saturn is theoretically a parent who gives conditional love in the form of the consequences of how we have handled the law.

Through consequences, we learn what we can do, what we can't do, and what we have to do to survive in this physical world.

Aspects between the Sun and Saturn can produce results ranging from a combination of love with the responsible use of power, to major battles over who wields the power and where and how it should be directed. Constructive relationships may lead to a family business or a shared profession. In the past, and still today in some cultures, the responsibility of raising a family and contributing to the needs of the society were typically shared in extended families. Western cultures today tend to have families limited to parents and children, not uncommonly with a single parent carrying most of the power and responsibility. The best expression of Sun-Saturn aspects is a blend of warmth and generosity with competence and disciplined accomplishments. While the daughter is still a child, the mother obviously holds more power. If she overcontrols, the daughter will resist or withdraw to whatever extent she can. In extreme cases, the mother may be totally dominating, dictatorial, and harsh. The daughter may feel that her every move is constricted and restricted and not okay.

Another form of overcontrol may be manifested by a mother who takes on too much responsibility. Her daughter may react by saying, "Mother wants to do it, so I will let her." Usually, life will eventually force such a child to grow up and carry her share of the responsibility. The opposite scenario combines an unusually mature daughter with an irresponsible mother, or a mother who does not really want to play the mother role, or one who simply cannot cope with the multiple burdens of too many children, a missing or inadequate partner, etc. The daughter may accept the parental role voluntarily, or feel compelled to take it on. Once grown, she may go on to mother her own children, or she may feel that she has done that sufficiently in caring for her siblings, and bypass being a parent.

Whatever the life details, if the mother and daughter can share the love of the Sun and the practical responsibility of Saturn, whether in the family or in a career, the relationship can be a bulwark of mutual support.

Sun to Uranus

The Sun and Uranus are "polar partners," signifying the opposing ends of several life principles. The Sun wants passion versus the Uranus desire for intellectual detachment. The Sun wants personal power while Uranus insists on equality. As with all oppositions in astrology, they need each other if we are to be "whole," handling all twelve sides of life. In healthy relationships, there is mutual love without an attempt by either person to coerce or possess the other person. The air element encourages the emotional expressiveness of the fire element. Aspects between Sun and Uranus can encourage spectacular creativity and innovation in any area of life to which they are directed. Along with aspects between the fire planets, this combination can stimulate unique excitement. If carried too far, both the mother and daughter may be adrenaline junkies and go to extremes in risk-taking.

As noted repeatedly, while the daughter is still a child, the mother normally holds the power position. If she attempts to coerce or possess a strongly Uranian daughter, the latter is likely to rebel or run away in whatever way she can. Conversely, if the mother is the more Uranian of the two, she may stay detached in some way, and the daughter may feel unloved. Either individual may want warmth and emotional expressiveness and feel that the other is cold and aloof. The Sun-Uranus contacts are only one of several ways that astrology can picture the "freedom-closeness" dilemma that is so common in life, especially in the Western world. In a healthy relationship, the mother and daughter become friends, able to share love and mutual interests as equals.

Sun to Neptune

With aspects between the Sun and Neptune, personal passion meets the mystical infinite. The result can range from encouraging spectacular artistic creativity or a talent for healing in either or both individuals in the relationship, to dramas that feature any of several forms of martyrdom. If either the mother or daughter is identified with the victim side of Neptune, a Sun aspect is likely to add dramatic emphasis. (Problems with drugs, alcohol, denial, deception, escapism, or feeling helpless may be played out with a larger-than-life flair.) One of the players in the drama may crave the personal love that supports a healthy self-esteem, while the other may be committed to saving the world, or may feel that all her love must be devoted to God, or to her artistic profession. Obviously, this scenario is most painful if a young daughter wants love while her mother has "higher" priorities. The roles can be reversed if an elderly parent is seeking emotional support from a grown daughter whose time is almost all committed to a more universal calling.

As with all aspects that involve the Sun, there may be power issues, and in all aspects involving Neptune, there may be tensions over beliefs, values, and goals. Since the ideals of Neptune are typically more subconscious than those signified by Jupiter, and since the Sun is primarily emotional rather than rational, it is especially important to bring in the intellect to become conscious and discuss the values held by each person in the relationship. Fire and water planets are both emotional, but normally fire will express the emotions while water will hold them in due to security needs. Bringing air (consciousness) into the picture should help, but the communication needs to be done with the empathy of Neptune and the love of the Sun.

Sun to Pluto

Both the Sun and Pluto signify the desire for passion, but the Sun seeks a power position in relationships, while Pluto, as one of the keys to partnership, faces the challenge of developing and maintaining equalitarian relationships. Letter 8—which includes Pluto, Scorpio, and the 8th house—can be experienced as a real double bind. Desires include wanting a mate, but also wanting power. It can be an intense challenge to maintain power over yourself without trying to control others or letting them control you. Consequently, most Sun aspects to Pluto will involve the issue of power (and violence is possible in extreme circumstances). Intense power struggles are common, or the weaker (for whatever reason) person in the relationship may retreat or may outwardly give in and try to manipulate the other person. Feelings of weakness may be related to age, physical size or strength, control of possessions, support by others, etc. Issues of privacy may be significant; either the mother or daughter may feel the other person is too intrusive or invasive in her life.

Where both individuals share common desires, whether for emotional passion or for sensual pleasures, there is a danger of excesses as they encourage each other's indulgences. Life areas may include eating, drinking, smoking, drugs, sex, spending money, collecting possessions, etc. Either the mother or daughter or both may be struggling to overcome addictions. Among the life goals of Pluto (and its sign and house) are self-knowledge and self-mastery, so a positive handling of a Sun-Pluto aspect can bring growth in either or both skills for either or both individuals in the relationship. With all water factors in astrology, but especially with Letter 8, it will sometimes be necessary to forgive and release the past. Dwelling on past hurts, or holding on to resentments and fantasies about vengeance, is similar to eating a little poison whenever we focus on such feelings. Letting go of these feelings is essential for soul growth. With the ability to release the past and to share love and power comfortably in the present, both the mother and daughter can move toward the ancient spiritual goal of becoming adepts.

Sun to Ceres

The asteroid Ceres seems like a Cancer-Virgo mixture—a nurturing, but practical, mother. Like the Moon, it may symbolize one's experience of being "mothered," whether by the blood-mother, a stepmother, a grandmother, a nanny, etc. It also shows one's capacity to "mother" others. Aspects between the Sun and Ceres tend to intensify the importance of the parental role since procreation is one of the Sun's primary forms of creativity. A mother-daughter relationship with one of these aspects may be deeply bonded and mutually supportive, or there could be subtle competition over who will play the (dominant) parent role. Truly stressful mother-daughter relationships may lead to the daughter deciding against becoming a parent herself. In such cases, healing requires forgiving her mother for her shortcomings. Often, the relationship with her mother can be improved once the daughter is grown. It should be possible to share love and nurturing with each other, and perhaps to make a joint contribution that helps others in need.

Sun to Pallas

The asteroid Pallas seems to signify Libra desires, which can range from wanting a personal partner in marriage to vocations such as counseling, law, and politics. There may be a strong sense of justice and concern with social causes, or an attraction to the graphic arts. Aspects between the Sun and Pallas can encourage emotional bonding between the two individuals, or can facilitate artistic creativity or shared social concerns. There is always an urge toward personal power with the Sun, while Pallas represents a desire for equality, so compromises are needed. Pallas can also express the competitive potential of Libra, so connecting it to the Sun's drive to be superior can add to the potential for rivalry in the relationship. The rivalry may be subconscious, and may be demonstrated in many different areas such as trying to impress others with clothes, makeup, popularity, or skills. However, in mutually caring relationships, the mother and daughter can be true partners, cooperating with each other and sharing the pleasures of life.

Sun to Juno

The asteroid Juno seems very Plutonian, capable of a passionate desire for a mate, but also on guard against being dominated. Aspects between the Sun and Juno are likely to bring up power issues, and to call for a compromise of wills. Questions of manipulation and emotional blackmail or excessive resentment may arise. In extreme cases, abuse is possible. As usual, the mother will normally hold the power position when the daughter is young, though there can be exceptions with an ill or otherwise inadequate mother. As an adult, the daughter can attain a more equalitarian relationship with the mother. Since the capacity for love is present with both the Sun and Juno, a positive goal of mutual support is possible with an enduring bond that permits a lasting partnership. At times, as with Pluto, either or both individuals may need to forgive and release the past in order to build a truly cooperative relationship. Sun-Juno aspects also may lead to emotional or sensual excesses, as either the mother or daughter or both encourage personal indulgences. However, with Juno, as with Pluto, there is a desire for self-knowledge and self-mastery, so what could be a challenge can be reversed, and the handling of power can become an asset. Sharing love and mutual goals brings healing peace.

Sun to Vesta

The asteroid Vesta is like the ultimate Virgo with tunnel vision. When Vesta is prominent, the individual can be so dedicated to an immediate task/goal that nothing else matters. When a mother and daughter are mutually supportive, the creativity and passion of the Sun can enhance the devotion and skill of Vesta to produce outstanding success that is potentially rewarding for both. There can also be enormous tensions in the relationship if love clashes with work. The daughter may feel unloved if her mother is obliged to work due to financial pressures or her own ambition. Later, the roles may be reversed if a grown daughter becomes too immersed in her career to give time and attention to her mother. The Sun is a natural leader while Vesta is focused on getting the job done well, but once a daughter is grown, the roles can be shared.

The Virgo focus on flaws in order to do one's job properly can also be a problem if it is displaced into relationships and threatens the self-esteem and need for love of the other individual. It is important to remember that all aspects can "work" both ways. The need to "do something worth doing and to do it well" and the need for love and approval will be present in both the mother and daughter. Either one may feel threatened if a basic need is denied. Defining another person as a "job," focusing on her flaws, and trying to change her is painful to the target, and if the latter fights back, the relationship can deteriorate into mutual criticism. A shared focus on seeing the assets in each other and offering emotional support for the practical skills of each other can build a team that makes a real contribution in the world.

Sun to Chiron

We think of Chiron as a "little brother" to Jupiter, with the potential of expressing either the Sagittarius or the Pisces side of Jupiter. Aspects between the Sun and Chiron can generate intense emotion, whether the fire or the water potential of Chiron is expressed. Both want more, whether a more ideal personal love, or greater power and fame in the world. A mutually supportive mother and daughter can enhance creative artistic talents or offer wisdom and healing in many forms. Both the mother and daughter may become sparkplugs and motivators for the enlightenment of others. As with all forms of Letters 9 and 12, the inner urge to reach the Absolute can lead to excessive expectations and disillusionment. If any fragment of life is overvalued, it becomes an idol and will let us down. Dashed dreams can result in the "wounded" feeling that is sometimes associated with Chiron. Overdoing anything may lead to crashing into victim roles. Extremes can range from overdosing on drugs in an effort to escape a miserable world, to trying to save the world and ending as a martyr. We need to "do our share," and then let go and trust our fellow humans and the Infinite Whole to help.

Sun to the Lunar Nodes

The lunar Nodes can be understood as two more Moons in the chart. Like the Moon, they seek emotional security. Human relationships, especially within one's family, are the most common source of this security, though we may also have pets, talk to our plants, cling to our homes and possessions, or overeat. Node aspects to any factors in the charts of other individuals are signs of emotional sensitivity, and they can stimulate intense feelings that run the gamut from attraction to repulsion. The Nodes are always opposite each other, so they are natural partners. We need to integrate their sign and house polarities, to find a balance between the opposing ends so we have room for both in our lives. Since the Nodes form an axis across the chart, an aspect to either requires an aspect to both. More individuals find the South Node a challenge. It may be experienced as a sense of self-doubt, or as indebtedness that calls us to go above and beyond normal obligations for someone or something. If the North Node is in Capricorn or in the 10th house, we may feel equally pressured there.

Aspects between the Sun and the lunar Nodes can deepen family bonds, increasing the need for love and closeness but also increasing the vulnerability if the relationships are conflicted. A power issue is always possible with the Sun. When properly used, personal power protects others as well as the self. The daughter of a mother who abuses her power may resist, or run, or give in outwardly while seeking to manipulate the situation. Once grown, such a daughter needs to build her own self-esteem to be able to learn from the past, and then to release it and use her own power wisely. There is little in life that can match the security that comes from a mutually supportive family. It is worth the compromises and patience needed to produce it.

Sun to the Ascendant/Descendant Axis

Like the lunar Nodes, the Ascendant/Descendant axis forms an opposition that can fall in any of the six zodiac sign polarities. All oppositions in astrology are natural partners that need to be integrated to allow room in the life for both. The Ascendant and the 1st house carry the meaning of Mars—a sense of personal identity, our right and power to do what we want. The Descendant and the 7th house are like Libra, and the Libra side of Venus shows our need for lasting, equalitarian relationships that can include cooperation and competition.

Depending on the rest of the horoscope, aspects between the Sun and these angles may encourage the fire desire to do what we please, or the hunger for love and companionship. In a mother-daughter relationship, accenting the fire can be exciting fun if both individuals have similar desires and each feels strengthened by the interaction. Conversely, especially if either person lacks self-confidence or if they have very different desires, there may be major power struggles. Either may see the other as much too self-centered and concerned solely with personal needs.

If either the mother and daughter or both place more importance on relationships, they may support each other's social needs, share friends, and maintain a partnership into later years. Conversely, either or both may seek to bolster a sense of self-esteem and personal power by competing for the approval of others, or one or both may put down the associates of the other. With mutual love and support, it is possible to build a deeply satisfying and lasting relationship.

Sun to the MC/IC Axis

Like the lunar Nodes, the MC/IC axis forms an opposition that can fall in any of the six zodiac sign polarities. All oppositions in astrology are natural partnerships that need to be integrated to allow room in the life for both. The MC and the 10th house carry the meaning of Saturn, while the IC and the 4th house carry the meaning of the Moon. They symbolize the parents in a child's chart and, once grown, the individual's ability to be a parent, caring for a home and family but also playing a role in the larger world. Horoscope angles are sometimes called *personal points* due to their rapid movement that is determined by birth time as the earth rotates on its axis. The MC/IC axis can be a major key to how one's parents coped with the balancing acts of handling home versus career, dominance versus dependency, conditional love versus unconditional love, etc.

In a mother-daughter relationship, the parent-child roles may be shared or alternated, even when the daughter is still relatively young. The mutual support can include emotional nurturing and practical responsibilities, caring for home and family and/or career activities. If either person takes on too much of the power and responsibility, even with good intentions, it can be experienced by the other as an ego threat, a denial of her personal competence. A daughter who is expected to carry too much of the family duties (perhaps acting like a parent to her own parent) may feel that she cannot look to others for support of her own needs. A mother who is determined to be a "superparent" or do everything herself may unconsciously cripple the daughter's confidence and ability to cope with real-world responsibilities and emotional demands. A healthy adult relationship can only be built with compromise and cooperation, but it is well worth the effort to provide lasting emotional and material security to both the mother and daughter.

Mother-Daughter Moon Contacts

Moon to Moon

The Moon and other forms of Letter 4 in our astrological alphabet are the central keys to the focus of this book. They represent our experience of being "mothered" and our capacity to "mother" others. Whether the mother who bore us, a stepmother, a grandmother, a nanny, etc., Letter 4 includes all forms of the person or people who, hopefully, gave us unconditional love when we were most helpless and vulnerable. Letter 10 signifies the other parent, and in "real" families the mother may be shown by Saturn, Capricorn, and/or the 10th house, and the father may be represented by the Moon, Cancer, and/or the 4th house. One parent may play both roles, and at different times in the life, the individuals playing the roles may change. But Letter 4 still remains the primary key to the home and family we are born into and the one we establish as an adult. We may also seek emotional security from other people, from pets, possessions, food, etc., and we may try to provide it to close relationships or to the world.

Aspects between the Moons of a mother and daughter show a strong emotional connection at the subconscious level that may or may not be conscious. Ideally, there will be an emotional bond that supports mutual security. Even a young daughter may feel protective of her mother, though the latter holds the main power in the relationship. If the mother is needy, whiny, or too dependent, the daughter may feel obliged to do too much, too young. If the mother is overprotective, the daughter may be weakened, failing to learn to do things for herself. Where either person feels insecure, lacking in protection, she may look to others for reassurance, or try to increase her own self-confidence, or turn to faith in a Higher Power. If both individuals are able to share their feelings of need without blaming the other for not meeting those needs, a more trusting and supportive relationship can often be achieved. Once lost, trust is not easily regained, but it is worth the effort to build a mutually caring life together, for the sake of each other as well as for others with ties to the home and family.

Moon to Mercury

Though nothing in astrology is guaranteed to be "good" or "bad," aspects between the Moon and Mercury tend to be helpful in mother-daughter interactions. Mercury signifies the ability to learn and communicate. The capacity for conscious rationality helps to broaden one's perspective, to handle equalitarian associations, and to "take things lightly." When both the mother and daughter are able to combine these talents with shared nurturing, their relationship may resemble one of mutually supportive siblings. If the protective instincts of the Moon are lacking, one or both individuals may see the other as too detached, too much in the head with inadequate empathy, or unable or unwilling to deal with feelings. One may be overly blunt, while the other ends up with hurt feelings. In a typical case of projection, one will want to "mother" or be "mothered," while the other prefers logical discussions. The "head" person will tend to be uncomfortable with emotions and retreat into even more intellectual detachment, while the one hungry for emotional reassurance clings and clutches more tightly.

Life is always a juggling act, since everyone has all twelve of life's primary drives/desires, but each will have her own emphasis. Remember to look for the repeated themes, for the same principles shown in the chart in many different ways. Unless the "intellect" versus "emotions" issue is indicated repeatedly in the charts, a Moon-Mercury aspect is usually an asset. It facilitates understanding, communication, and acceptance of each other, and these actions can help build lasting relationships that combine protective warmth without feelings of coercion or possession. Communication can be open and objective and also emphasize caring and sharing.

Moon to Venus

These aspects are usually interpreted as positive, encouraging mutual pleasure (the Venus desire) that is shared with home and family. However, it is also possible for the security needs and the pleasure seeking to lead to excesses, with each egging on the other to overdo. There may be overeating if food is a primary source of both security and pleasure, but overindulgence is possible in any area of life: homes, money, possessions, sensuality, etc. One daughter noted that her mother equated spending money with love. Even twenty years ago, when money purchased more, if this daughter spent less than $500 on her mother's birthday gifts, she was considered selfish and uncaring. Obviously, if the two individuals have different desires, there can be conflict. One may crave emotional satisfaction while the other is focused on material acquisitions. Especially while the daughter is young, the mother may have to work to provide her material needs, but the daughter might feel short-changed in the emotional area by a too-busy mother. The roles can be reversed with a retired mother longing for personal contact and attention from an ambitious, career-driven daughter. However, with similar pleasures and mutual emotional warmth and the practice of moderation, the relationship can help both the mother and daughter handle an often challenging world.

Moon to Mars

A Moon-Mars conjunction is a special case, since Mars is always a major key to one's identity. Either the parent or child or both will take the other as a role model, though the life details may be almost opposite depending on whether the other is seen as a positive or a negative role model. The reactions are largely subconscious, which generally makes them even more powerful. As a water factor, the Moon is always a key to the subconscious, while Mars represents actions that are so automatic and instinctive that they are also close to being subconscious, signifying habits from the past that are present from the beginning of life.

Though it would be logical for the child to be more influenced by the mother, at least while young, it is quite possible for the mother to want to be more like—or the opposite of—the child. The more emotional of the two may wish she could take things more lightly or be more practical. Or the matter-of-fact one with solid common sense may secretly admire the histrionic drama of the other who successfully manipulates the world with her feelings. Obviously, the dramatic individual would have strong fire and water in her chart, while the commonsense individual's chart would emphasize earth and air. (An element emphasis can be present in many different ways in astrology.)

Other Moon-Mars aspects can work harmoniously when the two individuals have similar desires, when they can do active things together that support the individuality of each without threatening mutual security. Different desires call for compromises. One major difference between the Moon and Mars is the desire for closeness versus the desire for personal freedom. A freedom-loving mother may need to understand a daughter who craves emotional warmth, while a freedom-loving daughter may struggle against the possessiveness of a clingy or just overprotective mother. Problems can result if either individual overdoes the self-centered potential of Mars. When carried to an extreme, temper tantrums and even violence are possible. Compromises that allow each individual to meet her basic needs for both individuality and security can provide the foundation to help build a mutually satisfying relationship. Both the mother and daughter can learn to respect each other's independence while simultaneously valuing and strengthening family ties.

Moon to Jupiter

These aspects connect faith to one's mother or to mothering. Relationships can range from life with an idealized mother figure to feeling disillusioned because she ought to have been ideal and wasn't. The mother may have wanted to be an ideal mother and tried very hard, or she might have wanted an ideal child but felt her daughter could not live up to her expectations. If the child and parent share ideals, they might make home and family the ultimate values in life, or they could expand horizons to seek to bring their vision into the world. The daughter might want to be a mother herself, as an ideal life role. Alternately, she might choose not to have children for fear of failing to be a perfect mother, or of being like a mother who "blew" the role or unlike a mother who handled it superlatively well. Such a fear might be subconscious and lead to infertility or miscarriages. If the mother and daughter can discuss their expectations of each other and of themselves, and can find shared beliefs and values and accept their humanness, they can develop a secure relationship based on mutual trust. If either individual is overly zealous, devoted to a rigid, dogmatic religion, her self-righteous behavior could alienate the other person, making it very hard to establish warm bonds and emotional trust. Somewhere, they need to find values they can share. If a shared religious commitment is out of reach, they may enjoy studying, writing, or teaching in related areas of interest, or love travel or sports, as long as they are headed in the same direction with reasonable expectations.

Moon to Saturn

With these aspects, the mother-daughter interchanges are combining maternal with paternal principles; theoretically, the unconditional love parent and the conditional love parent. Obviously, in life either parent can play either role, or they may alternate in the roles, or one parent may play both roles, or there may be no one in one of the roles. The lack of unconditional love is most common, or cutting it off too early before the child has developed adequate self-esteem through feeling secure and valued. On the other hand, if both parents persist too long in overprotecting a child, she can be very spoiled and have a rude awakening when she is out on her own. By receiving the consequences of our actions, from conditional love, we learn what is possible and necessary for survival in a material world. A healthy upbringing provides plenty of unconditional love in infancy and early childhood, followed by conditional love (consequence-based) as the child becomes old enough to accept responsibility.

Normally, our parents are our initial teachers, holding the power. If a daughter has felt unloved and unprotected by her mother, whether ignored due to the mother's other obligations and interests or subject to coercion and harsh discipline, it will take real effort to build a relationship of mutual support. Such a positive relationship becomes possible if the daughter can develop her own self-esteem to feel that she is worthy of love and protection. It can also be helpful if she develops other supportive relationships and the skills to protect herself. With mutual caring and respect, the mother and daughter may care for a family together or work in a profession with a blend of the nurturing Moon and the practical, responsible Saturn.

Moon to Uranus

These aspects often point to the common freedom-closeness dilemma. The mother may be overly possessive while the daughter wants more independence. Or the mother may be distant for any of many reasons, while the daughter yearns for a closer bond. The mother may be experienced as being erratic and unpredictable, hence a threat to security, or the daughter may become an impulsive rebel. As with all of the life dilemmas in the astrological model, we need all twelve sides of life and compromise is usually needed to be a whole person. A baby obviously needs much more protection, and a young adult has to make more decisions for herself even though she is at risk of making mistakes and receiving uncomfortable consequences. If a healthy mother-daughter relationship has been developed, the increasing distance and equality as the daughter matures can develop into a true friendship between two adults who care for each other, but also understand and accept each other without trying to change the other. Shared intellectual interests, hobbies, and friends can be helpful in building a relationship that facilitates mutual security without clutching; love with an open hand.

Moon to Neptune

Aspects between water planets show connections at the subconscious level of the mind. They point to increased sensitivity and, usually, empathy and compassion. But, as has been said repeatedly, the life details may be positive or painful depending on how the individuals handle the expanded sensitivity. Through the subconscious, we are connected to the Infinite. We are open to psychic impressions if we are able to connect the subconscious with the conscious side of the mind, to bring the subconscious awareness into consciousness. If we have faith in the Infinite, whatever name we give to the Higher Power, we can receive healing and inspiration. Whether or not we are able to become conscious of this subconscious knowing, aspects between water planets in the charts of the mother and daughter show an emotional connection that can be intensely powerful. With mutual caring, the bonding is wonderfully supportive. There may be a mutual love of beauty, shared mystical impulses, charitable instincts, or empathic tenderness.

Unfortunately, difficult relationships are also likely to be intensified, with either or both individuals subject to depression, anxiety, or other feelings connected to insecurity. Since Neptune is a key to faith in the Infinite and the Moon craves security from a human mother or mother-substitute, a threat to one's trust in either or both can be experienced in many painful ways. If the daughter feels that her mother failed to protect her as a child, and if the daughter continues to harbor resentment as an adult, it may take a major effort to forgive and release the past. The daughter needs to develop self-confidence, to realize that she is no longer a helpless, vulnerable child. Self-esteem can often be expanded by offering help to others.

Gaining more faith in a Higher Power can also be very helpful. If the daughter was looking to the mother to be perfect, to "play god" in her life, the daughter needs to realize that this is idolatry. She needs to find a "bigger god/goddess" and accept her mother's humanness.

An interesting flip in a mother-daughter relationship can occur if the mother is entrenched in a victim role and the daughter feels obliged to play savior. The mother might be alcoholic, ill, lost in fantasy, or unable or unwilling to cope with the material world. If the daughter is comfortable in her role, not resentful of being called to be an adult and deprived of much of her childhood, once grown she may simply continue in a helping profession. But it is also possible for the daughter to reject the rescuer role as soon as she can escape it, and to have to learn to control her oversensitivity to avoid continually attracting new victims into her life. We can escape excessive water vulnerability by focusing on more earth (tangible accomplishments), more air (detached intellect), and/or more fire (personal desire carried into action).

Since a positive bonding at the subconscious level is so strongly supportive of both individuals in a close relationship, it is well worth the effort to release old hurts and build mutual trust in each other and in a shared faith in the Infinite.

Moon to Pluto

As with the Moon and Neptune, this combination deals with the likelihood of subconscious connections and expanded sensitivity. But in contrast to the boundlessness of Neptune, Pluto represents the fixed quality of enduring self-will. Letter 8 in astrology shows where we are learning to share possessions, sensuality, and power with lasting, close, equalitarian relationships. Insecurity remains an issue whenever we have an emphasis on water factors, but the focus of both the Moon and Pluto is on fellow humans; relationships between parent and child and between potential mates. Feelings are usually intensified, but they can range from a bonded partnership that starts in childhood and continues long after the daughter is grown, to a lifelong power struggle with each individual seeking power for self-protection.

Where the mother and daughter care for each other, they are likely to easily give, receive, and share their pleasures, possessions, and power. They want to give satisfaction to each other and are mutually protective, slipping back and forth between the roles of parent, child, and equal partner in a comfortable interdependency. If either or both are insecure, they may fight for control, or retreat from the scene, or, if outclassed, give in outwardly but try to manipulate the situation. Manipulation, trying to get what we want without others realizing what is happening, is almost always a sign of weakness. It is usually connected to the water element in astrology, but may also involve earth if it is seen as a more practical alternative than openness to enable us to get what we want. Holding on to grudges and obsessing over emotional pain is a danger with double water aspects. Both the mother and daughter must learn to let go of old hurts and move on. Even when there has been severe abuse, maintaining the traumatic memories only maintains the hurts.

As with all water aspects, developing a mutually supportive relationship is so rewarding in the end that it is worth the effort to forgive and release the past and to look for areas of shared pleasure that can be strengthened.

Moon to Ceres

Aspects between the Moon and the asteroid Ceres connect two ways for astrology to signify the capacity to "mother" or be "mothered." They intensify the issue in the lives of both individuals, whether the mother and daughter are comfortable in their respective roles or one or both feel the other has failed her. The mother may need to work outside the home, or may be burdened with too many children, or illness in the family may stress it. Sometimes a strong, competent daughter may feel that she had to mother her own mother from an early age. But if the daughter rejects any kind of dependency that puts limits on her freedom, it is just as possible for the daughter to thwart a mother's need to protect as it is for the daughter to feel insecure when being raised by a parent who could not handle the responsibility of a child. In another variation, the mother may enjoy her protective role while her daughter is very young, but be very upset when the daughter starts developing her individuality. Even with a warm, loving relationship in the initial years, if the mother and daughter are too mutually dependent, they may have to learn how to let go emotionally once the daughter reaches adulthood. Codependency, where they are unable to function separately, may have to grow into a healthy interdependency where they can give, receive, and share, but also have the self-confidence to be individual adults. Feeling loved and protected is a deeply reassuring state of mind, so it is worth the effort it takes to find a balance between excessive dependence versus detachment. In its highest expression, this aspect shows that both the mother and daughter are supportive of one another, and each provides emotional security for the other.

Moon to Pallas

Aspects between the Moon and the asteroid Pallas call for a balance between "mothering" and sharing life as equals. Also, the Moon is deeply emotional while Pallas, like Libra, is more intellectual. The mother will obviously hold the power when her daughter is young, but when both the mother and daughter like each other, they can build a mutually supportive partnership that provides a bulwark of strength in a potentially challenging world. They may share many forms of pleasure, ranging from artistic interests, to friends, to supporting social causes. The relationship may resemble affectionate sisters to the point of sharing clothes and cosmetics.

With a lack of affection, a mother and daughter may engage in competition. Even a young child can be a rival to her mother, though the attitude may be subconscious in either or both individuals. Or they may just make dramatically different choices in fashion styles, hobbies, music, and associates. Unless there are major problems in the relationship, once the daughter is grown and especially after she has children of her own, a new understanding and acceptance can usually be developed. The tastes, the interests, and the causes may converge. With a little mutual good will and effort, the mother and daughter may become friends who respect each other.

Moon to Juno

Aspects between the Moon and the asteroid Juno are somewhat similar to Moon aspects to Pallas, but Juno signifies life areas of much deeper emotions plus a stronger will. Juno, like Pluto, wants a mate, but does not want to be controlled. Wherever Juno falls in a horoscope, we need to learn to give, to receive, and to share pleasures, possessions, and power for mutual gratification. We learn self-knowledge through the mirror of others, and self-mastery out of respect for the rights of others. The water nature of the Moon and Juno will intensify mutual emotional sensitivity that can range from highly supportive to highly conflicted. Security issues are crucial. As usual, the mother will initially have the power, and if she is insecure, she may abuse it in many ways. Alternately, she may simply be very possessive in the name of love for her daughter. If the mother has other emotional priorities, she may fail to handle the mother role effectively. Whether the mother's commitment is to a mate, to another child, or to her own mother, or is driven by financial pressures, sensual addictions, or other compulsions, she may be an inadequate parent.

As with Pallas, a competitive relationship may develop between the mother and daughter, and with Juno it is more likely to be below the level of awareness and thus harder to resolve. But with mutual good will and acceptance, by forgiving and releasing the past, the mother and an adult daughter can build a supportive partnership that may include a family business, shared interests and hobbies, or other pleasures. They can learn how to face the world as a team.

Moon to Vesta

Aspects between the Moon and the asteroid Vesta can be difficult if work, illness, or the critical attitude that is appropriate in a job interfere with the mother's ability to give her daughter unconditional love. Circumstances may force the mother to work outside the home. Illness may strike the mother or affect other family members, impairing the mother's ability to meet her daughter's needs. When the mother or other family members direct criticism at each other rather than keeping it focused on their jobs, the emotional climate in the home can be highly uncomfortable. If the mother makes the home her primary job, trying to keep it perfect at the expense of the emotional needs of the people in it, the latter will leave it as soon as they are able to. But with mutual good will, a Moon-Vesta aspect may signify a truly conscientious mother who does her best to be Supermom, meeting the needs of her family, sometimes at the expense of her own needs. If duties can be shared fairly, the load can be eased. Bringing in some humor or adding a light touch and some perspective can also help soften an overly serious approach to duties. Individuals dealing with Letter 6 in our astrological alphabet (Vesta, Virgo, the 6th house) often have to learn that not everything has to be done well. A family in which everyone combines compassionate caring with competence is demonstrating a constructive expression of Moon-Vesta aspects.

Moon to Chiron

Aspects between the Moon and the small planet (or comet?) Chiron can be similar to aspects between the Moon and either the Sagittarius or the Pisces side of Jupiter. The mother and daughter may idealize each other and share beliefs and values, or either or both may expect too much of the other and feel disillusioned. In the latter case, one or both individuals need to accept each other's humanness, and to try to find interests and goals that they can share. Idealism is always a two-edged sword. Excessive expectations inevitably produce frustration, while realistic aims that are sought together can lead to deeply rewarding bonding.

Sometimes one member of the pair will want more closeness, while the other prefers to explore a wider world. One may crave more personal emotional warmth, while the other feels that she "belongs to the transpersonal world." One may take a victim role and the other may feel obligated to be the savior yet resent the obligation. Healing can come if the mother and daughter can find similar interests and hobbies. They may teach, write, or travel together. They may share rescuing roles, seeking to create a more ideal world. Even if the shared values are simply focused into creating a loving home and family, the important key is that both are moving in the same direction, and moving together, without either one expecting the other to give her "Heaven on Earth."

Moon to the Lunar Nodes

The Nodes are similar in meaning to putting two more Moons in a horoscope, carrying the same desire for emotional security. They are frequently aspected in the charts of individuals who have close relationships. Since the Nodes are always opposite each other, an aspect to either one inevitably produces an aspect to the other. A conjunction with one produces an opposition to the other, etc. Nodal aspects to the Moon intensify emotional sensitivity in the relationship, though it will not necessarily be felt equally strongly in both the mother and daughter. Normally, the daughter will be more vulnerable while young, but if her nature is more practical, or more rational and detached, the mother may be the more sensitive of the two. Whether or not the emotional connection is conscious, it is highly important as a formative force in the relationship between the parent and child.

With mutual affection, the mother and daughter will often be deeply bonded. Once the daughter is grown, and even while she is still fairly young, they are likely to develop a positive interdependence with each contributing to the emotional security of the other. In difficult relationships, one may be overly possessive while the other seeks to establish greater individuality. Or one may pursue her personal security at the expense of the other person. They may look for security in different ways, with one trying to provide it through physical contact while the other expresses her affection verbally or simply by "doing" things for the other. But such minor character differences are relatively unimportant in a basically positive relationship.

With truly disturbed relationships, one or both may face a major challenge as they try to forgive and release the past. There may be tremendous pain, issues of abandonment, neglect, etc. Either the mother or daughter may associate the other with emotional damage. For those who believe in reincarnation, Moon-Node aspects may show past-life contacts, and since intense, shared emotions keep us connected, they can also hint at a return to future lives together. If this theory is even possible, it seems worth the effort to resolve issues in the current life. Even if one of the individuals is unwilling or unable to change, or if she has died, the other person can free herself from negative emotional bondage by forgiving the other. If both the mother and daughter want to create a mutually supportive association, amazing transformations are possible.

Moon to the Ascendant/Descendant Axis

These aspects bring in the principles of a cardinal T-square: the independence of the Ascendant (like Aries), the dependence of the Moon (like Cancer), and the equality of the Descendant (like Libra). With mutual caring and compromises, life is big enough for all three. In fact, to be a "whole" person, we need all twelve sides of life. When the daughter is young, the mother will normally have the power position, but as the daughter grows, she will express herself more, as symbolized by her own Ascendant, and the mother will usually need to ease up on the self-assertion of her own Ascendant so both can move toward the Descendant potential of a partnership between equal adults. On the negative side, the mother and daughter may compete or either may disrespect the other's choices in the realm of romantic partnership, or tastes in clothes, cosmetics, entertainment, etc. The central issue of the Ascendant/Descendant axis calls for finding a balance between assertion and accommodation, and fair play may be worked out in areas ranging from the distribution of domestic tasks to the handling of finances, to choices of television programs. When shared interests and pleasures are encouraged, a healthy interdependence can be developed. Each can give, receive, and share for mutual pleasure while respecting each other's individuality.

Moon to the MC/IC Axis

Letters 4 and 10 in our astrological alphabet represent the parents who oversee our early years, and our capacity to be parents when we become adults. The IC, 4th house, Cancer, and the Moon are theoretically the unconditional love parent who provides for the helpless infant, while the MC, 10th house, Capricorn, and Saturn are the conditional love parent who hands out the consequences of our actions, to teach us what we can, can't, and have to do to survive in a material world. Though most cultural traditions give the first role to the mother who gives birth to the infant, and the second role to the father whose work in the world supports them, it is not uncommon for these roles to be blurred, shared, or reversed in human families.

Aspects from the Moon to these angles reinforce the "mother" principle, but if a chart has greater emphasis on the "father" principle, it may outweigh the unconditional love, and the daughter may feel unloved and insecure. Both parents may have to work in the world. One parent may be gone, leaving the other to play both roles. There may be illness in the home, or too many children, or irresponsible or overly critical parents, or other pressures. The daughter may feel that she had to take a parent role while still young, or that her childhood was harsh, restricted, or constricted. Alternately, the parents may overprotect, so the daughter feels smothered. Once the daughter is old enough to encourage open communication with her parents, a more healthy balance can be sought between meeting emotional security needs and sharing responsible power. With mutual caring, the mother and daughter may build a solid foundation of support for their family, and may expand their "mothering" to the world by engaging in helping professions.

Mother-Daughter Mercury Contacts

Mercury to Mercury

Aspects between the Mercurys of two individuals tend to be helpful, suggesting the capacity to understand, communicate, and accept each other. However, nothing in astrology is guaranteed to be positive. The psychological principles of astrology show the life issues, so an emphasis on Mercury may indicate a need to communicate with, understand, and accept each other, rather than a mother and daughter who are already doing it. Problems are possible at any stage of the Mercury process. One or both individuals may fail to understand each other. Or one or both may understand but not communicate their knowledge, leading to feeling cut off and alienated. One may simply talk too much while the other clams up. Or one or both may fail to accept, using the knowledge and communication as a weapon to attack the other. Once the problem is recognized, the antidote is obvious. A major gift of Mercury is the ability to maintain perspective, a light touch, and a sense of humor. As long as there is mutual caring, communication can be kept tactful, human limits can be accepted, and a focus on the positive traits of the other person is likely to encourage her.

Mercury to Venus

These aspects, like Mercury to Mercury, tend to be positive, facilitating a pleasant relationship with friendly understanding, communication, and acceptance. Venus is always a key to one's pleasure, so Mercury-Venus aspects between the mother and daughter are often a sign of shared interests that are mutually rewarding. Venus pleasures include those involving the physical world and the world of relationships, so the mother and daughter may deepen their bond in almost any area by talking about, planning, and doing together any mutually pleasurable activity. They may make money together with a shared business, spend money together shopping at the mall, or engage in sports, entertainment, hobbies, social affairs, etc.

If the two individuals enjoy very different forms of pleasure, especially if either disapproves of the habits of the other, it will be important to strengthen the understanding and acceptance that is one of the potentials of Mercury. For example, if the mother adores classical music and the daughter adores rock music, they can agree not to play music when they are together, or they can stick to something neutral. Or they might find they both like folk music. As usual, with mutual good they can find compromises; some activities to enjoy together and some to be shared in other relationships. Since Venus is one of the keys to our choice of a mate, a positive relationship between the mother and daughter can produce a long-term adult relationship that is more like one between siblings and partners than parent and child.

Mercury to Mars

Conjunctions with Mars are special, since they indicate a sense of identification that takes the other person as a role model. With a positive role model, one will imitate the other, though this is often done subconsciously. With a negative role model, one will tend to do the opposite of the other. One may talk constantly while the other stays mum. One may be more studious while the other is more physically active. One may be rash and the other cautious. If there is mutual good will between the mother and daughter, they can learn from each other and move toward moderation in any area where they have tended toward excessive behavior.

Any aspects between Mercury and Mars in the two charts may face and deal with the same issues, working out a balance between thinking, speaking, and action. The astrological elements of air and fire tend to reinforce each other, encouraging humor, spontaneous, impulsive expression, and openness. If one person has strong air and fire while the other has a greater emphasis on earth and water, one may demonstrate the mind of a debater and a tongue like a sword while the other cringes inwardly or outwardly. Verbal strife or arguments are possible. An important potential with such aspects is the ability to achieve an objective understanding of anger, and to deal with it rationally. As always in astrology, the whole chart of each person must be considered. With a mother and daughter who care for each other, Mercury-Mars aspects can encourage mutual openness, fun, and really lively communication. Shared activities can include physical sports, mental games, hobbies, and productive tasks, including learning new skills.

Mercury to Jupiter

As with Mercury and Mars, we have air and fire again with these two planets, so they are likely to reinforce tendencies toward humor, excitement, creativity, and spontaneous action. Such feelings may lead to excesses, which could be physical, emotional, or mental. If the charts of both the mother and daughter are tilted toward spiritual interests, they may share a spiritual faith, or look for ways they can provide knowledge to improve the world. Alternately, they may just love to travel and be planning the next trip before they have ended the last one.

If the two individuals hold very different beliefs and values, there are likely to be problems. Our religion determines our ultimate goals in life; what we think is possible and morally right and desirable. Jupiter signifies the conscious form of this faith, while Neptune describes the subconscious faith. So, a mother and daughter with very different beliefs may face real problems. There is so much sensitivity and vulnerability connected to a deeply held faith that sometimes it is better to just not talk about such differences. The understanding and acceptance of Mercury can help, and silence on that topic may allow both the mother and daughter to avoid hurting each other while they continue a mutually supportive relationship in other life activities. On the positive side, a shared faith, and the values and goals on which it is based, is one of the strongest bonds that two individuals can enjoy. Mutual confidence can be built when each person can encourage and "talk up" the other one. In any relationship, one of the most healing actions that can be taken is to find ideals and goals that both individuals value, that, regardless of the past, can let them move on together.

Mercury to Saturn

Saturn always shows where we feel that life is serious. An aspect of Mercury to Saturn in the charts of a mother and daughter may be expressed by one person helping the other to "lighten up." Alternately, one may feel "dragged down" by the other's caution, insecurity, or anxiety, and may pull away from the relationship. If both tend to have an emphasis in earth and water planets, signs, and/or houses, they may end up reinforcing the security needs of each other and become prize worriers. With my Mercury octile my mother's Saturn, I did one version of a pull-away. She was heavily Capricorn, despite a Sun in Leo, and definitely a prize worrier. I always said, "I don't have to worry. My mother worries for me." But I was tactful enough not to say that to her. I just did not tell her anything that I knew she would worry about.

Mercury tends to show one's talent for abstract intelligence while Saturn shows the potential for practical intelligence, but both can be rational/logical. So aspects between them in mother-daughter charts can be used constructively to handle a family business or just the business of coping with a family. Since Mercury is one of the keys to siblings and Saturn signifies a parent, usually the responsible parent with the power, these areas may become life issues. The mother may have trouble being responsible, subconsciously taking a sibling role and turning the daughter into the parent. Or she may overdo her use of power. Parents who are too willing to play "Atlas" may invite their offspring to reject any share of family responsibility, leaving the parent to "do it all." As usual, once the daughter is old enough to share communication and family tasks, if both individuals care about each other, a strongly positive relationship can be developed. The Saturn urge for control and responsibility can be kept directed into the career, and the Mercury potential for communication, understanding, and acceptance can be an asset in the relationship.

Mercury to Uranus

Aspects between two air planets should encourage insatiable curiosity and free-flowing communication between the mother and daughter. Similar interests and friends can be shared, creativity can be enhanced, and life can be a constant search for new knowledge with each egging on the other. Brainstorming may produce truly original ideas. Of course, even with inherently compatible planets, if either the mother or the daughter is more conventional and security-minded, the other can challenge her traditional views. It is also possible for one to be cautious in some parts of life and willing to resist limits in other life areas, while the other person has different priorities. For example, one may need the approval of society and keep her unique personal ideas private, while the other may publicly flaunt her radical ideas yet actually live a traditional life. There can also be tension if a water emphasis in the chart of either the mother and/or the daughter shows excessive emotional sensitivity and if either or both are too blunt and outspoken. The air principle signifies the conscious side of the mind, including the ability to see the broad perspective, to be logical, and to talk. Water is the element of emotional sensitivity, with the capacity for compassion—literally feeling with others, and softening the openness of the air. But normally, Mercury-Uranus aspects show the potential for mutual understanding and acceptance; the ability to turn a parent-child relationship into a lasting adult friendship.

Mercury to Neptune

Aspects between air and water planets show the ability to integrate the conscious and sub-conscious sides of the mind. Between the charts of a mother and daughter, they are likely to enhance both verbal communication and psychic connections. If both develop this potential, they can "tune in" to each other at the subconscious level as well as consciously share interests and ideals. If either individual is overly sensitive and the other too blunt, the sensitive one will tend to retreat for self-protection. But if they share the Neptunian ideals of empathy and compassion, they can work out a compromise. One can work on not say-ing everything she thinks, and the other can work on not taking comments personally.

It is also possible for aspects between Mercury and Neptune to encourage an almost limitless imagination that may be expressed in either or both individuals. My Gemini Moon was conjunct my mother's Neptune and Pluto. Despite her strong Capricorn, her Leo Sun and Mercury and her Gemini Pluto, Neptune, and Jupiter managed to dramatize and exaggerate almost everything in life. With my heavy Virgo emphasis, I went to the opposite extreme of literal precision in all details. We had a clear case of projection, with each overdoing what the other was underdoing.

Mercury to Pluto

Mercury signifies the conscious side of the mind, but our Gemini expression of Mercury can be quite different than our Virgo one. Our Virgo skill can reinforce Pluto's capacity for obsessive detail, so the main danger associated with this reinforcement would involve over-doing the narrow focus sometimes called tunnel-vision. If both individuals have similar interests and pleasures, they might encourage each other's indulgences. It is not always true that if some is good, more will be better. If such excess is avoided, the relationship between the mother and daughter can be a positive and cooperative one. Shared intellectual inter-ests, tasks, and/or pleasures are possible.

If either the mother or the daughter is expressing more of the Gemini nature, the prin-ciples represent a natural quincunx, two sides of life that are almost totally different and not easy to integrate. Either individual in the relationship might emphasize a broad per-spective that talks a lot, but takes life lightly and values space. The other could feel deeply and crave more closeness, but hesitate to reveal her sensitivity. With mutual trust, caring, and respect, communication can be opened up and the mother and daughter may each contribute her own skills to build a partnership/sibling team.

Aspects between air and water planets can connect the conscious and subconscious sides of the mind, so the mother and daughter may be bonded on a psychic level that transcends words. Psychic sensitivity is a two-edged sword. With mutual good will, it builds powerful relationships that can be supportive bulwarks of strength in a challenging world. Where good will and/or trust are lacking, either or both individuals may be deeply threatened, often without any clear awareness of the reasons for the feelings. Sometimes increased communication can be helpful, offering reassurance to reduce the distrust. But if either or both individuals are too personally insecure to allow more openness, they may need to maintain some emotional detachment while attention is focused on strengthening personal self-confidence. As faith grows, a closer, more trusting relationship may become possible.

Mercury to Ceres

Ceres is one of the keys to our ability to "mother" or to accept being "mothered," so aspects between Mercury and Ceres should indicate the potential for mutual understanding and communication in mother-daughter relationships. Once the daughter is grown, they can take turns mothering each other or interact like mutually supportive siblings. Problems can arise if the mother insists on maintaining the parent role, forcing the daughter to stay in the child role. Alternately, an insecure or irresponsible mother may unconsciously push her daughter into being the parent, or a daughter who strongly identifies with the parent/power role may subtly push her mother into being the child in the relationship. Self-awareness and mutual good will can produce positive, supportive interactions.

Mercury to Pallas

The Libra potentials of Pallas can blend beautifully with the Gemini side of Mercury to develop a cooperative, friendly, expressive relationship that resembles affectionate siblings and partners. The mother and daughter may share clothes, makeup, hobbies, and friends. However, if either or both the mother and daughter are strongly competitive, the rivalry side of Libra may dominate, leading to verbal debates. Once the daughter reaches adulthood, if both individuals enjoy competition and the interaction is experienced as a game that is sometimes won and sometimes lost, the relationship may not suffer. However, if either person feels threatened, unable to take the game lightly, the insecurity and hurt feelings can lead to a more intense power struggle or to one or the other retreating. A positive bond can be built if mutual interests are developed that bring pleasure to both. They may range from a "cause" that both support (such as social justice), to an artistic skill, to similar tastes in entertainment, as long as both the mother and daughter enjoy the same activity.

Mercury to Juno

Like Pluto, Juno signifies a passionate need for a mate to share one's pleasure, while also wanting to feel a sense of personal control. If either the mother or daughter feels that the other is too controlling, the natural reaction will be a power struggle or a retreat. Since Juno describes a deep need for closeness, retreat is a "last resort." If the Mercury potential for equality, understanding, communication, and acceptance is developed, the relationship can become a truly positive partnership. However, if the detached coolness of Mercury is overdone, there can be hurt feelings of rejection, with a need for more warmth. When both the mother and daughter work together, they can gain mutual insight, combining the wide perspective of Mercury (as a key to consciousness) with the depth insight of Juno (as a key to the subconscious, intuitive side of the mind).

Mercury to Vesta

If Mercury is being expressed as its Gemini side, Vesta's Virgo nature intensifies a mental emphasis in a mother-daughter relationship. Both individuals may reinforce each other's intellectual curiosity and encourage each other's mental skills. They may combine the broad perspective of air with the productivity of earth, leading to shared accomplishments. Tension is possible if one is more tolerant and accepting while the other is more critical, and these roles may be reversed in different areas of life. For example, one may be a neat housekeeper but a sloppy thinker, while the other reverses the priorities. One may be committed to her work, while the other prizes social activities with friends. If both accept each other's differences and keep the critical Vesta potential directed into their jobs, the relationship can flourish.

Mercury to Chiron

Chiron can be expressed as the Sagittarius or the Pisces side of Jupiter, so its aspects to Mercury reinforce the mental sides of life. Connecting the conscious intellect to either form of idealism, the more conscious Sagittarius or the more subconscious Pisces, can be positive if the mother and daughter share interests, beliefs, and values. Obviously, there may be tensions if they hold very different values. They will need to expand the Mercury potential for understanding and acceptance of each other's differences. Chiron may also signify a problem with faith that can lead to anxiety and/or depression. If either the mother or daughter has a more secure faith, she may help the other move in that direction. If either individual has excessive expectations of life, the other may set a positive example of "going with the flow," of enjoying the journey toward the ideals. With mutual caring, the relationship can be truly rewarding as the mother and daughter share ideas and ideals and efforts to create a better world.

Mercury to the Lunar Nodes

The Nodes are similar to adding two more Moons to the chart, so aspects to Mercury connect the conscious and subconscious potentials of the mind. The mother and daughter will tend to be "tuned in" to each other, sensing each other's feelings and also able to communicate verbally. They may be deeply bonded, reinforcing each other's insights into life and enhancing mutual security. If either or both are overly sensitive, they may need to moderate the verbal bluntness of Mercury in their communication, or learn not to take casual comments personally. Lessons around who talks, who listens, what is said, how information is gained and shared, etc., are possible (especially if a conjunction to the South Node is involved). Once the daughter is grown, they may be naturally able to, or they may learn to, nurture each other and to relate as affectionate, supportive siblings.

Mercury to the Ascendant/Descendant Axis

The Ascendant, like Mars, shows our desire to express our own nature, while the Descendant shows our ability to share life with lasting, equalitarian relationships. Mercury aspects to these angles in the charts of a mother and daughter can lead to active communication between the two individuals and with others who share lasting relationships with them. The mother and daughter may enjoy discussions about people, relationships, and the dance between the self and others. Ascendant-Descendant aspects always suggest the possibility that individual freedom may need to be reconciled with the desire for companionship. As with all of life's dilemmas, compromises may be needed. The understanding and flexibility of Mercury can be helpful, allowing each individual the right to personal individuality as well as to other peer relationships. Depending on the whole chart, one person may be more insecure while the other is more self-confident and openly expressive, enjoying verbal competitive interactions. Developing tact that lets the confident one think, but not speak, on occasion, can lead to a more comfortable life. She can also direct her competitive instincts into alternative targets. The vulnerability of the less secure individual can be reduced if she engages in some kind of successful action. With mutual caring, the mother and daughter can share interests and companions to build a satisfying partnership.

Mercury to the MC/IC Axis

The MC/IC axis and the Nodal axis both point to the parental principle in astrology. In a caring relationship, a grown daughter and her mother are likely to take turns with the roles of parent and child. If either one insists on maintaining the dominant role or is unable to handle her share of the responsibility, there will be tensions in the relationship—particularly around issues of being heard, understood, acknowledged intellectually, etc. The serious tone of the MC/IC axis may have to be balanced with Mercury's skill at humor and lighthearted interactions. Mutual understanding and acceptance can lead to compromises. The open communication signified by Mercury is normally an asset, provided it is not used as a weapon. A mother and daughter who respect each other can work together effectively, whether in a job outside the home or in caring for a home and family.

Mother-Daughter Venus Contacts

Venus to Venus

As the pleasure principle, Venus to Venus aspects between a mother and daughter may be keys to shared pleasures or to areas where tastes and preferences differ. Enjoying similar activities will normally be an asset, helping build a positive relationship, though there is always the possibility that it can produce excesses if either or both keep encouraging the other to do more. Since Venus is a planet that rules both an earth sign and an air sign, the practicality of earth and the rationality of air can help understand and manage such possible excesses, though this may be more difficult if either individual has a strong emphasis on the emotional elements, fire and/or water, in her chart. Even in cases where there are major differences in the preferred pleasures of the mother and daughter, Venus aspects should help in a search for compromises that might involve hobbies, or friends, or just agreeing to avoid doing things when they are together that disturb the other individual.

In light of the competitive potential that is also present with Venus, we have to acknowledge that this may be a factor in a mother-daughter relationship. Instead of sharing their clothes, cosmetics, and friends, they may use them to compete against each other. With Libra, it is important to discriminate between partners and competitors. Shared pleasure is intensified, but fighting members of one's own team is counterproductive. It is fascinating that Venus was considered a war god by the ancient Mayans, and though Venus was considered female in the ancient Near East, Greece, and Rome, she was credited with some very nasty actions. To create a harmonious and mutually pleasurable relationship, a mother and daughter need to look for areas of life that they both enjoy.

Venus to Mars

Venus and Mars are keys to polar principles in astrology. They signify the confrontation of one's own personal desires, rights, and power with the desires, rights, and power of others with whom we have long-term, equalitarian relationships. All three air "sides of life" describe the conscious side of the mind and equalitarian relationships, but Gemini and Aquarius are more temporary and superficial once we become adults. Venus and Mars rule two polarities. With Aries/Libra, personal action on one's own terms confronts interaction with long-term equalitarian relationships. With Taurus/Scorpio, the control of personal pleasures and possessions confronts the need to deal with joint pleasures, possessions, and power. (Following its discovery after the development of telescopes, Pluto was recognized as a ruler of Scorpio, but Mars remains a co-ruler.) Aspects between Venus and Mars in the charts of a mother and daughter can intensify mutual pleasures, or they can be expressed in intense power struggles. If either individual is insecure, she may retreat for self-preservation. Obviously, this is most likely when the daughter is still young, but the roles may be reversed with an elderly mother and a grown daughter.

A conjunction of Mars with any factor in the chart of another person is a special case since it shows that the other individual is a role model for the Mars person. Role models may be positive, showing a desire to be like the other individual. Or they may be negative, indicating a desire, often subconscious, to be different from the other. If the feelings are conscious, they are easier to handle. We can choose to express them or decide against acting on them. A conjunction of Venus and Mars is more likely to be experienced as a positive identification with mutual affection, but astrology shows psychological principles that can always be manifested in a variety of ways. So competitive, power-struggle interactions are possible, and if a more harmonious relationship is desired, both the mother and daughter may need to look for areas of life that can be enjoyed together. Any active pursuit of pleasure may be helpful, and it becomes easier if each can gain a greater sense of self-confidence. Participation in physical sports where both the mother and daughter are on the same team is one possible way to build both self-confidence and mutual pleasure. Creating grace in motion (dancing, skating, tai chi, etc.) is another constructive option.

Venus to Jupiter

Since both Venus and Jupiter are generally associated with positive emotions, aspects between them in the charts of a mother and daughter are likely to encourage shared values and pleasures. Perhaps the greatest danger is that either or both will encourage the other to overdo the shared goals, leading to some sort of excesses. The results in the lives may still remain pleasurable unless they are carried to a real extreme, which brings the warning signal of pain. Even where there are major differences between the ideals of the two individuals, as long as there is a sense of mutual good will, it should not be too difficult to work out compromises. However, if beliefs become a rigid, limiting dogma held by either or both individuals, there is a danger of real alienation. One may end up praying for the other as a "lost" soul, or may overdo the sensual pleasures the other is denying herself for moralistic reasons. Such reactions call for a large dose of tolerance, which is not always easy when Jupiter is focused on religious convictions and associated ethics. The broad perspective, understanding, and acceptance of the air principle in astrology is needed to help build a more harmonious relationship. With mutual caring and some willingness to compromise, areas of shared faith and pleasure can be found.

Venus to Saturn

When a mother and daughter are cooperating with the Taurus potential of Venus and the career-oriented, practical, productive potential of Saturn, they can often be highly successful in dealing with the material world. They may actually work together, or the daughter may choose a field of work related to her mother's career, or they may just share similar ambitions and support each other's efforts in any area of life. An artistic focus is possible, or they might be collectors, or finances might be emphasized. If their ambitions or material tastes are in conflict, they will need to look for practical compromises if they wish to improve the relationship. In any effort to find compromises, common sense calls for seeking whatever pleasures can be found that are shared by both individuals while placing less emphasis on their differences.

If the Saturn side is overdone at the expense of Venus, either the mother or daughter may feel that affection (or money or sensual satisfaction) is limited, restricted, or controlled. If the Libra potential of Venus is more important in the relationship, close associates may be a source of either pleasure or tension. (Differences of opinion about partners and partnership are possible.) Alternately, there may be issues around dominance versus equality, or the balancing act between love and work and between ease and effort, especially after the daughter has become an adult. Saturn calls for the responsible handling of power, while the Libra side of Venus wants fair play, including taking turns in life activities. As usual, in any area of tension, compromises are needed if the mother and daughter want to increase mutual pleasure in the relationship.

Venus to Uranus

In contrast to aspects between Venus and Saturn, the nature of Uranus forms a natural trine to the Libra side of Venus while its nature squares the inclinations of Taurus. The air principle in astrology signifies the conscious side of the mind, learning, communicating, and feeling comfortable with equalitarian relationships. But the Taurus side of Venus can be quite uncomfortable with the readiness of Uranus to not just rock the boat, but sometimes to tip it over and risk all of its contents rather than stay in a boring rut. Since Venus shows where we really want pleasure, and Uranus indicates a capacity for intelligence and communication, even when a mother and a daughter are experiencing tension over differences, compromises should be possible. Obviously, compromise is a two-way street, requiring some "give" on both sides. If either the mother and daughter or both are too "fixed" in their wills, a ruptured relationship is possible. But a little tolerance (a Uranus talent) and affection (a Venus talent) can produce a wonderful healing.

Venus to Neptune

With aspects between the two major astrological keys to beauty, a mother and daughter may share talents and values that encourage and inspire each other. The focus could be in any area of the arts: painting, music, poetry, drama, etc. Alternately, they could focus on the counseling and healing potentials of Venus and Neptune, seeking to make the world more ideal. The hazard with all of the astrological keys to ideals, Jupiter, Neptune, and Chiron, involves excessive idealism. When expectations are too high, it can produce a kind of idolatry where we expect a part of life to be perfect or to give us "Heaven on Earth." Venus is capable of being more practical and more rational in contrast to Neptune. The latter, as a key to subconscious feelings, signifies habits that are harder to recognize and change. If both the mother and daughter can become aware of their subconscious ideals and goals, and can find even a few that they share, a mutually supportive relationship can be built that brings pleasure to both and may expand to help heal the wider world. If either the mother or daughter has given up the Neptunian search for infinite love and beauty and mystical oneness with the Whole, and has become a victim, sometimes the best the other can do is to set a good example and seek professional help for the victim. Trying to become a savior in a close personal relationship is more likely to produce a second victim. The savior often becomes a martyr. Setting a good example while continuing to love the other person and provide whatever practical help is possible may help heal her and the relationship.

Venus to Pluto

With aspects between two keys to pleasure, there can be an intense focus on this area of life. Where the Taurus side of Venus seeks personal pleasures, both Pluto (in its own nature) and the Libra side of Venus represent the capacity for shared pleasures. These may include money, possessions, and/or any sensual appetites, and the handling of power is often a major issue. A mother and daughter with aspects between these planets may simply have a deeply pleasurable interaction in any of these areas. Or they may encourage mutual excesses, running up debts, caught by addictions to tobacco, alcohol, drugs, sex, etc. Or they may struggle over the handling of finances, possessions, and pleasures. In extreme cases, litigation and/or physical violence is possible. Where the "enduring self-will" of the fixed "sides of life" are involved, compromise is often very difficult, but it is essential if what should be a partnership, the positive potential of both Pluto and the Libra Venus, has turned into a state of war. If the affection of Venus can be mobilized, as well as the self-knowledge and self-mastery potential of Pluto, real miracles can occur, even in a hostile confrontation. But it takes real desire added to the "fixed will" persistence of Taurus and Scorpio to escape the tendency to stay in a state of stalemate or to abandon the effort to revive a relationship once it has been given up as "dead." If there is still love on either side, the miracle is possible. The process is started by forgiving both oneself and the other.

Venus to Ceres

The asteroid Ceres is usually a key to one's ability to "mother" and be "mothered," so aspects between Venus and Ceres in the charts of a mother and daughter are often associated with affectionate relationships. The mother and daughter may enjoy similar physical pleasures or friends, or just feel like friends. However, if the mother is unable to relinquish her parental power and responsibility once the daughter is grown and ready to become more of an equal, tensions can develop.

Obviously, the total charts need to be considered. A single aspect can only be a small part of the picture. Since Ceres seems to have some Virgo qualities in addition to its Cancer overtones, there can also be issues around criticism that might be overdone by either the mother or daughter. But even where there is tension, mutual good will should be able to work out compromises to create a more harmonious relationship. A mother and her grown daughter can truly enjoy taking turns "mothering" each other, building a mutually supportive relationship.

Venus to Pallas

The asteroid Pallas seems to represent Libra tendencies, so aspects to Venus are likely to emphasize sociable, friendly interactions unless the competitive side of Libra brings rivalry into a relationship that should express teamwork. In such cases, finding areas of shared pleasure can help. The mother and daughter may share clothes, cosmetics, artistic interests, and friends. They also may share and reinforce in each other a concern for fair play and social justice, building a genuine partnership as they work for a "cause" that will help others. If competition is hard to eliminate, it can be handled more comfortably if both individuals have an outlet for it in sports or games that can be won sometimes, lost sometimes, and treated lightly. The air potential of Libra can be a major asset if it leads to mutual understanding, communication, and acceptance.

Venus to Juno

With its similarity to Pluto, aspects from the asteroid Juno to Venus can reinforce the potential for partnership between a mother and daughter. However, as with aspects between Venus and Pallas, they may also be manifested in rivalry and power struggles. In such cases, a focus on shared pleasures and less emphasis on differences will help. Or a competitive outlet in sports and games may keep the rivalry from becoming too serious. Mutual pleasures may simply deepen the enjoyment of both individuals, but they may also encourage excesses involving money, possessions, or sensual gratification that could lead to addictions. As with Pluto, if Juno's desire for self-knowledge and self-mastery is properly developed, the relationship of the mother and daughter can deepen into both respect and affection, to become a mutually supportive bond. Where there are differences in preferred pleasures, if both individuals are willing to compromise, power struggles can be avoided by focusing on shared interests and downplaying areas where tastes differ. Once the daughter is an adult, if both the mother and daughter can allow the other to be fully herself, a true partnership is possible.

Venus to Vesta

The asteroid Vesta seems to signify the "ultimate" Virgo, with a potential for total dedication that can produce a tunnel-vision focus on what is defined as one's "job." The "job" may be any immediate goal that gives a sense of accomplishment, something considered worth doing that can be done well. In the charts of a mother and daughter, aspects to Vesta from the Taurus side of Venus can facilitate shared accomplishments and pleasure from them. When the Libra side of Venus is involved, there is some danger of the work-oriented Vesta criticism being misdirected into the personal relationship rather than being properly kept focused on one's job. Once such a problem is recognized, the solution is easy to see, though not always easy to accomplish. Criticism is appropriately used to improve work efficiency, while human associates call for the air potential of understanding and acceptance.

An alternate possible problem between Venus and Vesta involves tension between work and relationships. A daughter may feel neglected if her mother chooses to work or if she has to work outside the home. The roles may reverse when an elderly mother feels neglected by a working daughter. As with any of the dilemmas that are inherent in life, compromise is needed to build more harmonious relationships. Carrying out joint projects, in work or with hobbies, can bring out the positive potentials of Venus and Vesta.

Venus to Chiron

Chiron's potential for being manifested as either the Sagittarius or the Pisces side of Jupiter can encourage deeply idealistic relationships between a mother and daughter. They may enjoy pursuing knowledge together, or travel, or share a set of beliefs about the world. Or they may have artistic interests or commitments to social causes in common. Where a mother and daughter have very different values and pleasures, both will need to allow the other to maintain her own ideals and try to find some areas of agreement. Another possibility with all of the astrological keys to idealism is the hazard that one or both individuals will expect too much of each other or of themselves. Disillusionment and alienation can follow if anything in life is expected to be perfect or to provide "Heaven on Earth." We need to keep our ideals, but to remember that they are long-range goals and we can enjoy the journey as we move toward them. When a mother and daughter share the journey, they can enhance the pleasure for both.

Venus to the Lunar Nodes

The lunar Nodes function as two more Moons in a horoscope, so aspects between Venus and the Nodes in the charts of a mother and daughter may lead to warm, mutually supportive relationships. The water factors in astrology symbolize the subconscious side of the mind, including the habits brought from past existences, so aspects to the lunar Nodes in the charts of others may be clues to past-life connections. Nodal aspects usually indicate areas in life where emotions are deep and where the mother and daughter are psychically open to each other. Positive emotions provide a bulwark of strength, while conflicting emotions can be a source of major challenges that call for serious attention to improve the relationship. Bringing subconscious feelings into conscious awareness can start the process of healing. We develop the air capacity for adult understanding and acceptance as we move from the baby feelings of the Moon and its Nodes into their mothering potential, from feelings of helpless dependency into the ability to nurture others. Taking turns in the mothering role can enhance comfort, cooperation, and pleasure for both the mother and daughter.

Venus to the Ascendant/Descendant Axis

These aspects in the charts of a mother and daughter call for the integration of personal desires with the capacity to enjoy the world with others. Astrology conceptualizes the inherent dilemmas of life as the confrontations between three major areas: personal needs and desires; interpersonal, face-to-face interactions with others; and transpersonal issues involving the larger world of nature, humanity, ultimate beliefs and values, and the "rules of the game." As seen previously, the Venus/Mars polarity (echoed by the Ascendant/Descendant axis) symbolizes personal desires versus face-to-face, interpersonal interactions with lasting, equalitarian relationships. In the charts of a mother and daughter, a mutually pleasurable partnership can be developed involving any or all of the Venus potentials of artistic interests, sensual gratification, and/or social activities. If rivalry develops rather than a cooperative partnership, compromises are needed so that each individual can feel able to meet her own needs without denying the needs of the other. By focusing on areas of similar tastes and interests and downplaying areas of differences, harmony can be enhanced to move toward a more comfortable relationship.

Venus to the MC/IC Axis

The MC and its polar opposite, the IC, represent the same principles as Saturn and the Moon, and the signs of Capricorn and Cancer. These parental principles signify the unconditional love mother and the conditional love father who enforces the law through the consequences of one's actions. Obviously, the real parents may differ enormously from these abstract principles. Either or neither parent may provide the unconditional love that is needed by the dependent infant, and judgment and consequences may be overly lenient, overly harsh, or inconsistent. With Venus aspects to these angles in the charts of a mother and daughter, the relationship with a constructive mother may be enhanced as the daughter matures to build a mutually supportive and pleasurable bond for life. Affection could be accented.

Where there have been serious tensions between the mother and daughter, major efforts may be needed to forgive and release the past, and to forge a more satisfying relationship based on mutual pleasures. Issues to be worked out might include the handling of dominance and responsibility, or excessive criticism. The mother's career may have interfered with her parental role, or either the mother or daughter might be in need of more emotional warmth and cuddling and feel deprived. Perhaps the balancing act between dominance, dependency, and equality is a challenge. Perhaps issues around money or sensual satisfaction are a bone of contention between the parent and child. With mutual caring, the past can be acknowledged and released and a more harmonious future can be achieved.

Mother-Daughter Mars Contacts

Mars to Mars

Mars is our primary key to our sense of personal identity, our feeling that we should have the right and the power to do what we choose. Mars aspects in the charts of a mother and daughter can range from feeling "I am my mother" to a determined effort to be her opposite. The mother and daughter may look and act like twins, or they may act like mortal enemies locked in a permanent feud. Or, most confusing to associates, they may fight each other when alone, but become a bonded team when confronting others. Shared desires and activities can strengthen the capacity for cooperation, and rivalry can be directed into sports and games and can remain constructive as long as they are not taken too seriously with a need to win at any cost. Humor is a great asset unless it is overdone in practical jokes that create real emotional or physical damage. The element of fire in astrology is a key to our life force, our vitality, enthusiasm, and confidence. With a positive relationship, a mother and daughter can fan the flames in each other and have fun together.

Mars to Jupiter

This double fire combination can be enormously energizing in a mother-daughter relationship. Action is the order of the day, whether carried out in physical sports or other activities, in emotional expression, in a search for knowledge, or in spiritual pursuits. Both may love to travel, write, or teach. Deeply satisfying relationships can be built if they share core beliefs about the nature of life and the world. If they hold conflicting beliefs and desires, especially if either or both hold rigid, dogmatic beliefs that her view of the world is final Truth, one or both may feel driven to convert the other to her own way of thinking. If a stalemate ensues, it may require a total avoidance of the topic of beliefs to sustain the relationship. Sometimes humor can help, but if beliefs are taken seriously by either or both individuals, humor can make the situation worse. Other factors in the charts should offer the air to understand and move toward tolerance, or the earth to be practical about the situation, or the water to be empathic, in order to mitigate the fire feeling that when we know what we want, we should be able to get it. As with any conflict in life, compromise is needed to move toward harmony and integration. It is worth the effort to turn loose the joy of the fire sides of life.

Mars to Saturn

These aspects in the charts of a mother and daughter portray a major life issue, the confrontation of personal will and power with the limits of personal power. Where personal will and attitudes about the rules of the game are in harmony with each other in the two individuals, the relationship can be highly productive and successful. Conflicts between freedom versus external power and limits can produce tempestuous struggles, and it is not always the child resisting the parent. An insecure mother dealing with a strong-willed daughter may feel impotent and trapped. Or she may feel responsible but guilty because she lacks the capacity to enforce her parental obligations. More commonly, it is the daughter who fights for more freedom, or runs away in some manner, sometimes by just giving up and becoming passive. In any conflict, both individuals need to look for ways to compromise. This is not easy if either is determined to dominate and the other is defiant. But, with mutual caring, demands can be moderated on both sides, and the mother and daughter can build a more constructive relationship.

Mars to Uranus

With two astrological keys that both signify resistance to limits, aspects between Mars and Uranus in the charts of a mother and daughter may reinforce each other's devotion to liberty and they may enjoy it together. This might lead to excessive risk-taking, from bungee jumping, to mountain climbing, to car racing, etc. They may need to call on other parts of their natures, on the earth sides of life, to maintain some practicality with at least one foot on the ground. If only one of the two is a risk-taker, there can be major tensions as the cautious one tries to restrain the more foolhardy one. Either the mother or daughter may play either role, or they may alternate in different areas of life. One may assert her freedom from limits by privately smoking marijuana while the other openly refuses to take orders from teachers or bosses. Projection is common in personal relationships, with one person overdoing an action that the other might subconsciously want to do (but is repressing the desire). Moderation can resolve the problem if both the mother and daughter can find activities that satisfy their need for creative self-expression without taking undue risks or inviting repercussions from the laws of nature or the society.

Mars to Neptune

One of the best outlets for Mars-Neptune aspects in the charts of a mother and daughter is through artistic or helping activities that build self-confidence in both. Dancing, singing together, sports that involve grace in action, hobbies involving craftsmanship, or idealistic causes that can be pursued jointly can all contribute to a mutually satisfying relationship. As with all of the astrological keys to idealism, Neptune aspects warn against setting expectations too high. Perfection is a long-range goal, and it is not much fun if we spend the journey berating ourselves or others for not being there already. The other principal danger with Neptune is a lack of faith in something beyond humans. This can lead to giving up the search for something more ideal and running away from life. Whether in excessive sleep, daydreaming, romantic fiction in print or in movies, or in the more damaging forms of escapism of alcohol, drugs, and psychosis, either the mother or the daughter might be running while the other tries to save her, or they could be encouraging each other's flight from a miserable world. A savior-victim relationship among family members is usually doomed to failure. The would-be savior can help more effectively by setting a good example personally and calling in a professional to assist the victim. Finding an activity that both can share while letting each be true to herself can work miracles in the relationship.

Mars to Pluto

These aspects in the charts of a mother and daughter may mark a major confrontation of wills. Where both individuals have similar desires, they may form a powerful, lifetime partnership. On the other hand, conflicting desires can lead to titanic power struggles. In extreme cases, the interaction can include vindictive, vengeful cruelty. The weaker one, who is not necessarily the child, is likely to give in or retreat. If a truly adult relationship is sought, compromises will be necessary. The Pluto potential for self-knowledge and self-mastery will need to be mobilized while any attempt of either person to dominate the other will need to be avoided. Competitive or physically demanding hobbies can provide a constructive outlet for this feisty combination. If shared desires can be discovered, the mother and daughter can pursue them together while placing less emphasis on their differences. Accepting differences, no matter how great, while allowing each person to be herself is the essential foundation on which a harmonious relationship can be built.

Mars to Ceres

The asteroid Ceres seems to portray one's potential to nurture or to accept nurturing from others, so it is usually a clue to one's experience of one's mother. A conjunction with Mars in the charts of a mother and daughter shows the tendency to be identified with one's mother as a role model. The daughter may want to be like the mother or her opposite, and the feelings are not always conscious, but may simply manifest in her actions. With positive feelings, the mother-daughter relationship is normally mutually supportive as each seeks to nurture the other in her own area of strength. It is possible for the critical potential of the Virgo side of Ceres to be misdirected against the people in one's life rather than kept properly directed into one's work. There can also be serious tensions if the mother overdoes her parental power, leaving the daughter feeling that her right to be herself is being denied. Sometimes this situation can be repeated with the roles reversed when a daughter who felt limited as a child becomes a bossy manager of an elderly mother. Each person is working on the balance between personal desires and the needs of other family members. A healthy adult relationship is attainable when the mother and daughter cooperate for mutual support while accepting each other's right to be a unique person.

Mars to Pallas

With its Libra potential, the asteroid Pallas should form a natural partnership with Mars when they make aspects in the charts of a mother and daughter. Their relationship can be strengthened and harmonized by teamwork in any activity that they both enjoy. They may share a love of sports, or artistic performances, or social occasions, or support of causes such as fair play and social justice. If rivalry is present, it can be handled if they avoid taking it too seriously, seeing life as a game in which we develop our skills by sometimes winning and sometimes losing. If there are major differences in the tastes of the mother and daughter, they can focus on the ones that they share and put less emphasis on the differences. However, if either feels that her right to be herself is really threatened, the relationship can produce serious power struggles or the retreat of the one who is more insecure. The latter will need to develop more personal self-confidence to counter the anxiety, and both might need more tolerance of each other's individuality. If each can comfortably allow the other to be herself and can appreciate her uniqueness, a relationship of mutual respect and affection can be developed.

Mars to Juno

Like Pallas, the asteroid Juno shows the craving for partnership, but with an intensity that is more like Pluto. So Mars-Pallas aspects in the charts of a mother and daughter face similar issues, needing to integrate personal desires with the desires of others who are emotionally close. Where the mother and daughter have similar tastes and desires, they may form a strong partnership that lasts throughout their lives. Conjunctions to Mars are especially important, showing the tendency to see the other person as a role model, whether we want to be like or the opposite of the model. The fire nature of Mars and the water nature of Juno (which is like Scorpio) can produce very intense emotions in any relationship. Where the mother and daughter have very different tastes and desires, and especially if either tries to dominate the other, a major contest of wills is possible. Retreat is an alternate potential if either one feels insecure. A strong-willed child can face down a weak parent. To move toward a more harmonious relationship, the insecure individual will need to gain more self-confidence and both will need to work together to find areas of shared pleasures that they can enjoy together. Mobilizing the Juno potential for self-knowledge and self-mastery can help, and where Mars is involved, it will always be important for each person to accept the right of the other to be herself.

Mars to Vesta

Vesta's Virgo potential can combine with the strong-willed drives of Mars to produce major joint accomplishments by a mother and daughter when they combine efforts. Alternately, it can produce disastrously alienated relationships. A critical attitude may undermine the self-confidence of either or both individuals. Even young children can be critical of parents. Strict enforcement of what is considered proper behavior or required chores may inhibit the daughter in her early years, and the latter may give in or she may rebel to prove her right to be herself. Sometimes with Vesta, health is an issue. A frequently sick mother may be a burden on her daughter, leaving her with little opportunity to do what she wants with her time and energy. Or a frequently sick daughter may be a burden on her mother, especially if the latter also has to maintain a job outside the home in addition to caring for her family. But these outer circumstances do not determine the eventual emotional relationship, since either individual may react to the denial of personal freedom with resentment or with a deeper love for the other in her care. Vesta shows the need for a sense of accomplishment, for something that is worth doing that we can do well. Caring for a loved one can be experienced as deeply rewarding when we are expressing the dedicated service of Vesta. To build a positive relationship, the mother and daughter need to find areas where they can share a sense of accomplishment with each feeling that the action is voluntary, an expression of their own identity.

Mars to Chiron

The little planet (or comet?) Chiron can manifest either the Sagittarius or the Pisces side of Jupiter. Whether it is acting as fire or as water, its aspects to Mars in the charts of a mother and daughter are likely to be emotional and to deal with idealistic issues. When the mother and daughter share ideals, they are likely to reinforce and energize each other. They may travel together, or study, write, teach, or seek to bring their ideals into the world. They might support each other's passion for sports, risk-taking, gambling, or for a healing profession. If they have different beliefs, values, and goals, they may clash, each trying to persuade the other to adopt her personal convictions. Or they may simply go their own ways, each determined to preserve her own freedom. If other factors in the charts reinforce the message of Mars and Chiron, the relationship is likely to be exciting and variable, open to creativity that is driven by a constant pursuit of something new and more.

Mars to the Lunar Nodes

Aspects from Mars to the lunar Nodes, which function as two more Moons in astrology, are likely to bring up freedom-closeness issues in mother-daughter relationships. Mars symbolizes the quintessential desire for personal independence while the Moon and its Nodes signify a deep need for emotional closeness: a home, family, food, and especially a caring relationship with a mother figure. When a mother and daughter have achieved integration of these two major life desires, they can be mutually supportive while allowing each other to be fully themselves. If integration is not achieved by a compromise that allows room in the life for both independence and emotional connections, projection often occurs. Either the mother or the daughter may overdo a demand for freedom while the other overdoes a hunger for closeness. One plays "clutch" while the other plays "run." If both individuals can become aware that both desires are essential parts of life present in everyone, compromises can be worked out so that neither need is denied.

A conjunction with either Node is similar to a conjunction of Mars with the Moon. The mother tends to be taken as a role model by the daughter, to be imitated if she is a positive model or opposed as an example of what not to do. In the latter case, it may take major efforts to find activities that both individuals can enjoy together to build mutual trust. Since the lunar Nodes, like all water factors, are usually an indication of deep subconscious connections between individuals that may stem from past-life bonds, there are often feelings of mutual vulnerability. It is worth whatever effort it takes to heal the relationship if occult teachings are right that unless it is healed in the current life, the two individuals will have to come back and work it out in future lives.

Mars to the Ascendant/Descendant Axis

Mars and the Ascendant represent the same principle in astrology, so aspects connecting them in the charts of a mother and daughter will reinforce the importance of their sense of personal identity and personal power. Since the Ascendant and Descendant represent an axis across a horoscope, all traditional aspects to either will produce an aspect to the other. (This will not be the case with some of the less frequently used aspects such as the septile, the seventh of the circle, and the novile, the ninth of the circle.) Aspects to the Descendant call for working with lasting, equalitarian relationships, so the mother and daughter will be seeking compromises between the desire of Mars and the Ascendant for personal rights and the Descendant need for others, which calls for respecting their rights.

Mars conjunct any astrological factor in another person's chart shows the likelihood of the other person becoming a role model. The Mars individual may want to be like or the opposite of the other person. With a positive identification, the mother and daughter are likely to react to life in similar ways, to enjoy the same activities, and to have fun together. This does not mean that they will agree about everything! They may also be intensely competitive on occasion, but then kiss and make up and face the rest of the world as a team. In contrast, a negative identification can produce a really destructive relationship that may even end in violence. It takes major efforts to heal such a relationship, to be able to permit, respect, and even learn to value the other person's independence, and to give her the right to be herself. But since each is seeing herself in the other, it is worth the effort as the only way to gain personal self-understanding and self-worth.

Mars to the MC/IC Axis

Since the MC and IC represent the same principles as Saturn and the Moon, conflict aspects to these angles from Mars in the charts of a mother and daughter produce the equivalent of a cardinal T-square. An octile (semisquare) of Mars to one angle and tri-octile to the other is a milder form of the same principles: a confrontation between independence, dependence/nurturing, and dominance/responsibility. These are all normal desires, present to some degree in everyone, but none of them can be expressed to the fullest extent without denying the others. Compromises are needed if we are to be whole persons, satisfying all twelve sides of life. When we are analyzing relationships, each of the two individuals may emphasize different desires, but each has the same twelve needs, and compromises are required to attain mutually satisfying interactions. Both the mother and daughter will be learning how to allocate their time and energy between personal desires, interests, and hobbies; the needs of home, family, and/or pets; and the demands of the outer world and making a contribution to society.

Sports or mental contests may provide a chance for each individual to occupy the "top dog" role by winning some of the time. A true contest helps develop physical or intellectual skills, depending on the nature of the game, and learn that losing is not the end of the world as long as we can play again and hope to win next time. If either individual wins all the time, the loser is likely to take flight in whatever way she can. If the mother and daughter can take turns nurturing each other, sharing responsibility while accepting each other's individuality, a mutually satisfying relationship can be achieved. Harmony aspects between

Mars and the MC-IC axis suggest that they may already have the capacity to handle such compromises, and can effectively help each other cope with the world.

Mother-Daughter Jupiter Contacts

Jupiter to Jupiter

Traditional astrology tends to assume that Jupiter will always function as a granter of wishes, a great benefic. Practicing astrologers normally learn rather quickly that the search for the Absolute that Jupiter represents can lead to quite destructive excesses. It is not always true that if some is good, more will be better. On the positive side, Jupiter to Jupiter aspects in the charts of a mother and daughter may signify shared beliefs, goals, and values that produce great good in the world. The mother and daughter may learn together, teach, write, travel, or work to save the world. But such aspects may instead encourage them to expect too much of themselves, each other, or the world, leading to constant disillusionment and depression. Alternately, the mother and daughter may share a lack of faith in a Higher Power, or they may believe in a harsh, punitive God who will send them to Hell for dancing or having a deck of cards in the house. Such beliefs or a lack of faith can produce chronic anxiety or outright fear.

Jupiter, like all factors in astrology, points to psychological issues in the life that may be handled well or badly, bringing pleasure or pain. Pain is always our warning signal, telling us that we are on the wrong track and need to change our habits. Jupiter aspects bring positive results in relationships when both individuals are clear and realistic in their beliefs and goals. Uncertainty or ambivalence about goals, or a lack of realism about what is possible or the effort needed to reach goals, is likely to produce only disappointment. When a mother and daughter agree on reasonable goals, they can make a joint contribution toward a more ideal world. They can help fulfill their own dreams and those of others.

Jupiter to Saturn

Aspects between Jupiter (which symbolizes our search for the Absolute) and Saturn (which describes the Laws, of nature and of human societies) highlight the transpersonal sides of life. Prior to the discovery of Uranus and Neptune, Jupiter and Saturn were rulers of the last four signs of the zodiac, and they remain the co-rulers of Aquarius and Pisces. Aspects between Jupiter and Saturn connect basic beliefs (the Jupiter principle) with learning to understand the consequences of our actions (the Saturn principle). Our beliefs determine our values and choices in life, leading to our actions and their resulting consequences. When a mother and daughter share the true wisdom of Jupiter, knowledge of and a faith in harmony with the Saturnian rules of the game in this physical world, they can be teachers of and examples for the world.

Conflict between these principles may manifest in many ways. A daughter's legitimate beliefs and goals may be opposed by a mother with overly rigid rules, or an overly permissive mother may fail to teach her daughter that there are rules in life and that they have consequences. A grown daughter with an elderly mother may also reverse these roles. I have seen a hippie mother from the '60s startled to have to deal with a daughter who converted to fundamentalist Christianity. Conflicts may involve differences of opinion in any area; over decisions on appropriate dress, health habits, friends, jobs, mates, the handling of offspring, etc. Our beliefs about the nature of life and reality shape our handling of it, so a mother and daughter with different beliefs are literally living in different worlds. If they care about each other, they will seek areas of life where they can share values, and hopefully they will both learn to be realistic enough to live voluntarily with the rules of the game.

Jupiter to Uranus

Grab the reins and hold on to your hats. Jupiter-Uranus aspects in the charts of a mother and daughter can be exciting. Of course, a single aspect is only a small part of the picture describing the potentials of a relationship, but if other aspects and sign/house placements support this one, innovative, creative interactions are likely. The mother and daughter may encourage each other's passion for new knowledge, new hobbies, new friends, and new experiences in general. Just don't try to predict what they may think of and do next. A general emphasis on fire and the cardinal quality in their charts will add to the dynamite and could encourage taking dangerous risks. An emphasis on air and the mutable quality will add to the intellectual focus with the danger of too many interests and a trail of unfinished projects. Boredom is the unacceptable state. Whatever it takes, get out of the rut.

Projection often occurs when earth and water are more emphasized in the chart of either the mother or daughter. One individual will be more security-minded, more cautious and traditional, while the other tries to light a fire and keep life moving. In projection, both individuals have the same basic life desires, but one overdoes one side of a conflict, while the other overdoes the opposite side. A daredevil daughter may terrify a protective mother, or an adventurous mother may push a timid daughter into emotional panic. Compromise is possible if both can move toward moderation. The risk-taker can develop more empathy with the cautious one, and the latter can gain confidence through small ventures beyond her security limits. Life is driven by the need to do more than we have done before, and much of our growth comes though the compromises called for by love in our close relationships. As we strive to widen our repertoire in life, mutual caring helps us make the effort to change our habits.

Jupiter to Neptune

In the charts of a mother and daughter, aspects between the two major astrological keys to the search for the Absolute can lead to extremes. Where both individuals share similar beliefs, values, and goals, they will encourage each other on the path. They may work together in any area to create a more ideal world. Typical choices include teaching and healing, but any form of service is possible. Where the conscious ideals of Jupiter and the subconscious ideals of Neptune reinforce each other, the greatest danger is a lack of realism about the limits inherent in the physical world that can lead to religious fanaticism, from inquisitions to martyrdom. But if the mother and daughter have adequate earth in their natures, they should be able to keep one foot on the ground while their souls reach beyond the sky.

When a mother and daughter are in conflict over beliefs, goals, and values, there are many possible variations. One may be more grounded and urge common sense on the other, while the latter seeks to convert the first to her vision of how life ought to be. Or they may have different beliefs and visions, and spend futile hours with each trying to convert the other to her view of the Truth about the world. Or they may join in a struggle to discover the meaning of life, guru-shopping, sampling different religions and cults, never feeling confident that they have found "The Answer." Or they may emphasize part of the mutable dilemma, one insisting on the Jupiter values of openness, honesty, and truth as the supreme values in life while the other elevates Neptune, making empathy and compassion the supreme values: "Tell it like it is" versus "Don't hurt anyone." As usual, compromise is needed if the mother and daughter want to maintain a positive relationship. If either or both hold a rigid, dogmatic set of beliefs, they may need to downplay that topic and focus on areas of life where they can be mutually supportive. Setting a good example rather than verbal persuasion is more likely to encourage conversion. A lifetime search for "The Answer" may be constructive as long as the journey is enjoyed and the seekers are functioning productively along the way. There are times when openness is really needed, and times when kindness is more appropriate. Plus the Virgo side of the mutable dilemma should be considered. To achieve one's goal, what action is most likely to be effective in the situation? Try to keep the ideals high, clear, and reasonable.

Jupiter to Pluto

Combinations of planets with the emotional elements of fire and water tend to express with extra intensity. Jupiter-Pluto aspects in the charts of a mother and daughter share that tendency, which can be manifested in many variations. Pluto (natural ruler of the 8th house) marks the end of the interpersonal section of life where we deal with face-to-face personal relationships, while Jupiter (natural ruler of the 9th house) marks the beginning of the transpersonal section of life where we define the faith that will guide our lives. We are currently seeing some of the tragic results of humans mishandling these principles in the Palestinian-Israeli struggle while Pluto transits the Jupiter sign of Sagittarius. Although the Moon is the primary key to the earth and the immovable homes and orchards on it, Pluto signifies all joint resources, including money and possessions and the capacity to share them for mutual pleasure. Where different groups are convinced that "The True God" has personally given them the same specific territory, compromise may become almost impossible and religious war almost inevitable.

When a mother and daughter can share joint resources, pleasures, and power (the Pluto side of life), and also share (the Jupiter) beliefs, values, and goals, they can stand together against almost anything in life. They may be totally unrealistic and hit the stone wall of Saturn limits, and they may choose to go up in flames together rather than compromise, but the courage of their committed conviction is formidable. Obviously, if they also have some earth practicality and some air flexibility and rationality, life is likely to be both more comfortable and more effective in coping with the physical world, and they may still demonstrate a remarkable bonded and idealistic partnership.

When a mother and daughter are in conflict over values, whether material, spiritual, or both, the struggle can be intense. Projection may lead to one being swallowed up in material possessions and pleasures while the other chooses a life of spiritual devotion and material self-denial and asceticism. One may just read a lot and the other party. One may spend herself into debt while the other pinches pennies and saves coupons. If each can allow the other to hold different beliefs and values without feeling personally threatened and trying to convert the other, they can maintain a mutually supportive mother-daughter relationship. But if either or both are rigid, dogmatic, or personally insecure, they will need to work to find life areas they can share comfortably. When intense feelings are involved, it is worth the effort it takes to find those comfort zones.

Jupiter to Ceres

The asteroid Ceres is one of the keys to relationships with mother figures, so aspects between Ceres and Jupiter in the charts of a mother and daughter connect ideals to mothering. They may idealize each other, or they may wish the other was ideal and feel let down. They may share beliefs, ideals, and goals, or differ strenuously. They may study, teach, write, or travel together, or one may choose to roam the earth or pursue knowledge while the other is a committed mother and homemaker. As long as they avoid rigid, dogmatic beliefs and the need to convert each other, they should be able to find shared warmth and maintain a mutually supportive relationship. They may pep each other up, provide supportive optimism and encouragement, and combine wisdom with caring.

Jupiter to Pallas

The asteroid Pallas seeks pleasure in equalitarian relationships, so when it aspects Jupiter in the charts of a mother and daughter, they often develop pleasant partnerships. As usual, the hazard with Jupiter is excessively high expectations, so either the mother or daughter may fall into that trap, but the air capacity inherent in Pallas with its Libra nature should encourage understanding and acceptance. Air sees the broad perspective and says, "It is okay to be human." Where ideals and values are shared, the mother-daughter bond is likely to deepen, and they may work together, as professionals or as volunteers, supporting causes such as social justice that create a more ideal world. Alternately, they may combine knowledge and artistic interests as teachers and/or practicing artists. Or one may make a profession of what was a hobby for the other, with both enjoying it. Competition is always a potential with Pallas, but it can be channeled successfully into sports or fighting for justice as long as there are also areas of life where both share values and goals.

Jupiter to Juno

Like Pallas, the asteroid Juno craves partnerships, but Juno is more like Scorpio than Libra, capable of intense passion. Jupiter-Juno aspects in the charts of a mother and daughter are a fire-water combination showing deep emotions that can idealize relationships but can also be deeply disappointed when they fall short of the expectations. When the mother and daughter share beliefs and pleasures, they can be deeply bonded in an adult, lifetime partnership.

When they differ in their beliefs and values, there may be power struggles or alienation and separation. One may seek knowledge or spiritual goals or may just want to stay free to follow her whim of the moment, while the other wants pleasures and possessions in the material world or sees emotional closeness as the ultimate value in life. If they care for each other and want to maintain a relationship, it can take a sustained effort to find common ground where both can enjoy the world together. Where there is love, it is worth the effort.

Jupiter to Vesta

The asteroid Vesta has some similarities to Jupiter in its capacity for dedicated commitment to a goal, but where Jupiter is searching for an abstract Absolute, for God in some form, Vesta is seeking an immediate sense of accomplishment in the material world, for a duty that is worth doing and can be done well. Of course, if Vesta is connected to Letter 9 or 12 in our astrological alphabet, or Jupiter is connected to earth factors or interpersonal needs, there will be a mixture of these basic desires and the individual can go in almost any direction, including alternating between options. For example, an individual with Vesta in Sagittarius or Pisces, in the 9th or 12th house, or closely aspecting Jupiter, Neptune, or Chiron, will frequently dedicate her life to a spiritual cause, while an individual with Jupiter in earth signs or houses, or conjunct earth planets, may make the material world (e.g., money, success, possessions) her ultimate value. An individual with Jupiter connected to the signs, houses, and planets that signify close interpersonal relationships may make them her ultimate value, or she may give up on them because she never found the perfect mate or was afraid of failing to be the perfect mother of a perfect child. The basic mix is looking for an ideal at the same time we are focused on present flaws, the two sides of the coin of perfectionism, so nothing is ever good enough. (Or, we may say, "If I cannot do it perfectly, I won't do it at all.") Astrology is enormously complex and we always need to look at the whole chart, to look for repeated themes, though linear language can only focus on one bit at a time.

Jupiter aspecting Vesta in the charts of a mother and daughter may be manifested in shared beliefs and values that draw them into similar work, seeking to make a more ideal world. Any service profession is appropriate, and they may share homemaking efforts together. The hazard of excessive expectations is increased since Jupiter shows where we are searching for ideals, while Vesta shows the tendency to look for flaws in order to correct them and do a better job. Jupiter and Vesta really epitomize the two sides of perfectionism. If the mother and daughter have adequate air in their charts, they should be able to keep the critical attitude focused on their work and use the broad perspective of air to understand and accept humans as human. But if the perfectionism is displaced into human relationships, there is a real danger of alienation. Of course, overdoing perfectionism is also possible in one's job. There is no perfect job. Some mistakes are inevitable. If we make our job into God, we miss out on a lot of other things in life. For a comfortable, lasting relationship where Jupiter is connected to Vesta, the mother and daughter need to share values and to accept humanness. The best expression is realistic mystics or practical idealists who work hard to bring their dreams into being.

Jupiter to Chiron

This combination, which is equivalent to connecting two Jupiters, reinforces the issue of beliefs, values, and goals in a mother-daughter relationship. If they share ideals, they are likely to move in the same direction in life. They just need to guard against being flagrantly unrealistic and overdoing the high expectations. If any part of life is turned into an Absolute so that we *have* to have it to be happy, it becomes an idol and it will let us down. Any area of life may become the target of the ideals. Money and material possessions are sometimes selected in our physical existence. Power, fame, or love may be the targets, but whatever the choice, sharing the goal will usually create a lasting, bonded relationship between the mother and daughter. Where there are major differences between their values and goals, either the mother and daughter or both may seek to convert the other, or they may simply go their own way in life. If they care enough about each other and can be reasonably flexible in their values, they can allow each other to have different beliefs and still be mutually supportive.

Jupiter to the Lunar Nodes

Jupiter-Node aspects in the charts of a mother and daughter often manifest as a mutually warm, supportive bond. Like the Moon, its Nodes symbolize our capacity to "mother" and to accept "mothering." Jupiter brings idealism into the equation, so the mother and/or the daughter may idealize each other and the relationship. Conversely, if either has inflated expectations or rigid beliefs, it will create problems. Bringing air into the picture can enlarge the perspective and facilitate understanding and acceptance of human limits. If the Nodes, like all water factors in astrology, are keys to past-life connections, it would explain the depth of feeling that is often experienced with lunar Node aspects between the charts of two people. It would also justify some extra effort to work out compromises in areas where there is tension, if only to avoid having to come back and face the same problem in the next life. Normally, there will be deep feelings on both sides, so it should be possible to forgive past hurts and build a more harmonious, mutually supportive relationship.

Jupiter to the Ascendant/Descendant Axis

Jupiter always brings ideals into the picture. Its aspects to the Ascendant/Descendant axis in the charts of a mother and daughter may be manifested in shared values and goals that can be jointly pursued and enjoyed. The mother and daughter may feed one another's faith, optimism, and ability to balance personal and interpersonal needs. Shared activities may be mental, emotional, and/or physical, including sports, trips, studies, artistic interests, friends, etc. If a mother and daughter hold very different beliefs and values, they will need to compromise. They could differ in their need for personal space, for companionship, or for the approval of others. They may disapprove of each other's choice of partner. They will need to keep their expectations of themselves and of each other reasonable, and to look for some areas of life where they are like-minded. Then they can build a mutually pleasurable relationship while allowing each other to be themselves.

Jupiter to the MC/IC Axis

The MC/IC axis carries the same significance as Saturn and the Moon, the keys to parents, so aspects between these angles and Jupiter in the charts of a mother and daughter connect idealism to the daughter's feelings about her parents or to the mother's feelings about her role as parent of her daughter. The MC and Saturn normally signify the parent who carries the primary power and responsibility, while the Moon and the IC signify the unconditional love parent who cares for the helpless infant. Obviously, real human beings may reverse these roles, or play both roles, or neither of them. With these aspects, the mother and/or the daughter may feel the other is ideal, or that she should have been and flunked the course. With shared values, the mother and daughter are likely to be able to share nurturing and responsibility in handling their relationship. Where their values differ widely, compromises will be needed if they want to maintain a positive connection. Often, there will be issues over power and responsibility versus dependence and vulnerability. On a very practical level, it is not easy to cope effectively with both a career and a family. But with some love, patience, and reasonable expectations, a mutually supportive relationship can be built.

Mother-Daughter Saturn Contacts

Saturn to Saturn

Traditional astrology tends to fear Saturn, and it is true that Saturn describes the rules of the game in this physical world, plus the consequences of how we have been handling the rules. But if we know the rules and live with them voluntarily, Saturn represents positive consequences. Saturn to Saturn aspects in the charts of a mother and daughter may be manifested through sharing a career in the world or joint responsibilities in the home. If both the mother and daughter respect each other and each functions competently in her own role, they can be highly successful in coping with the material world.

If either one tries to dominate, whether because she feels responsible or she only feels safe in the power position, there will be power struggles if the other individual is strong. Alternately, a weak mother or daughter may retreat. Of course, when the daughter is still a child, the mother will have the power unless she is chronically ill, and then she may use her illness to control the family. Once the daughter is grown, if she still feels weak but is mobile, she is likely to leave the scene. However, a mother who has been controlling her daughter with illness may be able to hold on to her by appealing to her sense of duty. Guilt is an important part of the Saturn principle. When we defy natural law or social regulations, the consequences mostly come from external forces. When we defy our conscience, we punish ourselves with guilt, and a needy family member can use it as a method of control.

An essential part of becoming fully adult is learning to own one's own authority. We achieve this through learning to cope with the material world, as each individual develops her own areas of expertise. To build a comfortable relationship, a mother and daughter need to find projects to which each can contribute in her own area of skill, and that develop their sense of competence and productivity in the world.

Saturn to Uranus

Once we have learned and accepted the Saturn rules that are required for survival in this material world, Uranus offers us the freedom to break or transcend the rest of what look like rules. We fly planes that are heavier than air when we learn some facts about gravity. Computers keep getting faster as we explore new materials and techniques. A mother and daughter with aspects between Saturn and Uranus may be highly successful if they cooperate to combine the Uranus openness to new knowledge with Saturn's practical ability to test the ideas and look at the consequences. Since both planets are associated with strong determination and a resistance to being dominated, if the mother and daughter are not willing to cooperate voluntarily, they are likely to have major tensions. The mother will initially have the power, but if she is more Uranian, she will be reluctant to use it. If she is more Saturnian, she is more likely to try to restrain her rebellious offspring. Typically, one will be more identified with the urge to innovate, while the other is more committed to tradition. A conservative mother may be shocked by a daughter who challenges the mores of society. A mother who grew up in the '60s, lived in communes, and explored inner space with psychedelic drugs may be astonished to find herself with a cautious, conventional daughter. However, unless one tries to force the other into her own lifestyle, it is possible to maintain a pleasant relationship by focusing on the activities where both are comfortable. A little tolerance goes a long way.

Saturn to Neptune

Aspects between Saturn and Neptune in the charts of a mother and daughter call for integrating the capacity to deal with the material world with a search for ideals, for infinite love and beauty and mystical oneness with the Whole. If the mother and daughter agree with each other in these areas of practicality and ideals, they will be able to support each other in surviving in the world while also contributing to its improvement. If one individual is more focused on physical obligations, power, and responsibilities, while the other is more a dreamer, inclined to the path of artist or savior, there may be tensions. If each can allow the other to be herself while maintaining some joint activities that are mutually satisfying, they can maintain a comfortable relationship. Neptune aspects always call for individuals to guard against having unrealistic expectations. If any part of life becomes so necessary that we feel we can't be happy without it, it has become an idol and will let us down. High ideals are long-range goals. They are only a problem if we are unable to be happy until we get there, or we are so exclusively focused on them that we neglect other valuable parts of life. If the mother and daughter support each other in a realistic journey toward joint ideals, they can build a beautiful and effective relationship

Saturn to Pluto

Like Saturn with Uranus, aspects between Saturn and Pluto in the charts of a mother and daughter involve strong wills on both sides, and a resistance to being controlled. One aspect is only a small part of the picture, but assuming that it is supported by other patterns in the chart, if the mother tries to dominate her daughter, she is likely to be met with stiff resistance. If both individuals are equally stubborn, a long-term stalemate is possible.

The struggle may be open, with both conscious of the issues, but often one or both will be acting with minimal conscious awareness, displaying what psychologists call passive-aggressive behavior. For example, an object treasured by the other person may be "accidentally" lost or broken. If both individuals are able to give up any attempt to dominate the other person, and if there is at least a little love between them, a real partnership is possible with a cooperative sharing of responsibilities and power. Any activities that are mutually pleasurable can be used to build a more harmonious relationship. They might garden together, study investing, design clothes and sew, collect things, try gourmet cooking, or just enjoy similar movies and music. Where they have different tastes, they will need to allow each other to be different. A focus on the areas they both enjoy can build a really positive relationship once the power issue is handled, when both the mother and daughter can be secure enough to relinquish any need to be in control.

Saturn to Ceres

Since the asteroid Ceres provides a key to one's relationship to a mother and "mothering," aspects to Saturn connect the parent principles. Ceres seems to symbolize a Virgo-Cancer mixture, an "Earth Mother" that is more practical than the Moon, our major key to the mother principle. A mother and daughter with these aspects between their charts may take turns with the parent roles even when the daughter is still young. If the mother tries to take on too much of the power and responsibility, the daughter may rebel, or she may give in and consciously or subconsciously decide to "let mother do it all." Since individuals with either a Virgo/Ceres/Vesta or a Capricorn/Saturn emphasis are only happy when they feel productive, it is important to let them develop skills early in their lives. Parents who do too much for them, or who stand over them dictating exactly how to do everything, are not helping such children. A more comfortable relationship can be developed when the mother and daughter carry out projects together and feel a sense of joint accomplishment. Hobbies, crafts, duties in the home, or service that helps others are all suitable activities to develop skills that increase feelings of competence in both the mother and daughter and also help improve their relationship.

Saturn to Pallas

As usual, aspects to Saturn call for a middle road that avoids taking on too much or too little power and responsibility. With such aspects in the charts of a mother and daughter, the mother will, or course, initially be caring for a helpless infant. However, as soon as is practical, she should look for opportunities to share pleasurable activities with her daughter that fit the nature of the asteroid Pallas. They may enjoy picking out clothes together, or find they like the same music, movies, or games. As the daughter matures, they can move toward a partnership that shares both Saturn duties and Libra pleasures, including expanding contacts with other people. If the mother tries to maintain her control too long, insisting that her daughter do everything her way, or if she tries to do everything for her daughter, preventing her from discovering her own ability to be productive, there will be tensions in the relationship. The daughter may eventually rebel against the control, or she may "let mother do it all" and remain dependent, delaying her full maturity as a responsible adult. Shared pleasures can help build a lasting, comfortable partnership.

Saturn to Juno

Saturn aspects to the asteroid Juno are similar to those to Pallas, but Juno is more intense, resembling Scorpio more than Libra. Juno-Saturn aspects in the charts of a mother and daughter can lead to a positive partnership if both individuals avoid trying to control each other. Obviously, this is not an issue when the daughter is a baby, but as she grows, her mother needs to look for activities that can be shared with mutual pleasure. Juno can be a key to deep attachments, and if the mother and daughter can avoid power struggles, a lasting, satisfying peer relationship is possible once the daughter is grown. If either feels that the other is trying to control her, a stalemate is likely or the relationship may be ended. Issues may develop around the handling of money, sensual appetites and sexuality, possessions, or relationships with other people in the lives of both individuals. While Saturn shows the need to develop skills in the physical world, Juno is focused on the need for a mate, setting up a possible contest between love and work. If a mother and daughter differ in their emphasis on these different areas of life, they will need to accept each other's differences in order to achieve a comfortable relationship. Then they can concentrate on mutually pleasurable activities.

Saturn to Vesta

With a double emphasis on work, aspects between Saturn and the asteroid Vesta in the charts of a mother and daughter call for facing this part of life. Both the mother and daughter will need to avoid being overly critical of themselves or each other. They will need to keep the critical attitude directed into the work, where it is appropriate and helpful.

Though the mother will initially carry the responsibility for the daughter as a baby, as soon as the daughter is old enough to help, the mother should let her join in productive activities that develop skills and feelings of accomplishment. It will be counterproductive if the mother tries to do everything for her daughter, or if she orders her to do things and/or stands over her telling her exactly how to do them. Individuals with a Virgo/Vesta emphasis or a Saturn/Capricorn emphasis need to feel competent in order to feel good about themselves and life. Practice enhances skills and strengthens abilities. Projects can include homemaking, gardening, crafts of all kinds, or work outside the home. Cooperative efforts with family members can help build the self-esteem of both the mother and daughter, as well as build good relationships with each other and with the family.

Saturn to Chiron

Like Jupiter and Neptune, Chiron symbolizes a search for ideals. Aspects between Saturn and Chiron in the charts of a mother and daughter can be integrated if both individuals can do practical things that help them reached shared goals. Whether their careers are related or they do different things for related goals, the relationship will be strengthened if they can feel that their activities are in synchrony. If the mother and daughter differ widely in their coping skills and/or in their ideals, there are likely to be tensions. Compromise is possible if they avoid the Chiron pitfall of excessive expectations and if each is able to respect the other. If the mother continues to try to dominate a grown daughter, or to be "Atlas" and absolve the daughter of all responsibilities, the daughter is likely to rebel against the control or to let her mother be Atlas while she becomes increasingly irresponsible. A harmonious relationship can be achieved if each carries a share of the Saturn power and responsibility while contributing in some way to mutual ideals.

Saturn to the Lunar Nodes

Aspects that emphasize the two parents in the charts of a mother and daughter will obviously increase the focus on that area of life. Saturn symbolizes the traditional father role as the provider who enforces the rules by meting out consequences. The lunar Nodes are equivalent to two more Moons in the chart, signifying the unconditional love mother who cares for the helpless infant. Of course, the real parents may reverse these roles, or one may play both roles, or neither may play them. Many children are never given unconditional love, and a smaller number are overindulged and grow up to become irresponsible adults. A lack of unconditional love results in a harsh, punitive, restricted, or overly controlled childhood (Saturn overwhelming the Nodes). The mother or daughter may feel a sense of karmic (extra) pressure in regard to guilt, a parent or parental roles, career ambitions, or family obligations. We need to learn when to ask for assistance, to temporarily accept a dependent role, and when to be strong, able to cope. If a mother and daughter can share love and responsibilities, a lasting, positive family bond is possible. With mutual support, they can build a sense of security for each other, and perhaps extend it to help meet the needs of others in the world.

Saturn to the Ascendant/Descendant Axis

These aspects between the charts of a mother and daughter call for integration of personal desires, interpersonal relationships, and the handling of responsible power in the world. Where the mother and daughter are both able to satisfy all of these natural life desires in moderate ways, they can readily learn to do them cooperatively. If either or both individuals put too much emphasis on one or two of these basic life desires, they will tend to short-change the other one or two, and have problems in those areas. One may take on more responsibility while the other only wants to party with friends. One may demand more freedom while the other wants more closeness. Judgment and/or dominance may confront equality in the form of either competition or cooperation. Compromises are needed to make a place in the life where each of the basic desires can be satisfied. If both the mother and daughter can share in these efforts, they can achieve a mutually supportive relationship.

Saturn to the MC/IC Axis

As with Saturn aspects to the Moon and/or to its Nodes, this combination emphasizes parental issues, but in this case there is a double focus on the father figure and its association with power and responsibility. If the mother takes the power role and is overly controlling and responsible, her daughter may rebel. Alternately, the daughter may retreat if she is too insecure to resist. If the mother is weak and insecure, the father or a surrogate person may dominate the family. If there is a power vacuum, a strong daughter may fill this vacancy while she is still quite young. If the family is "all chiefs and no Indians," a lasting power struggle may ensue. It will help if each individual can identify his or her areas of expertise, and they can use their individual skills wisely. For a harmonious mother-daughter relationship, they will need to take turns nurturing and handling responsibility. A family farm or business, or other related careers or professions are possible. With mutual caring and willingness to work, they can build a supportive relationship that enhances security for all.

Mother-Daughter Uranus Contacts

Uranus to Uranus

Uranus aspects between the charts of a mother and daughter can be mutually stimulating, reinforcing their readiness to investigate anything new. The basic urge symbolized by Uranus calls for going beyond previous limits. When this urge is satisfied by expanding the boundaries of scientific knowledge, it can be very constructive. When it takes the form of fighting the rules of nature or of the society, it can be highly destructive. Outcomes can range from university scholarships and successful inventions to ending up with impaired health or in jail. When a mother and a daughter share constructive interests, they can encourage each other to develop new hobbies, make new friends, and contribute to humanitarian causes. They may need to draw on some earth potential in order to finish at least some projects. If the daughter is more restless, impatient, or rebellious, the mother may need to encourage her to persist long enough to complete some activities, and to live voluntarily within the rules of society. More rarely, these roles may be reversed with a grown daughter if her mother has managed to become a senior citizen without acquiring some common sense. Moderation is the secret to integrating our different desires, learning to be a whole person who is able to handle all sides of life, including harmonious relationships with our loved ones. The great gift of the Uranus principle is the ability to understand, accept, and even appreciate everyone's uniqueness.

Uranus to Neptune

Aspects between these two transpersonal planets in the charts of a mother and daughter are likely to encourage them to focus on the world. Humanitarian causes may be supported, artistic talents may be developed, the pursuit of new knowledge may be facilitated, or the mother and daughter might just enjoy widening their circle of friends and experimenting together with new forms of fun. With any contact to Neptune, it is important to keep the expectations reasonable. The intelligence and broad perspective of Uranus as an air planet may facilitate this acceptance of humanness, but the potential desire of Uranus for a radical revision of the world's traditions might, instead, just add to the utopian urges of Neptune. A mother who is idealistic but also adequately grounded can set a good example if her daughter is inclined to be too "far out." More rarely, these roles might be reversed if a grown daughter sees her mother sliding over the edge. If an excessive Neptunian hunger for the ideal ends in escapism such as alcoholism or drug addiction, professional help should be sought for the "victim." Trying to "save" a close relative is more likely to end with the "savior" becoming a martyr, which is another form of victim. Less grave, but still painful, it is possible for a mother and daughter to have tensions if one overdoes the abstract intellect of Uranus, maintaining a cool distance that the other interprets as blunt, uncaring, and emotionally painful. Balance can be restored if the more Uranian person develops a little more Neptunian empathy and compassion, and the more Neptunian person becomes a bit more detached and able to take life somewhat lightly. As with all of the different parts of life, moderation allows us to be whole, to express all of our drives, including mutual pleasure with close relationships.

Uranus to Pluto

These two planets rule signs that square each other, so the desires they describe tend to be incompatible; in this case, part of the fixed dilemma. The issue of freedom versus closeness is the most common problem when aspects between these planets are present in the charts of a mother and daughter. Power struggles are also likely if either person tries to control the other. The fixed sides of life can be highly creative, but want to change on their own terms. They all possess an enduring will that resists being controlled by others. Uranus represents a tendency to rebel against all limits, including bonded human relationships. Friends are enough. Pluto symbolizes the desire for a passionate, committed partnership, but also the goals of controlling oneself and avoiding being controlled by others. The incompatibility of the principles is strong and obvious, and moderation and compromise are required to achieve a lasting, comfortable relationship. It is possible to have a cooperative partnership if both the mother and daughter avoid any attempt to coerce each other.

One of the most destructive outcomes can occur if the Pluto potential for mastery of the appetites is not developed, and the Uranus defiance of limits is added to the Pluto desire for shared pleasure. It is possible for a mother and daughter to share an addiction to food, tobacco, alcohol, drugs, gambling, or even just shopping beyond the budget, operating as a partnership in which they egg each other on and defy the standards of the rest of the world. Yet that destructive pattern can be reversed and they can encourage each other to move toward mastery of the appetites. Substituting a variety of constructive pleasurable activities that they share can make a real difference. Artistic action such as dancing, gardening, music, dramatics, yoga, tai chi, etc., can replace passive indulgences, with each individual encouraging the other to persevere in the new skills. The mutual determination of the fixed sides of life can support a new and better life for both.

Uranus to Ceres

Aspects between Uranus and the asteroid Ceres in the charts of a mother and daughter can be manifested as a real friendship between parent and child, with each respecting the other as a unique and interesting individual. There also may be tensions with one individual wanting more freedom while the other wants a traditional parent-child relationship. Or, warmth and compassion may clash with independence and detachment. In the latter case, joint projects in the home, or with friends outside the family, may help the mother and daughter gain a sense of cooperation. Taking turns, each nurturing the other at her own level of skill, can facilitate the sense of equality desired by Uranus while satisfying the service inclinations of Ceres.

Uranus to Pallas

A mother and daughter with these aspects between their charts should be able to form a pleasant, cooperative relationship focused on activities that both can enjoy. Shared interests could include fashion, movies or other entertainment, social activities with friends, artistic crafts, etc. They might also become involved in social causes, working for greater justice in the world. If the competitive potential of Pallas becomes a threat to a harmonious partnership, it can be directed into sports and games that develop personal skills and self-confidence while learning to see that life is a game. We learn to win sometimes, lose sometimes, and take it lightly. We learn to compete when it is appropriate, and to cooperate when we are members of the same team. A mutual interest in expanding human knowledge can be an important asset in developing a harmonious, lasting partnership.

Uranus to Juno

With Juno's similarity to Pluto, aspects between them in the charts of a mother and daughter may manifest many of the same potentials. There may be tensions if either the mother or daughter wants more closeness while the other wants more independence. As with all the dilemmas that are inherent in life, compromise is needed to develop a comfortable relationship. If a mother and daughter reinforce each other's desire for sensual pleasure in the physical world, they will increase the danger of addictive behavior. If the Uranian and Plutonian tendencies to resist outside control are added to addictions, the problem can be increased. It can be reversed if constructive pleasures are substituted for the passive indulgences. Dancing, swimming, singing, gardening, etc., can be pleasurable and healthy. Teamwork in activities that are mutually pleasurable and also constructive can produce a partnership that is also a friendship.

Uranus to Vesta

Engaging in innovative work together will help a mother and daughter who have aspects in their charts between this planet and asteroid. Projects are needed that include variety and intellectual challenge for Uranus and that produce a sense of accomplishment for Vesta. Voluntary teamwork describes a keynote of these astrological factors. If the mother over-does the Vesta inclination to focus on flaws and to criticize her daughter's efforts, or the mother just does things for her because she can do them better, the daughter might rebel and insist on doing them her own way or not doing them at all. Alternately, the daughter might just give up and let her mother do everything, thereby failing to develop her own skills. If illness is a problem within the family, it may derail the urge for independence that Uranus represents. If either the mother or daughter is overly focused on practical work while the other only wants to party with friends or to pursue abstract intellectual interests as a spectator, they will need to understand and accept their differences. A positive relationship can be developed by keeping criticism directed at their work rather than at each other, and through teamwork with a variety of interesting activities that build skills to produce success in the world.

Uranus to Chiron

Aspects between these factors in the charts of a mother and daughter are likely to stimulate mutual intellectual activity, innovation, and creativity. The transpersonal focus of both the big gas planet and the little body that may be a comet will encourage interest in the world of ideas, ideals, and universal principles. If the charts of both individuals support these interests, the relationship can blossom into one of shared learning and teaching. If either the mother or daughter is less attracted to the world of the mind, the differing values may lead them in different directions in life. Both Uranus and Chiron can signify an urge toward freedom, so both individuals may be comfortable with maintaining a friendship with occasional, fairly impersonal interactions. However, if either is more invested in personal family contacts, the other person may feel rejected and hurt, and compromises may be needed. Chiron carries the potentials of both Jupiter and Neptune, and with all of the astrological keys to idealism, there is always the danger of having unrealistic expectations. If either the mother or daughter has serious problems involving her faith in a Higher

Power, and she has slipped into a victim/martyr role, the other person may be drawn into playing savior. In such cases, seeking professional help is advised. Finding areas of faith, values, and goals that lead both individuals in the same direction, can strengthen and harmonize the relationship. Allowing each other to be human and maintaining a sense of humor can also help build a mutual and lasting adult friendship.

Uranus to the Lunar Nodes

These factors may warn of a freedom-closeness dilemma when they are aspected in the charts of a mother and daughter. One individual may fight for more personal space while the other clutches at her, requiring compromise to prevent a rupture of the relationship. Emotions might war with the intellect. Issues around abandonment, neglect, or excessive eccentricity are possible. Yet, the urges represented by Uranus and the Nodes can also be expressed in ways that produce wonderful relationships. A mother and daughter may be friends who take turns nurturing each other. The lunar Nodes, like all water factors in astrology, point to subconscious connections that may stem from past-life relationships. There is often a deep emotional bond between the two individuals, including psychic openness so they can be aware of each other's feelings. Uranus also shows the potential for awareness that reaches beyond traditional channels, so aspects between it and the lunar Nodes may accentuate this openness. If the mother and daughter care about each other, a deep and lasting bond is possible, providing mutual support with mutual respect for each other's individuality.

Uranus to the Ascendant/Descendant Axis

With mutual respect for each other, these aspects between the charts of a mother and daughter can encourage pleasurable activities including shared studies, social gatherings, and artistic expressions. Even when the daughter is still young, suggestions are likely to be more effective than orders. Reasons are preferable to arbitrary declarations. If either the mother or daughter is overly independent, the other may feel rejected and need to be encouraged to develop other relationships to satisfy her need for companionship. If a competitive relationship develops between the mother and daughter, it can be channeled into sports, games, or finding a social cause that both individuals can support. Sharing a search for knowledge, expanding opportunities for peer relationships, and encouraging mutual artistic interests may all help build a positive relationship that can evolve into a true friendship and partnership between the mother and daughter.

Uranus to the MC/IC Axis

For a successful resolution of these aspects between the charts of a mother and daughter, a friendship needs to be built between the parents and their child. The MC and IC carry the same meaning as Saturn and the Moon, while Uranus symbolizes the drive for equality, the right to be uniquely oneself, and a tendency to resist all limits. Obviously, a full integration of these principles is only possible once the daughter approaches adulthood. A small child needs the Moon's protection and Saturn's lessons about rules and consequences. However, a start needs to be made much earlier by respecting the daughter's right to be an individual. If she is overly Uranian and rebels against any attempt to limit her freedom, her mother will need both patience and firmness, setting a good example while pointing out the reality of the physical world, which sets limits and inflicts painful consequences if they are ignored. It is possible for these roles to be reversed with an elderly mother who resists the need for proper food, exercise, sleep, etc. Her daughter may set a good example, but may also need to take stronger measures to persuade her mother to cooperate with the rules of life in a physical body. Activities that can be carried out together, that are mutually supportive and pleasurable, are the most effective way to enhance harmony and affection. A cooking class together that teaches good nutrition, or an exercise class together that acknowledges the reality of one's age, may help develop new, constructive habits. With mutual caring and moderation, the mother and daughter can both move toward their full potentials.

Mother-Daughter Neptune Contacts

Neptune to Neptune

In light of Neptune's slow motion, only a few aspects are possible between the charts of a mother and daughter, but the basic astrological principles can be applied to other relationships such as a grandmother and a grandchild. The search for infinite love and beauty and mystical oneness with the Whole is likely to be intensified and expanded when such aspects connect the charts of two individuals. The search can find an artistic outlet in music, dancing, drama, poetry, etc., or it can be expressed in activities that seek to create a more ideal world. Any area of healing is appropriate, but we can feed people, clothe them, shelter them, or inspire them in many ways. The biggest hazard with Neptune is the risk of giving up the effort to improve the world and turning to some form of escapism. Milder forms include excessive television viewing, daydreaming, reading romantic fiction, and sleeping a lot. More serious efforts to run away from our disillusionment include alcoholism, drug addiction, chronic illness, and psychosis. When a mother and daughter hold very different ideals, there can be major tensions, and compromise is necessary to build a more harmonious relationship. With the astrological keys to idealism, it is also always important to avoid excessive expectations of oneself and of others. Neptune activity is normally mostly subconscious, which makes it harder to reach and to change. Introspection and meditation can help, in addition to finding something we can do to make a better world. If Neptune aspects between a mother and daughter are directed into shared artistic or service action, the relationship can be a deeply satisfying one and they can also make contributions to the world.

Neptune to Pluto

With two water planets aspecting each other in the charts of a mother and daughter, they are likely to be extrasensitive to each other's feelings, connected at the subconscious level. This ability to "tune in" to another person can be both an asset and a hazard. Oversensitivity is often experienced as vulnerability and one or both individuals may retreat, emotionally or even physically, for self-protection. On the positive side, a mother and daughter can be enormously helpful to each other with such extra insight. Zip's life was saved when her mother had a psychic vision and insisted that a doctor perform surgery on her in the middle of the night. He said that she would have died if he had waited until the next morning. There were strong water connections between the charts, including a Moon conjunct Pluto and the Neptunes sextile each other. As usual with all Neptune aspects, excessive expectations need to be avoided to attain a comfortable relationship. Mutual pleasures can enhance the harmony. Pluto is a key to joint resources, including debts, taxes, return on investments, and inheritance. If a mother and daughter give, receive, and share, each in her own area of skill, both can benefit. When they cooperate in acting on their ideals, the world can benefit.

Neptune to Ceres

These aspects in the charts of a mother and daughter may be expressed through mutual idealism in a loving relationship that helps the world. Or Ceres as the "mother" asteroid may want to have, or to be, an ideal mother. If either the mother or daughter or both want the other person to be more ideal, they will be dissatisfied when she is human, and the relationship will suffer. Alternately, if one person is more focused on practical, immediate action that copes with the physical world, while the other has her head in the sky dreaming of utopian plans to save the world, the mother and daughter may need to meet somewhere in the middle, to find a place in the life for a little of both. Reasonable expectations, plus joint activities that promote shared ideals, can go a long way toward healing the problems and building a harmonious relationship.

Neptune to Pallas

Shared artistic activities are a great way to work with Neptune and Pallas aspects in the charts of a mother and daughter. The asteroid Pallas seems to carry the Libra love of the graphic arts such as photography and designing in many areas, but it can also focus on fair play and social justice or just crave an active social life. A mother and daughter can build a positive relationship by engaging in any of these activities, with the impetus of Neptune's search for ideals adding to the potential of their making a real contribution to the world with their talents. It is always important to keep the expectations reasonable when astrological keys to idealism are involved in the horoscope patterns. A true partnership is possible for a mother and daughter when they accept each other as equal humans, moving together toward shared ideals.

Neptune to Juno

Like Pallas, the asteroid Juno indicates a desire for partnership, but Juno is more like Scorpio than Libra. The desire for a mate is more intense, and Neptune wants an ideal one. These aspects in the charts of a mother and daughter may lead to a long-term adult association that can be highly valued by both if their expectations are reasonable, or it can be painful if either or both are focused on the shortcomings of the other. One example was shown in a recent PBS documentary about Harry Truman that included material about his wife, who remained attached to her mother for most of her life. A mother and daughter can build a mutually satisfying relationship by sharing pleasures on all levels, physical, emotional, and spiritual. With compatible ideals, they can also combine their efforts to help create a better world.

Neptune to Vesta

This combination is equivalent to the Virgo/Pisces polarity, appropriate for an artist or savior who seeks to make a more ideal world, but who may neglect human relationships in a single-minded devotion to her service. When this planet and asteroid aspect each other in the charts of a mother and daughter, human relationships may require attention, especially when the daughter is young. If the two individuals have similar ideals and values, they may build an enormously positive relationship as they share their efforts to help others. If either the mother or daughter is more focused on the work that is required to survive in the physical world, while the other is prone to fantasy or following a utopian vision designed to save the world, they will need to find a middle ground that allows some room in their lives for realism and idealism. They will also need to avoid the pitfall of perfectionism, which can produce chronic frustration and which carries the danger of being displaced into human relationships. As long as we direct our criticism into our jobs, we increase our skills and efficiency. It is destructive to expect ourselves or our fellow humans to be perfect and to focus on their flaws. If other patterns in the charts repeat and emphasize the Neptune-Vesta theme and the mother and daughter have very divergent ideals, they may simply go their own ways once the daughter is grown. However, if they can cooperate in practical accomplishments that move the world a little closer to their mutual ideals, they can build a positive relationship and improve the world.

Neptune to Chiron

When two keys to idealism are connected in the charts of a mother and daughter, the search for the Infinite is accentuated. If both individuals share a basic faith and its concomitant values and goals, they may reinforce each other's commitment to create a more ideal world, and may continue to be seekers, helpers, and healers together. Very different beliefs may produce an unbridgeable gulf if either or both take their beliefs seriously. If they care about each other and want to maintain an ongoing relationship, they may have to agree that religion will not be discussed. They can focus on the areas of life where they share interests and values. Artistic talents, hobbies, studies, and travel may provide areas for mutual satisfaction. Reasonable expectations of each other and of life in general will help them maintain a comfortable relationship.

Neptune to the Lunar Nodes

As with aspects from Neptune to the Moon in the charts of a mother and daughter, Neptune-Node contacts can encourage warm, mutually supportive, idealistic relationships. If both individuals can nurture and accept nurturing, even a young daughter can be a comfort to her mother. As with all aspects to Neptune, excessive expectations can be a hazard, leading to disillusionment when the other individual is found to be human. There will also be tensions if a mother and daughter hold very different ideals, and compromises will be needed. Since water factors in astrology symbolize the subconscious side of the mind and may be keys to past-life contacts, such aspects usually show extra sensitivity and possible psychic openness between the individuals who have them. Sensitivity is a two-edged sword; it is potentially an asset and also a danger. While we occupy a physical world, we need to know when to be open to the sensitivity, but also when and how to shut it down for self-protection. If the mother understands these areas of life, she can teach her daughter. If neither understands, they may suffer needlessly. One of the tragedies of materialism is its ignorance of the fact that the physical world is only a fragment of reality. The larger spiritual reality is not understood by materialists. Parapsychology research demonstrates experiences beyond the information received by the physical senses and logic. If a mother and daughter care about each other and hold similar ideals, they can build a powerful relationship that will provide emotional support for both and also help heal others.

Neptune to the Ascendant/Descendant Axis

These aspects in the charts of a mother and daughter call for the usual caveat to avoid having excessive expectations of oneself or others. They also remind us of the need to hold on to our utopian dreams without losing the ability to meet our own needs and the ability to relate comfortably in close relationships. To be a whole person, we need to handle all twelve sides of life. When a mother and daughter care about each other, they can cooperate in meeting these inherent challenges in life, which we call the dilemmas. The areas of life we call personal (our own desires and needs), interpersonal (one-on-one interactions), and transpersonal (the big picture, greatest good for greatest number) are all important parts of the picture. Aspects between Neptune and these horoscope angles connect one factor from each of the three major areas. A mother and daughter who accept each other's right to be an individual, who are mutually supportive, who share pleasurable activities with each other and with other associates, and who contribute toward a mutual vision can be a bulwark of strength for each other and for the world.

Neptune to the MC/IC Axis

These aspects connect idealism to the parental axis in the charts of a mother and daughter. They can signify beautiful relationships between a daughter and her parents if they hold similar but also reasonable ideals. Expecting too much of oneself or of others is a sure road to disappointment. If conflicting ideals and values are held by family members, compromises will be needed. One individual may make sports the most important area of life. Another may choose intellectual pursuits over everything else. Still another may elevate her career into her "absolute value," or make friends the essential in her world. With mutual tolerance, different values can be accommodated. If the mother is more focused on the material world, whether on her career or on security within the home, she may need patience and empathy to deal with an overly idealistic daughter. If the mother has her head in the sky to the extent that she fails to meet the practical needs of adequate food and shelter or other protections for her daughter, the latter will learn through painful experience about the need to integrate the different sides of life. Even if a difficult start has been made, a better relationship can be developed if some shared ideals can be identified. Any conflicting ones that remain can be downplayed while the mother and daughter cooperate to move together toward the mutual ideals.

Mother-Daughter Pluto Contacts

Pluto to Pluto

Pluto's slow orbit about the Sun means that few mothers will have mutual Pluto aspects with their children. However, though this book is written especially for mothers and daughters, the principles of astrology can be generalized and applied to any relationship. Since Pluto's orbit is elongated, more aspects will be possible, including a Pluto square Pluto, for individuals born during its faster periods such as the last half of the twentieth century.

In the charts of a mother and daughter, Pluto aspects will emphasize its nature, which symbolizes the ability to give, receive, and share possessions, pleasures, and power with lasting, close, equalitarian relationships. An important part of this capacity is the development of self-knowledge, partly gained through the mirror of a mate, and self-mastery, partly learned through respect for the rights of a mate. When a mother and a daughter share Pluto aspects, they may develop a true partnership throughout their adult lives. They may share sensual pleasures, material possessions, and deep emotional warmth. Problems will develop if the pleasures are mutually reinforced to become addictions. They can include excesses involving monetary extravagance, food, alcohol, tobacco, drugs, sex, gambling, etc. In extreme cases, power struggles can result that may range from litigation over inheritance and debts to violence. Obviously, for such extreme developments, many factors in the chart would be needed to repeat the theme and show the potential danger. One aspect is only a small part of the picture. A positive relationship can be developed if the mother and daughter can substitute constructive pleasures for the passive indulgences. They might garden together, learn to sew and crochet, take up gourmet cooking that emphasizes healthy nutrition, or join a dance, golf, or tennis club. The more active pleasures we have in our lives, the less we are likely to overdo any one to the point where it becomes destructive. When Pluto's positive potentials for self-knowledge and self-mastery are developed, a mother-daughter relationship can be an impressive, lasting partnership.

Pluto to Ceres

These aspects connect mate and mother potentials, so when there is mutual caring, they encourage a lasting mother-daughter relationship that extends into the daughter's adulthood. If the positive sides of the principles are present, there will be deep bonding with each supporting the other at her own level of ability. If the mother has been overly controlling when the daughter was young, or if the daughter was overly emotionally dependent and possessive, it may take time and effort to loosen the grip of the one doing the more active clutching in order to move toward a more equalitarian relationship. If such an effort is not attempted or is unsuccessful, psychology labels the two individuals as codependent. The relationship may still be helpful if both individuals remain basically dependent and if each is able to give something to the other so it is not totally one-sided. Even a chronic invalid can give love and gratitude to her caretaker.

Growth may occur if either or both can increase her ability to cope with the material world in ways that will increase her self-confidence, and/or if she can expand her contacts with other individuals to develop equalitarian associations. If only one person is growing, the other may become even more insecure and anxious, and the former will need understanding and patience to help the latter find ways to also enlarge her life. With mutual caring, both can expand their range of pleasures that are shared with a wider circle, without losing the important sense of mutual support and security provided by their special relationship.

Pluto to Pallas

Both this planet and this asteroid show the desire for a partnership, so aspects between them in the charts of a mother and daughter can be expressed in cooperative activities. Finding areas of mutual pleasure will strengthen a positive relationship. Where there are different tastes and interests, compromises can help and remaining differences can be downplayed. Mutual caring is important to encourage such compromises. If competition becomes a major part of the relationship, it can be channeled into sports, games, and fighting for social causes that both individuals support so they are drawn together by the effort. Based on Greek mythology, some astrologers associate Pallas with issues involving the relationship between a father and daughter, but our focus is on the mother-daughter relationship. If the mother has overcontrolled her daughter when she was young, it may take time and patience to persuade her to let go of some of the power and to move toward more equality. It is worth the effort to achieve the full potential of Pluto and Pallas—a relationship that is experienced by both the mother and daughter as reliably supportive and pleasurable.

Pluto to Juno

Pluto and the asteroid Juno seem to signify the same basic principles, so aspects between them in the charts of a mother and daughter will reinforce them in the relationship. With mutual caring, a deeply loving partnership can develop with both individuals sharing pleasures, possessions, and power. If the mother initially overused her power, it may take time and patience to persuade her to release some of the control and move toward a more equalitarian relationship, but it is worth it if it allows both the mother and daughter to continue a mutually supportive association. If the mother is unwilling or unable to allow her daughter more independence, there is likely to be a power struggle with the daughter eventually leaving. When the daughter remains really dependent, neither individual can reach her full potential, able to freely give, receive, and share pleasures and possessions. They are also less likely to develop the capacity for the self-knowledge and self-mastery potentials of Pluto and Juno. The latter abilities become especially important if the mother and daughter have been reinforcing each other's appetite indulgences, perhaps even slipping into addictions to alcohol, tobacco, etc. It is worth the effort to find more constructive pleasures that can be shared while building a loving, mutually supportive, equalitarian partnership.

Pluto to Vesta

Pluto shows the desire for a lasting, peer relationship while Vesta shows the need for a sense of accomplishment through productive work. Aspects between this planet and asteroid in the charts of a mother and daughter can be mutually rewarding if both can enjoy cooperative work. If the mother tries to overcontrol her daughter, giving orders or telling her exactly how to do the job, it is likely to damage the relationship as well as interfere with her daughter's development of necessary skills. Individuals with a prominent Vesta need to do something they feel is worth doing, and to do it well, in order to develop a sense of personal self-esteem. Sometimes illness is part of the challenge to be mastered, or may be used by either the mother or daughter to manipulate the other. If either the mother or daughter is too critical, the relationship can also be damaged. The search for flaws is valuable in one's job, but counterproductive when directed against fellow humans. An alternate danger occurs if either the mother or daughter is almost totally focused on her job while the other craves a warm relationship. When young, the daughter may feel rejected if her mother is too absorbed in her job. Later, an elderly mother may feel neglected by a daughter whose work requires most of her time. Compromises with time and energy, and shared projects that use the skills of both, can help increase the harmony and build a mutually supportive relationship.

Pluto to Chiron

Aspects between an interpersonal planet and a transpersonal one in the charts of a mother and daughter are connecting two very different areas of life. Interpersonal interactions involve face-to-face contacts between two individuals, or small group activities. The transpersonal sides of life, Letters 9 through 12 of our astrological alphabet, deal with conscious and subconscious belief systems, values and goals, natural and cultural laws, and human societies and life in general. Pluto's orbit is mostly outside of Neptune's, while Chiron orbits the Sun between Saturn and Uranus. But Pluto has a moon (Charon) as a partner, and it is clearly symbolic of Scorpio with its challenge of learning to share possessions, pleasures, and power in lasting, close relationships. Chiron may be a comet, but it is clearly a key to both conscious and subconscious faith, and thus part of the transpersonal area of life.

If a mother and daughter have similar beliefs and values, aspects between Pluto and Chiron may be manifested as a deep and lasting bonded relationship built on shared pleasures and goals. If either individual has excessive expectations of herself, the other person, or life in general, tolerance is needed to attain mutual acceptance. With shared love, they can find areas of life that are rewarding for both. Without love, the emotional intensity of a fire-water mixture added to the finality urge signified by Pluto, and to the absolutist tendency typical of Chiron, may lead to a permanent severing of the relationship. Neither Pluto nor Chiron is noted for a willingness to compromise, and compromise is called for. If the mother and daughter care for each other, they can focus on activities that both of them value and enjoy, and can build a lasting companionship.

Pluto to the Lunar Nodes

Aspects between water factors in the charts of a mother and daughter will usually be experienced with above-average strength. Pluto shows the desire for a mate, and the Moon and its Nodes seek baby-mother relationships. Where there is mutual love, the mother and daughter can build a deep, lasting partnership with each individual feeling emotionally supported by the other. If the mother overcontrols or overprotects her daughter initially, it may be difficult to move into the equalitarian relationship that is appropriate for Pluto after the daughter reaches adulthood. It is worth the effort, since it can help build a partnership where both individuals can give, receive, and share mutual pleasures and possessions. Occasionally, the mother and daughter may be so bonded that they remain essentially married and develop few outside relationships. Sometimes, it is only after the death of the mother that the daughter is able to form new attachments. Alternately, if either one does establish another committed relationship such as marriage, either one may feel compelled to end the tie to the other. The married individual may feel this is necessary to maintain her new partnership, or the other individual may feel rejected and retaliate by ending contacts. But, short of such extreme cases, a loving partnership between a mother and daughter can provide mutually rewarding support for both while still allowing space in their lives for other people and activities.

Pluto to the Ascendant/Descendant Axis

With mutual caring, aspects between Pluto and these horoscope angles in the charts of a mother and daughter can produce a positive partnership. There may be freedom-closeness issues if either individual requires a level of personal independence that leaves the other feeling lonely and rejected, but through compromise they can work out a solution. The handling of power may also need attention and compromises, especially after the daughter becomes older. Finding activities that both individuals enjoy can enhance harmony. These may include artistic interests, hobbies such as collecting, social interactions, financial concerns such as investments, etc. If competition comes into the picture, it can be channeled into sports, games, and fighting for more fair play in the world, as long as both individuals are able to take it lightly and know when it is appropriate to cooperate. Since both Pluto and the Descendant signify a need for sharing life with others, it is worth the effort it takes for a mother and daughter to build a mutually supportive relationship.

Pluto to the MC/IC Axis

Connecting Pluto with these horoscope angles in the charts of a mother and daughter tells us that the desire for partnership and deep emotional bonds will be affected by attitudes about parents. The mother and daughter can work out the power issues if they learn to share power. Then, they can build a mutually supportive partnership that includes taking turns nurturing each other and handling responsibilities. If the mother is unwilling or unable to relinquish attempts to control her daughter, there can be power struggles, or the daughter may sever the association, or she may give in, become passive, and let her mother play Atlas. If both can find pleasurable activities that they can enjoy together, including shared appetites and possessions, the mutual pleasure can help harmonize the relationship. If one individual is more work-oriented and the other more in need of emotional interactions, they will need to compromise to salvage the association. The mother may be more invested in her career or may need to work long hours to support her family, leaving her daughter feeling lonely and rejected. An elderly mother may mourn for more time with a busy daughter. In balancing the different sides of life, compromise is always needed to find a middle path that leaves space for all of our basic desires. It is worth the effort to work out compromises in order to build a comfortable partnership between a mother and daughter that both can find mutually supportive.

Mother-Daughter Ceres Contacts

Ceres to Ceres

Aspects between the "mother" asteroid Ceres in the charts of a mother and daughter can manifest as the ability of the individuals to nurture each other. This capacity will be encouraged if the mother allows her daughter to join her in home activities at a young age. It is important that the activity be voluntary rather than coercive, so the daughter feels a sense of personal investment in the accomplishments. If the mother simply tells the daughter what to do, or if she does everything for the daughter, the latter's work efforts are less likely to be effective in developing her skills and her sense of self-confidence. Any activity that helps the home and family can be useful, whether setting the table, weeding the garden, or caring for younger siblings. If a warm, cooperative relationship is developed early, the mother and daughter may continue it long after the daughter is grown.

Ceres to Pallas

The principles of mother and partner are connected when there are aspects between these asteroids in the charts of a mother and daughter. If a cooperative interaction is developed while the daughter is young, it is likely to be carried on into later years, and to be a source of mutual reassurance and support. Shared activities can focus on meeting the needs of home and family, or they can include fun with others outside the home, artistic interests, mutual hobbies, and competitive games as long as they are accepted as recreation to be taken lightly. Where there are different interests, the mother and daughter will need to allow each other space to include other associates. If one individual is more invested in actions that produce useful results, and the other is more interested in human companionship, as long as they accept their different tastes and have some pleasures that they enjoy together, they can continue a comfortable relationship.

Ceres to Juno

Like Pallas, the asteroid Juno wants to share life with others, but Juno is more like Scorpio than Libra. These aspects in the charts of a mother and daughter can indicate mutually rewarding and supportive relationships if both individuals accept each other as equals once the daughter is older. If the mother is strongly invested in her parental role, relinquishing it to be more of a partner may not be easy, but it is worth doing to create a lasting, deeply warm, mutually protective relationship that both can enjoy. Different tastes may call for compromise, and it is important to allow space for such differences. If either the mother or daughter is too possessive or jealous, there may be problems. Shared actions that both individuals find pleasurable will facilitate the development of a lasting, harmonious association that is more like a partnership than a traditional parent-child situation.

Ceres to Vesta

Mother and work are connected by these aspects in the charts of a mother and daughter. If the mother is too absorbed in her career, or has to work long hours to support her family, her daughter may feel rejected. Also, it can create a problem if the mother is too critical, if an attitude that is appropriate in her job is displaced into her fellow humans. The relationship can be helped if the mother explains her need to work and keeps her critical attitude limited to improving her job efficiency. The roles may be reversed if a grown daughter spends long hours on her career and her elderly mother craves more support. Compromise can usually help bring more satisfaction into the relationship. Projects that can be shared, that give both the mother and daughter a sense of accomplishment, can also be helpful. Some type of service that helps people or life in general is appropriate to both Ceres and Vesta. A focus on health concerns may be part of the picture as a profession for either or both individuals. Alternately, one might need help that the other could provide. If both the mother and daughter enjoy caring for pets or gardening, these activities can contribute to a mutually pleasurable relationship.

Ceres to Chiron

Mother-daughter aspects between the asteroid Ceres and Chiron, which may be a comet, connect idealism to the urge to provide service in the charts. With mutual caring, both individuals may idealize each other and enjoy helping each other. If expectations are too high, idealism becomes a hazard, leading to one or both feeling disappointed that the other did not live up to her ideals. Accepting the reality that humans are human (and fallible) can solve the problem. Finding joint projects that are in harmony with the ideals of both, and that provide a sense of accomplishment, will usually enhance their satisfaction. The activities may center in the home, or may expand to help and heal humanity. They may want to help homeless children, or to save dolphins or the rain forest. It is just important that both the mother and daughter share their idealistic goals and their efforts. Such shared actions can contribute to a positive relationship that both experience as mutually supportive.

Ceres to the Lunar Nodes

It's "mothering" all the way when a mother and daughter have these aspects between their charts. The emphasis on these closely related astrological principles can produce highly positive relationships in which each individual supports the other, contributing to feelings of profound security for both. However, if one of them is more invested in the need for such security, the other may feel stifled or smothered by too much togetherness. Alternately, the Ceres need to be productive may compel one to work outside the home, whether by choice or out of economic necessity, and the other may long for more home time and activities together. It is important that each individual be able to give something to the other, depending on her level of skills. Especially once the daughter is older, a relationship that is too one-sided may remain on the parent-child level. The parent may end up resenting her burden and/or the child may resent her dependency. Truly shared activities, in which each helps meet the security needs of the other, can contribute to a mutually rewarding relationship.

Ceres to the Ascendant/Descendant Axis

Aspects of the asteroid Ceres to these angles connect the urge to nurture or to be nurtured to the personal identity and the ability to handle lasting peer relationships. A mother and daughter who have these aspects between their charts may build warm, mutually supportive partnerships if each is able to accept the individuality of the other person. A conjunction of any astrological factor with the Ascendant is equivalent to one with Mars, an indication that one person is a role model for the other. With a positive role model, there is a desire to be like the other person, while a negative role model leads to wanting to be the exact opposite. Finding areas of life where both the mother and daughter can help each other, each at their own level of competence, can increase the potential for a pleasant relationship. Shared artistic interests, social activities, service assistance to others, etc., can deepen relationship bonds. Compromises may be needed if either the mother or daughter has a greater need for human attachments while the other craves more independence. With mutual caring, both the mother and daughter can build a partnership that includes mutual support and space for individuality.

Ceres to the MC/IC Axis

With aspects between the charts of a mother and daughter that involve astrological factors that are all associated with parents, this area of life is highlighted. Once the daughter is grown, it will be important for both the mother and daughter to take turns with the power and responsibility that are part of the parental role. If the mother hangs on to her control too long, or even if she overdoes it when her daughter is still young, the relationship will have problems. She could demand too much of her daughter, or go to the opposite extreme of trying to do everything for her daughter. In either case, the mother may end up resenting her burdens, and/or the daughter may resent her dependency. The daughter may also feel rejected if the mother works long hours, either due to her own ambition or to financial necessity. The roles may be reversed if a grown daughter is very absorbed in her career and her mother feels neglected. Occasionally, a chronically ill mother can also thrust a young daughter into such a role reversal. Sharing power and responsibilities provides a way to build a positive adult relationship between a mother and daughter. With mutual caring, both individuals can help each other and be helped. The shared activities could center on the home, or a mother and daughter could choose to use their skills to provide service to a wider world.

Mother-Daughter Pallas Contacts

Pallas to Pallas

A double focus on the asteroid Pallas in the charts of a mother and daughter can encourage a delightful partnership with mutual interests in artistic pursuits, social activities, or almost any action that people can do together for mutual pleasure. If the relationship includes a competitive spirit, this can be directed into sports, games, or a shared fight for social causes. Obviously, the equality demanded by the Pallas principle will be easier to attain once the daughter is past childhood, but even when she is young, her mother can treat her with respect and they can reach joint decisions when this is feasible. Since a single aspect is only a small part of the picture, other factors in the charts may point to problems in the relationship, but with mutual caring and a shared commitment to the fair play that is so important to Pallas, the mother and daughter should be able to sustain a comfortable and lasting partnership.

Pallas to Juno

The theme of partnership is emphasized when these aspects are present between the charts of a mother and daughter. With its Libra nature, Pallas shows the ability to view the broad perspective, while Juno is more like Scorpio, inclined to be more passionate. Thus, though each individual will want the companionship of others in her life, one may be more possessive and emotionally needy. If each can accept their differences and focus on their common needs, they should be able to enjoy many areas of life together, including artistic interests and a variety of pleasures with other people. If a divorced mother remarries, or if a grown daughter chooses to marry and establish her own family, and she and her mother have developed a deep bond, a new adjustment in their relationship will be needed. If either tries to cling possessively to the other, it may take love and patience to work out more open but still caring ways to interact. Shared pleasures are still the key.

Pallas to Vesta

Cooperative work can provide a good foundation when a mother and daughter have aspects in their charts between these asteroids. Projects that can be done together, that give both a sense of accomplishment, can help build a constructive partnership. If either the mother or daughter is more invested in practical achievements while the other is focused on pleasure with other people, compromises may be needed to manage a reasonable balance. If the mother has to work outside the home while her daughter is young, she can explain the situation and still make quality time for some shared pleasures. Aspects to Vesta are always a reminder that critical attitudes should be directed into one's work and not displaced to assault our fellow humans. A mother and daughter might enjoy sharing activities such as sewing, gardening, a variety of crafts, or volunteer work that helps others. If the competitive potential of Pallas slips in, they might need to discuss it and agree on when it is appropriate to compete and when teamwork is needed. If either has health needs, the other might be there for her. With mutual respect and caring, an effective and satisfying partnership can be achieved.

Pallas to Chiron

Idealism is connected to the need for human companionship when there are aspects between these factors in the charts of a mother and daughter. A strongly idealistic sharing of life is possible, but having unrealistic expectations could leave either or both individuals feeling disappointed. If both the mother and daughter accept each other as humans, they can focus on their joint values and move toward achieving their mutual goals together while enjoying the journey through life. They might study together, or write, or teach, or be planning the next trip before they have finished the last one. They might both be interested in healing or in volunteer service to others. If a competitive spirit is part of the picture, sports or games may be a good outlet. Sharing efforts to fight for a more ideal world is also possible. Once the daughter is grown and a more equalitarian relationship is established, if both cooperation and competition are present, an agreement on when to compete and when to cooperate, and the ability to take both lightly, can maintain a mutually comfortable camaraderie.

Pallas to the Lunar Nodes

A need for close relationships is emphasized with these aspects in the charts of a mother and daughter. The desire of Pallas for equality and the dependency/nurturing instincts of the Nodes (which function as two more Moons in astrology) can be harmonized if the mother and daughter take turns helping each other. Even when the daughter is young, shared activities are possible that provide mutual pleasure and security feelings. These may focus on home and family, or may include friends. Social pleasures, artistic interests, or cooking, sewing, or gardening together, etc., may be part of the picture. If either the mother or the daughter has been uncomfortable in the dependent role, it may take time and patience to achieve a comfortable equality once the daughter reaches adulthood, but it is worth the effort to build a lasting companionship that provides security and pleasure to both individuals.

Pallas to the Ascendant/Descendant Axis

These aspects in the charts of a mother and daughter call for working out areas for cooperation while each allows the other to be a unique individual. With a Pallas-Ascendant conjunction, either or both may be taking the other as a role model, tending to imitate her or to do the opposite. If the relationship is tilted toward competition, it will help if they can maintain a "game-playing" attitude, able to win some, lose some, and take it lightly. To build a truly constructive companionship, they will need to find activities that both can enjoy together. Artistic hobbies, shared entertainment, fashion, cosmetics, jewelry, etc., might be common interests. If one wants more independence and the other more time together, compromise will be needed, but with some Pallas agreement on fair play, the mother and daughter can build a positive relationship.

Pallas to the MC/IC Axis

The principles of parents and partnership meet when there are aspects between these factors in the charts of a mother and daughter. If the mother is strongly identified with her role as the responsible caretaker, and the daughter would like a more equalitarian relationship, there are likely to be tensions. Sometimes the mother is able to relinquish her role when the daughter is older, but sometimes it takes a struggle or even a rupture in the family. If the mother is able to move toward a peer relationship as her daughter grows, a positive companionship can be developed that is founded on mutually pleasurable activities. Sharing artistic hobbies, social interactions, projects that benefit the home and family, etc., can encourage a cooperative partnership. Engaging in such activities is also helpful if the mother has to work outside the home and the daughter either feels rejected by a mother not there for her, or she feels pressured by having to take on duties not being carried out by parents. If the mother and daughter can develop a mutual give and take that includes both duties and pleasurable activities, they can build a reciprocal, supportive relationship.

Mother-Daughter Juno Contacts

Juno to Juno

Mutual Juno aspects in the charts of a mother and daughter may be a key to an intense relationship. This can range from a devoted partnership to an unrelenting power struggle. Obviously, when the daughter is young, her mother holds most of the power, but Juno's Scorpio potential can be amazingly manipulative, even in a young child. Water factors in astrology signify the subconscious side of the mind, which may quietly attain goals without the open confrontations typical of air and fire. If both the mother and daughter care for each other, a warm, mutually supportive companionship can be developed with both enjoying a variety of activities. Sensual pleasures and possessions may become an important focus, including clothes, jewelry, cosmetics, money, etc. If other factors in the charts support the tendency, it would be possible for a mother and daughter to reinforce each other's indulgences up to the point of addiction. But self-knowledge and self-mastery are also Juno potentials, so they could also share a passion for depth psychology or occultism. If a deeply bonded partnership is formed, it might even threaten the ability of one or both to break the relationship in order to get married. But if the mother and daughter can love each other without the need to possess, they can maintain a lasting, cooperative partnership that also has ample room for others in their lives.

Juno to Vesta

These aspects invite a working partnership when they are present in the charts of a mother and daughter. They might help each other in the home, and once the daughter is grown, they might engage in a family business or work in a related field. If one is more invested in a career and the other is more focused on personal relationships, they may need to work out compromises. If the mother is away at work for long hours, a young daughter might feel rejected and lonely. The roles might be reversed if a grown daughter is absorbed in her career and her mother feels neglected. As usual, Vesta aspects also remind us to keep our critical attitudes directed into our work, not at our fellow humans. Juno aspects call for a mutual give and take, avoiding any attempt to control what should be peer relationships. If the mother and daughter can enjoy projects that give both a sense of accomplishment and pleasure, they can build a positive, mutually supportive partnership.

Juno to Chiron

Juno's need for a mate connected to Chiron's idealism in the charts of a mother and daughter may call for some easing of emotional intensity and expectations of each other or of life. When both individuals share similar beliefs, goals, and values, they may develop a lasting, deeply bonded partnership. Differing beliefs and values may lead to a tense relationship, or to their going their separate ways. Neither Juno, with its Plutonian tenacity, nor Chiron, with its lofty aspirations, is enthusiastic about compromising, but with mutual caring, the mother and daughter can find interests and activities that both can enjoy. They may find pleasure in the material world of collectibles, investments, or fashion. Or they may share an interest in travel, reading, or altruistic endeavors. With the Juno need for emotional closeness and the Chiron hunger for a more ideal world, it is worth the effort to build a partnership based on pleasures that both individuals enjoy and that make a contribution to the world.

Juno to the Lunar Nodes

Togetherness will be emphasized when these aspects occur in the charts of a mother and daughter. Water factors in astrology signify the subconscious side of the mind, so both individuals may be psychically open to each other, sensitive to feelings and sometimes even picking up thoughts. Emotions tend to be strong, so positive relationships can be very positive, while painful ones may also be intense. In light of the power of subconscious habits, which control a major part of our lives, becoming conscious of our inner driving tendencies and their consequences is the first step toward undertaking the efforts needed to change habits that are producing undesired results. Shared activities that both enjoy may include the home and family focus desired by the lunar Node principle, or the pleasure from artistic interests, social activities with other people, attention to finances, etc., that are associated with Juno. Compromises may be needed in areas where tastes differ. With mutual caring, a mother and daughter can build a lasting, mutually supportive partnership.

Juno to the Ascendant/Descendant Axis

Both Juno and the Descendant show our need to deal with long-term peer relationships, while the Ascendant is a primary key to our sense of individuality, our right and power to live life on our own terms. Aspects between these factors in the charts of a mother and daughter may strengthen their bonding to create a lasting, cooperative partnership that both enjoy. If either or both feel that their freedom is threatened by the other person, the tensions will require compromises. As usual with Juno, shared activities that both enjoy are needed to increase harmony. They may discover similar tastes in entertainment, fashion, sports, financial investments, etc. Even with a young daughter, suggestions rather than dictatorial orders are advisable, and obviously once she becomes an adult, both individuals will need to respect each other's right to be themselves. With mutual caring, a mother and daughter can develop a lasting, pleasurable partnership.

Juno to the MC/IC Axis

A parent-partner companionship is possible with these aspects between the charts of a mother and daughter. Juno shows our need and capacity for lasting, equalitarian relationships, while the MC/IC axis shows how we relate to our parents and our ability to handle being a parent. Tensions are possible for a variety of reasons. The mother may be too protective of her daughter, or overly domineering, interfering with the child's movement toward equality and/or toward learning to handle her share of power and responsibility as she approaches adulthood. The daughter might respond by becoming passive, allowing her mother to "do it all," or by fighting for her share of the power and eventually severing the relationship. If both individuals can find areas of life where they share pleasures, responsibilities, and mutual nurturing, they can build a lasting, harmonious partnership. A family business or a related profession would be among the options, and an extended family sharing a home is common in more traditional societies.

Mother-Daughter Vesta Contacts

Vesta to Vesta

Aspects in the charts of a mother and daughter that connect this "workaholic" Virgo asteroid can encourage mutual competence in tasks in the home or in crafts that provide a sense of accomplishment. There is an additional bonus if the activities also develop skills that will facilitate success in the world once the daughter reaches adulthood. Hazards include a displacement of the critical attitude that is valuable when directed into a job, looking for ways to improve efficiency, with the result that either or both individuals become critical of each other. Alternately, the mother may be so absorbed by her work outside the home that the daughter feels alienated. It is possible for both the mother and daughter to become intensely involved in different areas of life and to simply drift apart, even if their interests are not actively in conflict. But if they develop closely related interests and skills, they can work together, whether with gardening, hobbies, or caring for family members, etc. Team-work may also extend into later years with a family business or profession. Individuals who fail to find an area of work that provides a sense of achievement are in danger of developing health problems. If the Virgo need to do something worth doing and to do it well is not satisfied, the subconscious mind can escape guilt through illness. Finding self-esteem through some type of achievement may help improve health. If either the mother or daughter has health problems, the other may satisfy the Vesta urge toward service by caring for her. In general, Vesta aspects are most comfortable when both the mother and daughter are sharing projects that give both a sense of accomplishment.

Vesta to Chiron

Aspects between these factors in the charts of a mother and daughter connect the work ethic with idealism. As is the case with all of the astrological keys to idealism, Chiron (like Jupiter and Neptune) reminds us that having inflated expectations will lead to disappointment. Vesta's hazards include involvement with an activity that is so personally consuming that other important parts of life are neglected, and one's fellow humans may be alienated. Since both Vesta and Chiron are often associated with healing, this might be a feature in the relationship. Either the mother or daughter might be involved in healing others or in need of healing. If both share similar interests, whether providing service to a home and family or to the public, joint efforts that help others can strengthen bonds and lead to a fulfilling relationship.

Vesta to the Lunar Nodes

The work ethic and the need for emotional closeness and security are connected when these aspects are present in the charts of a mother and daughter. Productive work can provide material security, but the Moon and its Nodes also show the craving for emotional support. With mutual caring, a mother and daughter can cooperate in projects in the home or in the world that provide both the Vesta need for a sense of accomplishment and the mutual warmth that is important to the Nodes. Vesta hazards include one or both people being too critical, and the other feeling hurt. Too much tunnel vision in either individual may result in neglect of other important parts of life. Health challenges are also possible. Another danger stems from either the mother or daughter overemphasizing a job at the expense of emotional ties. This can occur when a mother has to work out of financial necessity, but the roles can be reversed if an adult daughter is absorbed in her career and her elderly mother feels neglected. If both continue to engage in activities that give them a sense of accomplishment while making room in their lives for emotionally supportive contacts, the mother and daughter can maintain a mutually satisfying relationship.

Vesta to the Ascendant/Descendant Axis

When aspecting major angles in the charts of a mother and daughter, the drive to be productive that is a keynote of the asteroid Vesta may lead to developing skills that help the family or that are extended into the world. If both individuals have similar interests, they can work together and both can gain satisfaction from their accomplishments. When the mother and daughter are invested in very different areas of life, they may simply drift apart. Vesta hazards include one or both being too critical, and the other feeling hurt or too much tunnel vision or the need to master health challenges. The Ascendant/Descendant axis represents one form of the freedom-closeness dilemma. Either the mother or daughter may feel that her individuality and personal freedom is threatened by the other, or that her need for emotional closeness is not being met. Even a few shared projects that give both individuals a feeling of achievement can help a mother and daughter increase their sense of mutual respect and affection, and they can develop a satisfying partnership.

Vesta to the MC/IC Axis

Aspects in the charts of a mother and daughter between the asteroid Vesta and the parental angles can facilitate the development of skills that give both individuals a sense of accomplishment. Both Vesta and the MC highlight the work ethic, which may be directed into service to the home and family or into a career in the world. If the mother is overly protective, or too controlling, taking on too much of the responsibility or telling her daughter precisely how to do things, she may inhibit her daughter's development of her own skills. The daughter may respond by becoming passive and letting her mother do it all, or she may struggle for her own share of the power. Illness can be a hazard when Vesta is strongly aspected, if the individual is unable to gain a sense of competence and achievement in the world. The subconscious escapes guilt by being unable to work. Joint projects where both the mother and daughter work and accomplish together can help to build a mutually supportive relationship that provides security to both.

Mother-Daughter Chiron Contacts

Chiron to Chiron

Subconscious faith, goals, and ideals are highlighted by these aspects between the charts of a mother and daughter. Shared ideals can strengthen and deepen their bonds as both individuals move in the same direction in life. Whether they are focused on artistic interests, health concerns, or searching for knowledge and sharing it with others, they can reinforce each other's values and contribute to making a more ideal world. If the mother and daughter have very divergent beliefs and values, they need to accept their differences and look for some areas of life that can be shared. If either or both hold rigid, dogmatic beliefs that they are unable or unwilling to compromise, or if either seeks to convert the other or condemn her, they may be unable to maintain a relationship. Mutual tolerance for differences and attention focused on interests that both value can help develop and enhance a harmonious relationship.

Chiron to the Lunar Nodes

Idealism and emotional security needs are connected by these aspects in the charts of a mother and daughter. If both individuals value home and family ties, they may retain a deep bond throughout their lives. If the shared beliefs and values extend beyond the family, they may join in efforts to create a more ideal world. They might volunteer to help save homeless children, rescue wildlife, protect the environment, or choose other areas where they can make a contribution. If the mother and daughter hold very different beliefs and values, they will need to compromise, accepting each other's differences and seeking some areas where they hold similar ideals. For example, one might be committed to efforts in the transpersonal world of humanity and nature, while the other is almost totally absorbed in the immediate family. To be a whole person, we need to include all twelve parts of life. Making a little time for each can help a mother and daughter build a mutually supportive relationship.

Chiron to the Ascendant/Descendant Axis

Aspects between a key to idealism and these major angles in the charts of a mother and daughter call for reasonable expectations and the ability to integrate the life urges for both freedom and closeness. Where beliefs and values differ, both individuals will need to accept the differences while finding some areas of shared goals that let them move in the same direction some of the time. It is also important for both to accept each other's right to individuality and some personal freedom, while shared pleasures provide mutually rewarding interactions. Life is a juggling act, learning to integrate twelve primary drives. When a mother and daughter can each allow the other to be herself while sharing some primary ideals, they can maintain a lasting, pleasurable partnership.

Chiron to the MC/IC Axis

Ideals connect to parents when these aspects are present in the charts of a mother and daughter. If the mother tries to impose her beliefs and values on her daughter, or tries to "buy" her conformity with overindulgence, there may be tensions when the daughter becomes old enough to question the principles. The role of the father may also be a complication in the situation. If either parent or the daughter expects too much of one other, they will need to accept that it is okay to be human—on the way to perfection, but allowed to enjoy the journey. When a mother and daughter share ideals and goals, when each is able and willing to handle her share of the power and responsibility, they can cooperate to build healing relationships in the family and in the world.

Mother-Daughter Lunar Node Contacts

The Lunar Nodes to the Lunar Nodes

Aspects between the Nodes in the charts of a mother and daughter point to a deep, subconscious connection that implies a possible past-life relationship. Water factors in astrology show the potential for psychic awareness, so both individuals may be open to each other's feelings and thoughts. The need for emotional closeness is likely to be reinforced, and with mutual caring, the mother and daughter can be truly supportive of each other. However, if they have come from a hostile past, or if either or both are inwardly deeply conflicted, it may require intense probing to become conscious of the sources of the tensions and to resolve them. In really serious cases, professional help might be needed. Issues of abandonment, neglect, or "smothering mothering" are possible. A more common issue can be present if other patterns in the chart of either person put more emphasis on the need for independence or on career aspirations. It may take time and effort to find compromises that allow both some closeness and some freedom for other activities in life. It is worth the effort, since Nodal aspects invite deeply caring, mutually supportive relationships.

The Lunar Nodes to the Ascendant/Descendant Axis

The freedom to be an individual versus the need for closeness is the issue with these patterns in the charts of a mother and daughter. Where both individuals can accept each other's uniqueness and share pleasurable activities while remaining mutually supportive, they can enjoy a lasting, satisfying partnership. The astrological principles are equivalent to a cardinal T-square, symbolizing independence, dependence/nurturing, and equal sharing. The mother and daughter are learning to balance time and energy in terms of personal interests and hobbies, home and family (including pets), and equal, one-on-one relationships. Even when the daughter is young, an accepting mother can encourage growth toward a peer relationship with shared artistic interests, pleasure with friends, and a sense of fair play. With mutual caring, the mother and daughter can develop a lasting companionship.

The Lunar Nodes to the MC/IC Axis

Aspects between these factors in the charts of a mother and daughter connect variations on the parent principles in astrology. The MC/IC axis signifies the unconditional love parent who cares for the helpless infant and the conditional love parent who teaches us the rules of the game through the consequences that follow our actions. Obviously, either parent may play either role, or neither. If parents are too permissive and protective, we may not learn that there are limits in the world, or learn to handle responsibilities until we reach adulthood. If parents are too dominant or punitive, we may struggle to learn to trust and to find a sense of security. Parents who set a good example with a balance between supportive love and realistic limits can help their daughter learn to integrate these sides of life. Letting the daughter develop her skills by sharing the power and responsibilities that are appropriate for her capacity (and age) will prepare her for becoming a mother in her turn and/or for a career in the world. It can build a relationship in which a mother and adult daughter take turns parenting each other, whether in the home or in work in the larger world.

Mother-Daughter Contacts to the Angles

The Ascendant/Descendant Axis to the Ascendant/Descendant Axis

Connecting these major axes in the charts of a mother and daughter highlight the self/other issue in astrology. We all want to live on our own terms, but we also all need associations with others. With conjunctions, there is usually a very intense involvement between the two individuals. Conjunctions between the two Ascendants indicates that one or both individuals see the other as a role model, whether she wants to imitate her or to do the opposite. The simultaneous conjunction of the Descendants shows a similar tendency, with each looking for a partner who is like or the opposite of the choice of the other person. Where the Ascendant of one is on the Descendant of the other, both individuals feel like natural mates to each other. Unfortunately, this may or may not be a positive partnership. It is possible to have truly harmonious cooperation, or to have an intense power struggle with either or both competing with or trying to control the other. An emphasis on air and fire would tend toward open, conscious competition, while an emphasis on earth and especially on water might stay underground, with water tending to remain subconscious. Initially, the mother would have the advantage, but if a positive relationship is desired, compromises would obviously be needed. Other aspects between the angles are less intense, but still important. A sextile/trine combination would encourage harmony, but even with conflict aspects, it is possible to develop a cooperative partnership if both the mother and daughter can accept the other as an individual and can share mutually pleasurable activities.

The Ascendant/Descendant Axis to the MC/IC Axis

With squares between these axes in the charts of a mother and daughter, we have a complete, natural cardinal dilemma. Independence vies with dependence/nurturing and competes with equalitarian relationships versus power and responsibility in the world. All are vital parts of life. We can engage in them alternately, or compromise in the middle to have a little of each, but if any of them is denied or overdone, it will make trouble for us. A mother and daughter with these aspects may project onto each other, with one overdoing one or two of these areas of life and the other person putting too much emphasis on different areas. Compromising, to let each person satisfy each of these life urges, is usually the best solution. However, differing emphases are quite possible at different stages of life. It is also practical to recognize and make allowances for diverse skills. Regardless of the nature of the specific aspect, the mother and daughter are learning together to balance their time and energy between personal development, the ties of home and family, the needs of a committed partnership, and the duties of a career or contribution to the outer world. Accepting each other's individuality and learning to share nurturing, responsibilities, and pleasurable activities can help them maintain a lasting, mutually satisfying partnership.

The MC/IC Axis to the MC/IC Axis

With these aspects in their charts, a mother and daughter may need to learn to take turns being the parent once the daughter is grown. If the mother is able to relinquish her power and responsibility as her daughter develops the capacity to handle her share of them, they may easily move in this direction. Tasks in the home, family obligations, mutual interests that enhance security, etc., can encourage this development. If the mother is unable or unwilling to give up her power, the daughter might become passive and let her mother carry the whole load, or there could be power struggles. Alternately, less often, a weak or inadequate mother might stay in the child role, perhaps unconsciously pushing her daughter into assuming the responsible parent role while the latter is still young. If shared activities are developed and maintained, they can evolve into a family business or a related profession, with both the mother and daughter continuing to contribute to each other's emotional security and effectiveness in the world. Each learns to be comfortable caring for others, asking for and receiving assistance, and taking on appropriate responsibilities—neither too much nor too little.

PART FOUR

Case Studies

SIX

Astrological Interpretations and Personal Experiences of Mother-Daughter Pairs

In these case studies, we will first present the horoscopes involved, followed by the astrological interpretations, and then the personal experiences—in their own words—of the mother-daughter pairs. After that, we will suggest sections in chapter 8, "Healing Options," that might be helpful for the daughter to read to reach more resolution of her relationship with her mother, to transform negative feelings or behavior patterns into positive ones. It is interesting to us to note that each generation does better than the previous one in the cases we have studied.

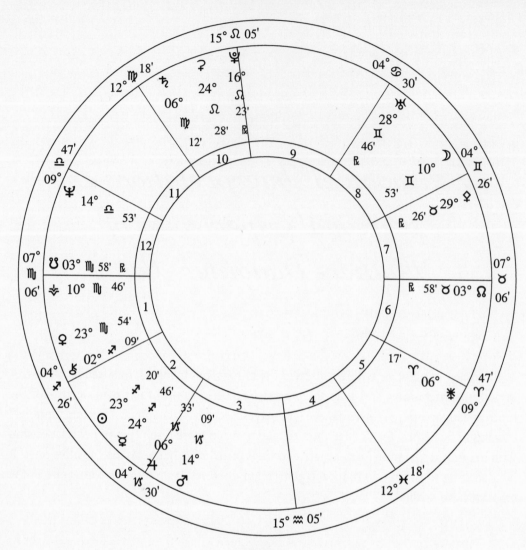

Ms. A
Natal Chart
December 15, 1948
3:25 A.M. CST
Chicago, Illinois
41N51 87W39
Koch Houses

CASE STUDY 1

Our first case study involves three generations (with a peek at a fourth). We'll call them Ms. A, Ms. A's Mother, Ms. B (Ms. A's daughter), and Ms. C (Ms. A's granddaughter).

Ms. A

Looking at the natal horoscope of Ms. A,[1] we notice a strong focus on power issues in the horoscope as a whole, and in the significators that apply to parents. The major power "letters" of the astrological alphabet are 5 (Sun, Leo, 5th house), 8 (Pluto, Scorpio, 8th house), and 10 (Saturn, Capricorn, 10th house). Letter 1 (Mars, Aries, 1st house) does not seek power over others (as can 5, 8, and 10), but is very forceful, assertive, and willing to fight against outside power or control. If linked with Letter 5, 8, or 10, Letter 1 can add to the power drive.

In regard to the parental picture, we see:

1. Pluto (a power planet) is the most elevated planet—closely conjunct the Midheaven in the 10th house (of power and the authority parent).

2. Both Saturn and Pluto (two potential "dictator" planets) are in the 10th house (of parents). Ceres (a key to the mother or nurturing figure) is also in the 10th house, which suggests that the mother owns at least part of that 10th house, although Saturn there implies that the father also owns part of that 10th house.

3. Ceres is in Leo (a power sign).

4. Although the Moon is in Gemini (a sign that is *not* oriented toward power), it is in the 8th house, reinforcing the power motif.

5. Just the fact that the 10th house is occupied (two planets and an asteroid) and the 4th house is empty suggests that conditional love (10th) may have been more significant in the early childhood than unconditional love (4th). If rulers and other factors belie this, we can change our minds.

6. Uranus (ruler of the 4th) is in the 8th house.

7. The Nodes (secondary keys to nurturing/emotional security issues) are across Scorpio (power) and Taurus.

1. Ms. A is knowledgeable in astrology and uses Koch houses for her and her family's charts, so we did as well.

The contraindications for power-oriented parents are Sun (ruler of the Midheaven) conjunct Mercury in Sagittarius (emphasizing idealism, mental stimulation), Moon in Gemini (curiosity and communication), and Sun in the 2nd house (earning a living; providing material security). Saturn in Virgo also implies a hardworking parent.

We get the picture of a parent (probably Dad) who is hardworking (Saturn in Virgo in the 10th; Sun in the 2nd—lots of focus on earth). One or both parents may have been bright and talkative (Sun conjunct Mercury; Moon in Gemini). However, we would expect at least one parent (more likely the mother) to be oriented toward power, control, and running the show. If she did it well, she would have been a mover and shaker, and would have channeled her drive and ambition into work, efforts to change the world, competitive sports, games, etc. If she did it poorly, she could have tried to dominate and control her child(ren). In extremes, cruelty, violence, and emotional blackmail and intimidation are possible.

Although communication, truth-seeking, and curiosity are also strongly emphasized for Ms. A herself (Mars in the 3rd house; Moon in Gemini; Sun conjunct Mercury in Sagittarius), we notice that the indications of what Ms. A "meets and greets" when first coming into life are almost all connected to power issues:

1. Scorpio rising

2. An asteroid (Vesta) and a planet (Venus) in Scorpio occupying the 1st house

3. Ruler of the Ascendant (Pluto) conjunct the Midheaven in Leo in the 10th house

4. Co-ruler of the Ascendant (Mars) in Capricorn

5. Ruler of the 4th house (Uranus) in the 8th house and opposite the Sun

If the power parent was insecure, the strength of Ms. A (which could have been manifesting at an early age) may have been interpreted as a threat. We notice that Ms. A also strongly continues the hardworking motif that relates to at least one parent: Ms. A has Vesta, the workaholic asteroid, conjunct the Ascendant in the 1st house. Mars (personal identity, drive, and action) is in ambitious, dedicated, disciplined Capricorn, along with Jupiter, a key to values and ideals. Pluto, the Ascendant ruler, is in the 10th house of career and contribution to society, and Saturn in its "natural" house (10th) emphasizes hard work, duty, and responsibility.

Although Vesta rising often symbolizes a strong drive for personal competence, it can also point to alienation. Some people with a prominent Vesta deal with harsh criticism or judgments. With Vesta conjunct the Ascendant, the individual is prone toward self-criticism and has to learn to value and appreciate herself. Extremes are possible when Vesta is in the picture. Pluto on an angle reinforces the potential of all-or-nothing experiences. The South Node conjunct the Ascendant can also indicate self-doubts. The karmic issues of the South Node, when involved with the Ascendant, can sometimes point to issues of physicality as well as personal identity, desire, and power. Occasionally, just staying alive is the karmic challenge. The keys to personal competence and hard work can also indicate being hard on one's self: Mars in Capricorn; the Ascendant ruler in the 10th house.

The aspects appear to confirm this picture. The Moon (usually a key to the mother) is square Saturn. This can indicate differences or conflict between Mom and Dad, Ms. A's struggle to balance work (Saturn) and domestic needs (Moon), and/or tension between compassion and the bottom line. On the negative side, Saturn-Moon conflicts can also indicate that Ms. A felt that nurturing was limited and restricted, or that nurturing was more an issue of dominance and control. The Moon is also quincunx the 1st-house Vesta, which pulls in the Ascendant. This indicates a potential pulling apart, separation, psychological distance, or alienation between the Moon (mother figure) and Ms. A (planets in the 1st house and on the Ascendant). The Moon is also quincunx the Jupiter/Mars midpoint, with Mars being another Ascendant ruler (again indicating potential differences between Ms. A and her mother, especially concerning beliefs, values, and moral and ethical principles).

The Moon does make a trine to Neptune, which could facilitate either faith, sensitivity, and artistic skills, or deception and secrets. The Moon is also sextile Juno, reinforcing Pluto motifs of intense emotions, and holding the positive potential for partnership and the negative potential for power struggles or abuse.

Ceres (the Earth Mother asteroid) squares the 1st-house Venus (fixed squares indicate challenges in learning to share power, possessions, and pleasures), but trines the Sun and Mercury in Sagittarius (reinforcing the quest for knowledge and understanding of life's meaning).

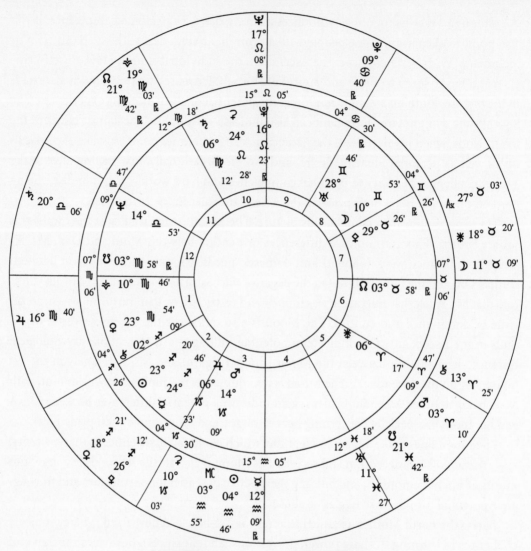

INNER WHEEL
Ms. A
Natal Chart
December 15, 1948
3:25 A.M. CST
Chicago, Illinois
41N51 87W39
Koch Houses

OUTER WHEEL
Ms. A's Mother
Natal Chart
January 25, 1923
12:00 P.M. CST
Suburb of Chicago, Illinois
41N53 87W47
Koch Houses

Synastry

Ms. A's Sun and Mercury are conjunct her mother's Pallas (potential partnership on the positive side; competition on the negative side). Ms. A's Sun squares her mom's Nodes of the Moon, suggesting strong emotional ties, possible past-life connections, and probable power issues within the nurturing matrix.

Ms. A's Moon makes many aspects to her mother's placements, again suggesting that Mom had a very strong emotional impact: Moon semisextile Pluto (power issues); quincunx Ceres (differing approaches to nurturing); trine Mercury (probable reinforcement of curiosity and the need to communicate); square Uranus (freedom versus closeness; attachment versus separation); and sextile Chiron (emphasizing questions of meaning and ultimate values).

Ms. A's Venus is sextile/trine her mother's lunar Nodes, which can point to mutual support and comfort. Again, karmic ties are implied.

Ms. A's Mars is semisextile her mother's Mercury (again, a focus on thinking and learning), square Chiron (highlighting concerns around ideals and values), and sextile Jupiter (again, an emphasis on metaphysics, goals, and values).

Ms. A's Ceres is trine her mother's Pallas (potential parent/partner connection) and quincunx her South Node (intense emotional connection; possible karmic lesson).

Ms. A's Ascendant is square her mom's Sun (power issues, questions of ego and self-esteem), quincunx Mars (issues around anger, assertion, and violence), trine Uranus (questions of individuality and self-expression), and trine Pluto (upping the intensity meter).

Ms. A's Jupiter/Mars midpoint is conjunct her mother's Ceres (nurturing tied to issues of assertion, anger, moral and ethical principles, and values) and opposite Pluto (intensity, power).

Ms. A's Jupiter squares her mother's Mars, so beliefs and values are highlighted once more. The positive potential is active idealism, and the negative potential is religious wars or clashes over faith and principles.

Ms. A's Saturn makes a yod (double quincunx) with her mother's Sun (ego and power issues) and Mars (assertion, anger, courage).

Ms. A's Neptune sextiles her mother's Neptune, highlighting issues of compassion, sensitivity, and beauty, or deception and martyr/victim motifs.

Ms. A's Pluto and Midheaven conjunct her mother's Neptune and oppose her mother's Mercury. (Power issues continue, along with a more mental emphasis and issues of idealism, dreams, and sensitivity, or lies and fantasy).

Summary of Synastry

The contacts between the charts appear to reinforce issues around power and control (and possibly anger, aggression, and violence). Ms. A's experience of her mother also seems to include a strong Neptune factor (positively would be spiritual, idealistic, or compassionate; negatively would be deceptive or involved with victimhood, addiction, etc.). There is also a strong emphasis on Ms. A's quest for meaning, understanding, beliefs, and values. The intensity of Ms. A's Scorpio rising and Pluto at the Midheaven seems to be echoed in many of the contacts between her chart and her mother's chart.

Ms. A's Own Words about Her Mother

From my earliest childhood memories until my mother died when I was twenty-seven, she was an emotionally and verbally abusive alcoholic. During my childhood, I never experienced any affection or caring from her, and during my teenage years her resentment or hatred of me escalated to severe physical abuse, which lasted several years (but I was the only one of four kids that she abused). Beatings were followed by a warning that if I told my father or anyone else, the next one would be worse. Everything was to be kept a secret (Neptune in my 12th house, hmmm . . .). Several times when I had bruises and cuts on my face, my father and other relatives were told that I was involved in street fights.

The only time that her secret got out was when a neighbor saw through the window that I was covered in blood and she was on top of me with a butcher knife in her hand. He flew in through the door and grabbed the knife, and then called my father at work to tell him what had happened.

I moved out of the house shortly after high school, and our relationship did *not* change—even when I had two kids of my own, thinking that being a grandmother would change her in some way. She was not allowed to be alone with my kids after what happened one time when she had promised to watch them one evening. When I arrived home after only two hours, I found her drunk in a chair, with both kids crying, hungry, and in dirty diapers.

After suffering a stroke and a couple of heart attacks—all alcohol-related—she died at the age of fifty-two. I was twenty-seven at the time and, sad to say, felt relieved.

Messages/scripts

You're stupid. You're unlovable. You deserve to be hit/beaten. You will never make it on your own. You need someone to take care of you. Never show your emotions ("You cry and

I'll really give you something to cry about." Any expression of anger was followed by physical abuse.) I have only two memories in my life of being touched kindly by my mother: once at age four when she held my hand in a store, and once when I was seventeen and asked her to put suntan lotion on my back (and her hands shook the whole time) So, for the most part, the only touch I experienced was painful, a message I registered as "Touch is bad."

How was she a positive role model?

Unfortunately, I can't think of a single way that she was a positive role model for me.

How was she a negative role model?

She was an extremely negative role model in every area for me—as a mother and a grandmother, in her communication skills, and as a woman (helpless, codependent, with beliefs that may have been a reflection of the times in which she grew up). As a wife to my dad, she was extremely jealous and paranoid. In addition, her alcohol abuse created such a negative impact on me that I still have a problem being with people who are "normal" drinkers.

Where did she have the greatest impact and how?

I have spent many years working through a lot of the issues related to my mother. It took being involved in two abusive relationships before I really was able to release the message that I deserved to be treated badly. Some things remain. For example, I still have a lot of fear when I'm around angry people or when I walk into a dark room (which, as a child, was the first sign that I would find my mother drunk). Learning that it's safe to express emotions is an ongoing task (reflected in my Moon-Saturn square?) as is feeling comfortable with touch.

I also had to "prove" to my mother that she was wrong about me (even long after her death): I went back to school and maintained a 4.0 GPA ("You're stupid"), and raised two kids by myself with no child support ("You'll never make it on your own"), etc.

On a positive note, many of what I consider my strong points are a direct result of my relationship with my mother. Having to take care of things (because she didn't) has made me an extremely responsible person. Being independent and self-sufficient is a direct result of not having someone to take care of me.

In addition, I have consciously chosen to be the exact opposite of my mother in many ways. For example, my kids and grandkids are the most important part of my life. Not only did I decide that I would never hit or spank my kids, I have always treated them with respect, communicated with them openly and honestly, and tried to build their self-esteem and to teach them to value their own feelings and judgment. My kids and I are still very close and I think that we always will be. I feel that I'm a good mother (and a fantastic grandma!), but I also know that there are ways that I could be a better mother. Not expressing emotions has, unfortunately, applied to both negative and positive emotions. I rarely express my positive feelings about my kids to them verbally, although, logically, I am aware that even though I had parents who never once said they loved me, etc., it is not an excuse to continue the pattern.

The hardest part of dealing with or resolving problems in my relationship with my mother is that she died by the time I was old enough to start my healing process. As a small child, I assumed that I was bad and that it was my fault she didn't like me, which progressed as I got older to wondering, "Why me?" (and not my sister or brothers). Later, I tried to figure out what kind of psychological problems would cause her to be so abusive. Now, at the age of fifty-two, I have reached the point of questioning my reasons for choosing her as a mother and trying to determine how our interactions relate to the lessons I am to learn in this lifetime.

Healing Options

We would suggest that Ms. A focus on Letters 5, 6, 8, and 10 in chapter 8 if she wishes to further heal her internal relationship with her mother. The major issues for Ms. A revolve around power (Letters 5, 8, and 10) and channeling the hardworking/critical focus of Vesta (and Letter 6) in a positive direction.

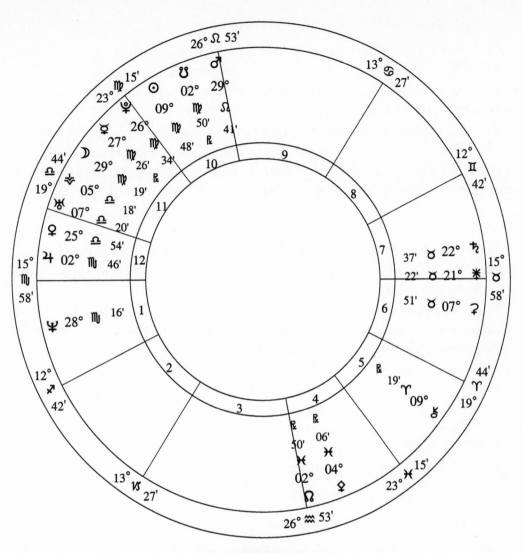

Ms. B
Natal Chart
September 2, 1970
12:02 P.M. CST
near Chicago, Illinois
42N00 87W50
Koch Houses

Ms. B

Looking at Ms. B's natal horoscope, we notice some fascinating similarities (and differences) with the chart of her mother (Ms. A). They both have Scorpio rising, with Leo/Aquarius across the MC/IC axis. They both have a strong personal identification with hard work and with power issues.

One major difference, however, is the strong focus on independence that is present in Ms. B's horoscope. Although Ms. A does have a Sagittarius Sun and Mercury, much of her potential adventurousness and love of freedom was overshadowed (at least in the early years as indicated by the "meet and greet" placements as well as everything in and ruling the 4th and 10th houses) by the issues of dominance, control, and clashes of values and beliefs.

Ms. B has a stellium in the 11th house, indicating a strong urge for individuality and independence. The stellium includes Uranus in its natural house and Pluto (the Ascendant ruler) in the 11th house.

Where Ms. A's Moon was quincunx (a separative aspect) her Vesta/Ascendant, Ms. B's Moon is conjunct her Mercury and Ascendant ruler (Pluto). The implication is that Ms. A was separated from experiencing nurturing and support, whereas Ms. B was getting it directly from day one.

Ms. B does have power issues in her chart, for both herself and for at least one parent. Her own power motifs are shown through the following:

1. Scorpio rising

2. A planet (Neptune) in Scorpio occupying the 1st house

3. Mars (co-ruler of the Ascendant) in Leo (power sign) in the 10th house (dominance)

4. Sun (ego, self-esteem) in the 10th house

Ms. B's parental keys do reflect issues around power, authority, and control, although that motif is much less emphasized than the motif of hard work and competence. The power/parent themes include:

1. Sun in the 10th house

2. Mars in Leo in the 10th house

3. Moon conjunct Pluto

4. Leo Midheaven

The work/parent motifs include:

1. Moon conjunct Vesta (the workaholic asteroid)

2. Moon in Virgo

3. Sun in Virgo

4. Ruler of the 4th house (Uranus) conjunct Vesta

5. Ruler of the 10th house (Sun) in Virgo

6. A planet (Sun) and a Node in the 10th house occupying Virgo

7. The Nodes (secondary keys to nurturing) across Virgo and Pisces

8. Ceres (the Earth Mother asteroid) in the 6th house of work

Mind/communication motifs are also very strong in Ms. B's parental picture. In fact, the Mercury-Moon conjunction by itself is enough. (Remember, the planets are the strongest form of the astrological alphabet.) Ms. A has her Sun-Mercury conjunction tying Mercury motifs to the father figure; Ms. B has Mercury strongly linked to Mom. We also see Moon in the 11th (air) house, and Uranus (ruler of the 4th house) in Libra (air) and in the 11th (air) house. The Sun (a key to parent) is also in a Mercury-ruled sign (Virgo). Pallas (a Libran asteroid) occupies the 4th house of parents and is conjunct the North Node.

Air is the most equalitarian of all the elements, so there is a definite implication that Ms. B's mother—although very strong (and possibly dominant and forceful)—was also very willing to be a partner (Letter 7), friend (Letter 11), and sister (Letter 3) to her daughter. Naturally, any letter combination can be used well or poorly. If Ms. B's mother manifested the negative side of these combinations, she could have demanded power when she wanted it and expected equality in terms of wanting her daughter to do things, perhaps even before they were age-appropriate. Generally, however, air is connected to intellectual understanding, objectivity, and tolerance.

So, we have a picture of an extremely hardworking mother, a mother who treated her daughter like an equal, emphasized curiosity and communication, was somewhat unusual, and who was strong and forceful.

Just to reiterate the conjunctions (because they are the strongest aspect), we have Mom as a personal role model (particularly for assertion and action) with the Midheaven and Node conjunct Mars. We have Mom as a communicator and someone who is endlessly curious (Moon conjunct Mercury). We have a parent who is a very hard worker (Uranus, ruler of the 4th, conjunct Vesta, and the Moon very widely conjunct Vesta). We have a parent as partner and equal (Pallas conjunct Node in the 4th) and Mom as powerful person (Moon conjunct Pluto). With the father out of the picture, as is the case here, Mom takes over Saturn as well, so Saturn conjunct Juno repeats the power and the partnership focus.

The other aspects reinforce this picture. The Moon is semisextile Mars (reinforcement of assertion, strength) and sextile Neptune in the 1st (support for idealism; potential harmony between Mother and Ms. B). Ceres, the Earth Mother asteroid, is trine the Sun and sextile/trine the Nodes of the Moon, suggesting general support (particularly in regard to practicality and earthy accomplishments). Ceres is exactly quincunx Uranus (and Vesta). Since Uranus is a ruler of the 4th house, this is one key to potential separation between the parents. The Nodes of the Moon across the 4th and 10th houses can also indicate separation, although often it is just parents who are struggling to find a balance between their public and private lives. The Moon is also in a wide quincunx to the North Node in the 4th house. The Sun in the 10th is quincunx Chiron (in Aries in the 5th), so we can speculate that Ms. B's father left very early on, presumably to follow his own dreams with the Chiron involvement.

Mars in the 10th is closely square Neptune in the 1st. Any 1st/10th square can (but does not have to) indicate strife between the individual and authority figures (including parents). In this case, the potential concerns would involve power (fixed signs) and idealism or compassion (Neptune) versus personal desires (Mars). This combination can be positively channeled by fighting for a cause or putting grace into action.

Power struggles with Mom are certainly possible, but there are lots of placements that suggest that Mother could be a great partner and confidant as well.

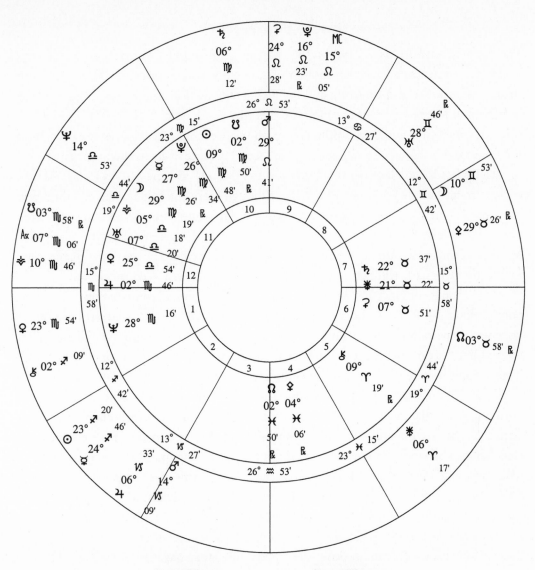

INNER WHEEL
Ms. B
Natal Chart
September 2, 1970
12:02 P.M. CST
near Chicago, Illinois
42N00 87W50
Koch Houses

OUTER WHEEL
Ms. A
Natal Chart
December 15, 1948
3:25 A.M. CST
Chicago, Illinois
41N51 87W39
Koch Houses

Synastry

The contacts between Ms. A's and Ms. B's charts reiterate familiar themes.

Ms. B's Jupiter is conjunct her mother's South Node and Ascendant, which emphasizes the intense emotional connection and highlights faith, action, and courage. Ms. B's Midheaven (and Mars) conjunct her mom's Ceres (the Earth Mother asteroid). The balance between conditional and unconditional love, and between personal desires and protection, is emphasized, although activating a mother's Ceres is more likely to elicit nurturing.

Ms. B's late Virgo placements (Pluto, Mercury, Moon) all trine Ms. A's Pallas (asteroid of partnership) in the 7th house of sharing, although Mars, the Midheaven, and the Nodes are square that Pallas, and Neptune is opposite it. We would expect that two such strong personalities might still occasionally butt heads or have disagreements, particularly with Ms. B's Ascendant square her mother's Pluto and Midheaven. The partnership and communication emphasis will help a great deal to resolve power issues constructively.

Ms. B's Sun is conjunct Ms. A's Saturn. This is another "power" combination. When done poorly, either can feel that the other is a drag, a burden, or constrictive/restrictive. When done well (especially in Virgo), both provide solid support for one another and are willing to work hard to do what must be done. When Saturn connections are expressed positively by the people involved, they add to the endurance and longevity of the relationship.

Ms. B's Pluto, Mercury, and Moon are square her mother's Sun and Mercury. Since both have Mercury involved, communication is still emphasized (especially in mutable signs). Clashes are possible with this combination, unless both people have established a clear balance between the idealism and quest for something grand (Sagittarius) and the hard work and effort (Virgo) required to make it real. In this case, we have already noted that both Ms. B and her mom are extremely hardworking individuals.

Ms. B's Uranus (and Vesta) are trine her mother's Moon, so her mom could have nurtured her freedom and individuality. They both square her mother's Jupiter, however, so issues of idealism (perhaps seeking the impossible—that Sagittarius feeling that "over there" is always better than right here, right now) could be a challenge. Ms. B's Uranus is also opposite her mother's Juno (marriage asteroid), so a freedom-closeness dilemma is suggested. Even as independent and competent as Ms. B's chart suggests she is, she could have felt neglected occasionally if her mother worked as hard as the chart certainly suggests.

Despite all of the Virgo in Ms. B's chart (and there is a lot!), much of the earth in her chart is tied to other people: most of the Virgo is in the 11th house of friends; Saturn, the major earth planet, in the 7th house of partners and other people; Vesta is conjunct the 4th-house ruler, etc. There is the danger that, when Ms. B was younger, if her mother was very hardworking and supercompetent (as the horoscope suggests), Ms. B may have dis-owned some of her own earth and projected it onto her mother. She may have seen her mother as the superresponsible, capable, achievement-oriented person. If she overdid that, she might have identified too much with her 1st-house Neptune (dreamy, drifting, not pushing too hard) and the water sign rising (internally rather than externally oriented). As she got older, however, she would inevitably start to manifest her own earth, especially once she started working. Then the earth in the 10th and Ceres in Taurus in the 6th would start kicking in.

Summary of Synastry

We have the picture of a mother who is an important role model in many ways, particu-larly in terms of power, initiative, courage, communication, hard work, partnership, and individuality. Of course, role models can be positive or negative (although much looks constructive here). We see a daughter who is also strong and competent but may have underappreciated and underutilized her talents initially, especially if her mother was doing the Supermom role early on.

If used negatively, we could see the issues of dominance, control, and anger from the previous generation carried forth. If used positively, we would expect a good partnership between the mother and daughter, an enduring tie that continues even when the daughter is an adult. They stay in one another's lives and communicate regularly. They work well together.

Ms. B's Own Words about Her Mother

I was raised by a single mother in a time when it was not politically correct to do so. She was always the "cool" mom, and everyone wanted to be at my house. Sometimes I felt like I was the mom and we had actually switched roles—she was out playing with the kids more than I was. No matter what I was doing in school my aunt would say, " When your mother was your age, she was doing this or that . . ." (always something more exciting and hip than what I was doing). We could never get away with any of the typical teenage stuff because she had already done it and knew what we were trying to pull. She always tried to make our lives fun, to make us feel like we weren't missing out on anything. I saw how she struggled and worked three jobs to support the children she chose to raise, and yet she never com-plained or let on how desperate she sometimes felt. She never really voiced her opinions (unless I asked), but let me make my own decisions and stuck by me whatever the deci-sions were. As an adult and mother myself, I see how much I am like her. One of her favorite phrases is "Get your own life, please," because I have come to duplicate many parts of her life—things I knew about, like having my children less than two years apart like she did, and things I wasn't aware of, such as craving strawberries while pregnant. She is still my best friend, next to my husband, and I speak to her every day because I truly like her as a person.

Messages/scripts

My mom always had a list of things she wanted to try—truck-driving, being a police officer, playing with baby tigers, etc.—and she has completed every one of them. Her biggest message to me was that of limitless possibilities. Anything I wanted to achieve or bring into my life was possible. It took a letter she wrote to me for a youth retreat in high school to realize just how proud of me she was (is). She was not a real "mushy" person when I was growing up, choosing to express her affection in late-night bakeoffs and slumber parties rather than through terms of endearment or physical affection. I always knew she loved and supported me, and she makes sure she extends that affection to my children on a daily basis as well. Her daily question to my kids is, "How much does Grandma love you?" Their response is to stretch their arms open as wide as possible.

How was she a positive role model?

The ways in which my mom was a positive role model are obvious. I couldn't have asked for a better example of how to be a mom. She taught me to be strong, and how to take care of myself. She taught me that I am the one who decides what I want in my life and I am the one who can go out and get it. She made me strong and independent. My husband is in the military and travels extensively. Being raised by my mother has given me the ability to survive and take care of myself while he is gone. She did not have a wonderful childhood. I know this from what she tells me and what I vaguely remember of her parents. She taught me that we do not have to follow in our parents' footsteps, but can overcome negative events and correct them in our own lives. I always had a wonderful "family" around me when I was growing up, yet not one of those people were related to me. I learned that "family" does not mean blood, but rather love, respect, and support. My mother raised me with the understanding that I could say anything to her, that we could talk about anything. This lead to a wonderful bond between us and is the main reason I grew up without dropping out of high school, getting pregnant at sixteen, doing drugs, or a million other things I saw happening to people my age. I see myself passing these traits along as I raise my children. I have been told that I am a good mother by other people. That is just as much a compliment to my mother as it is to me. I strive to have kids who like me as much as I truly like my mom.

How was she a negative role model?

My mom was a strong single mom. Because of her negative upbringing, she undid that with me by never spanking, drinking alcohol, or using harsh words with me. I grew up wanting to be like that. It never occurred to me to want to be married or to have a dad involved in my kids' lives. I can honestly say that feeling stayed with me well through high school. It took a lot of work to allow someone in my life to help me take responsibility for everyday events and to have someone to depend on. From all the social work and childhood horror stories my mom told me, I could rattle off warning signs of abusers, alcoholics, etc., and was probably a very hard person to date. It took a lot of work to realize that not all men are horrible, that not all of them leave their wives and kids, and that you can live "happily ever after" with someone instead of having to make it all happen on your own. I still send a red flag up if my husband has more than two beers in one night because I grew up in a home where there was absolutely no alcohol around. I am working on that one.

Where did she have the greatest impact and how?

My mom is the closest person in my life. She and I have the same religious beliefs and the same child-rearing beliefs, and she can still make me laugh easily and often. She helped me deliver my daughter when my husband was gone (she even had phantom labor pains—now there's a connection for you!). She taught me about unconditional support, strength, and independence, and how to stay true to myself no matter what comes up. She taught me all these things by example: how she lived her life, how she raised us, and how she is with my children. My kids are lucky to have her in their lives on a daily basis, to learn the same lessons from her that I did.

Healing Options

Clearly huge progress has been made in one generation in this family! If, however, Ms. B feels that there is even a little healing to do in her relationship with her mom, we would suggest referring to Letters 6, 8, and 9 in chapter 8.

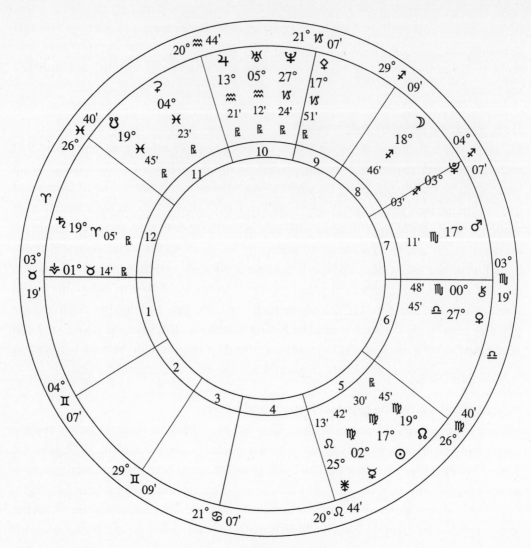

Ms. C
Natal Chart
September 9, 1997
9:03 P.M. PST
San Diego, California
32N42 117W09
Koch Houses

Ms. C

Ms. B has a daughter of her own, who we will call Ms. C. She is too young to give her impressions of her mom, but we are including her horoscope here for people to see the four generations in action.

As you can see, Ms. C's chart includes the familial Vesta emphasis (her mother has Vesta conjunct the 4th-house ruler and Moon; her grandmother has Vesta conjunct the Ascendant, and her great-grandmother had Vesta conjunct the North Node). The hardworking focus continues with Ms. C: two planets and a Node in Virgo, and Vesta rising. The 10th-house focus is also present. In her case, the 10th-house Uranus seems to reflect her mother's 11th-house stellium, while the 10th-house Neptune echoes her mother's Neptune in the 1st. Ms. C's Moon is in Sagittarius and Ceres is in Pisces, so she sees her mother primarily as an idealist, although a little of the power motif continues with the Moon in the 8th house, the Capricorn Midheaven, and the 5th-house focus with the Sun there. The theme of Mother as potential friend is reinforced by Uranus in the 10th, two planets in Aquarius in the 10th, and Ceres (the Earth Mother asteroid) in the 11th.

The Venus-Venus conjunction between the charts of the mother and daughter is potentially very loving and sweet, and the Ceres-Pallas conjunction is also likely to denote a partnership between the mother and daughter.

It appears that the idealism, imagination, and willingness to work hard have been passed on to the next generation quite strongly!

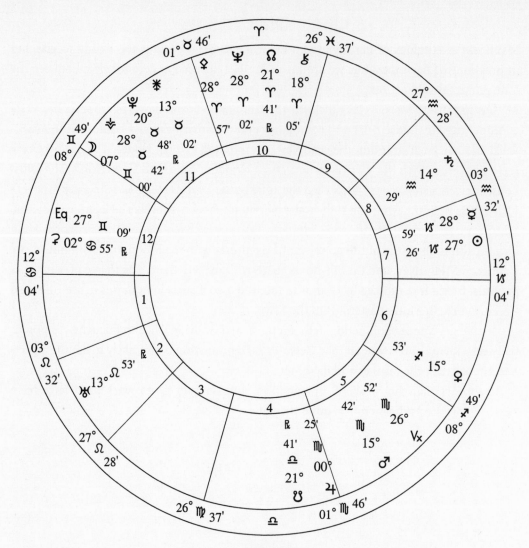

Ms. GG
Natal Chart
January 17, 1875
4:00 P.M. LMT
Columbia County, Georgia
33N28 82W12
Placidus Houses

CASE STUDY 2

This four-generation case study involves a deceased great-grandmother and her daughter, (the grandmother), plus a living mother and her adult daughter. We will label them GG (great-grandmother), G (grandmother), M (mother), and D (daughter).

Ms. GG

The major theme in GG's chart seems to revolve around the issue of power. Letters 1 and 2 describe potential power over personal action and possessions. GG certainly wanted that, with stellia in both the signs of Aries and Taurus. She also had a strong Letter 5 drive with her Uranus in Leo and Mars in the house of Leo. She wanted to be a leader and influence others. Jupiter and Mars in Scorpio and Saturn in the house of Scorpio call for her to share power with lasting, close peer relationships. Letter 10 brings in a focus on executive power, so GG's Sun and Mercury in Capricorn, and her Aries stellium in the house of Capricorn, indicate a strong urge to be in charge. Finally, Letter 11 points to resistance to being controlled by others. GG's Saturn in Aquarius and five factors in the house of Aquarius, most of them in Taurus, reiterate the power theme in her chart. (The fifth factor is the Antivertex. Most computer programs print out the Vertex—see the 5th house here. We consider the Antivertex, the opposite end of the axis, more important. The Antivertex signifies personal identity and action, while the Vertex—like the Descendant and West Point—represents aspects of ourselves that we meet in relationships.)

Many of the preceding factors are also keys to GG's parents, though some suggest the potential of a power issue with a mate. The Mars rulership of signs in both the 10th and 4th houses fits the military crisis of the Civil War that devastated much of the southern United States during the lifetime of GG's parents. Her mother, born on January 14, 1851, had many shared patterns with GG, including an Aries stellium, Sun in Capricorn, Moon in Gemini, and Venus in Sagittarius. We do not have a birth time for her mother. (GG's grandmother—born January 9, 1814—also had the Sun in Capricorn. So, GG was the third generation of strong, Southern women with Sun in Capricorn.)

GG's 4th and 10th houses suggest that she saw both parents as strong. They may have had a power issue with each other as well as with GG, and she with either or both of them. The Aries stellium in the 10th house participates in a (mostly) cardinal T-square with the 7th-house Capricorn and the South Node and Jupiter in the 4th house. Jupiter is an "out-of-sign" part of the T-square, in Scorpio, a fixed sign. Jupiter might be in the end of the 4th house or the beginning of the 5th. GG's birth town is no longer in existence, so both her birth time and place are approximate. Mercury, ruler of the IC, and a Libra lunar Node in her 4th house are keys to her mother. Mercury is in the 7th house, showing that Mom was a role model for a mate. Saturn, the natural key to the father, is in the 8th house, so Father was also a model for GG's choice of mate. She apparently experienced both her parents and her mate as power people. Pallas, a key to partnership, is in the 10th house of father to repeat the theme. It certainly looks like a family that is "all chiefs and no Indians."

GG may have loved her mother, with the conjunction between their Venus positions, but GG acted on her Aries, Sagittarius, and Aquarius, the "freedom" Letters, by eloping soon after her sixteenth birthday. She chose an older man as partner, a "father figure," to fit her mixture of factors connecting parent and partner. Her earth and water were strong enough to signify a need for security with her Sun and Mercury in Capricorn and four factors in the 10th (Capricorn) house, plus four factors (including the Antivertex) in the Taurus sign, one in the Taurus (2nd) house, and one in the Virgo (6th) house. She was able to be practical, but had a clear conflict between her fire and Aquarius need to be independent, able to act on impulse, and do what she pleased, and her earth desire for stability. GG's water factors included a Cancer Ascendant and Ceres, a strong identification with her mother as a personal role model, and with her role as a mother. Her Scorpio Mars in her 5th house, and Jupiter in either the 4th or 5th house, connected her identity and values to home and family, and her lunar Node in the 4th house reinforced the importance of that area of life. GG also had a Pisces MC for additional water.

There is no doubt that GG wanted power. Her strong stellium in Aries is in the natural house of Capricorn where it could be expressed as a feeling that "My will is or should be the law. I should be in control, either because that is the only way I feel safe, or because I am responsible and if I do not make the world do what it should, my conscience will get me." Her need for freedom, to avoid being ruled, is emphasized by the Aries and by the strong Aquarian (11th) house, which includes the Moon, ruler of her Ascendant, so it is a key to her basic identity and sense of personal power. Uranus in Leo in the Taurus (2nd) house adds to her determination with its fixed emphasis. It holds a grand trine in fire signs and earth houses, a potential steamroller combination. Mars, always a key to identity, is also in a fixed sign and house, the (Leo) 5th house, to add to her sense of personal rights and power. This was a potentially powerful lady.

But there is enough potential for projection of her power into others to show that GG may have actually not had much personal control of it. As already mentioned, GG had her

Capricorn Sun and Mercury in the 7th house and Saturn in the 8th house, the two houses of partnership. Projection is possible in most areas of life, but it is most common in the 7th and 8th houses, where individuals often choose mates who express part of their nature for them, and usually do it to excess. GG's Pallas, an asteroid that is a key to partnership, was in the 10th (Capricorn) house, and Juno and Pluto, also keys to a mate, were in a fixed sign and house in a grand cross with her Uranus, Mars, and Saturn. She was likely to pick a mate with equal determination, possibly an older one as well, and being a female in the culture of the last quarter of the nineteenth century in the southern United States, she certainly had a power issue in her life.

GG's odds for being in control may actually have been slim to none, except in the area of her children, where she would have wanted to be a perfect mother with Ceres in the Piscean (12th) house. Jupiter in the 4th house would have wanted a perfect home, or if it was in the 5th house, it would repeat the desire to be a perfect mother of perfect children, and in Scorpio would want to be and/or to have a perfect mate. But she also had lessons in the home and in partnership with her South Node in Libra in the 4th house, while Scorpio is often associated with the need to learn what is enough and when to let go. With Letter 8, we learn to share power with others, with a mate, or, when it is in the 5th house, with children. Her tightly aspected fixed cross could have been manifested in power issues involving partners, children, or the physical world of money, possessions, or pleasures.

A major asset suggested in GG's chart is her intelligence and capacity to make friends that is especially shown by her Ascendant ruler, the Moon, in Gemini in the Aquarian house, but is also supported by the additional factors in Gemini, Aquarius, and Sagittarius, and the powerfully aspected Uranus. Both major keys to parents, the Moon and Saturn, are in air signs, so despite the indications of strong parents, they may have respected her intelligence and treated her as an equal, to the extent permitted by the culture of her day. GG's air and fire in her chart are strong enough to provide some humor and optimism in addition to her intelligence. Those talents should have supported her core strength, which could have been tested by life circumstances.

Synastry

GG's Sun (and, more widely, her Mercury) was conjunct her mother's Sun (in Capricorn), showing the potential for a loving connection, but also the danger of power struggles. GG's Neptune-Pallas conjunction (idealistic about partnership) was conjunct her mother's

Uranus-Pluto conjunction (freedom-closeness issues), while GG's South Node was conjunct her mother's Jupiter. Thus, the mother and daughter reinforced each other's cardinal T-squares. The balancing act between independence (Aries), equality (Libra), and power/control (Capricorn) was probably challenging for both of them.

The mother and daughter had their Venuses conjunct, which could have indicated mutual pleasure and affection or self-indulgence and focus on personal desires. They shared a Moon in Gemini (curiosity and communication skills), which may or may not have been conjunct due to an unknown birth time for the mother.

Although the mother and daughter had their Saturns sextile each other (good potential for sharing power), GG's Pluto was in a yod pattern—quincunx her mother's Jupiter (clash of values) and Venus (differences around money, pleasure, or partnership, such as choosing to elope at age sixteen). The Jupiter-Pluto clash is a "double whammy" because GG's Jupiter was opposite her mother's Pluto. GG's Uranus was also quincunx her mother's Mars, again emphasizing the "runaway" and freedom factors, and the quincunx between the mother's Juno (marriage asteroid) and the daughter's Juno again suggests differences of opinion around intimacy, shared resources, or marriage. (GG's Uranus squared her own Juno within a one-degree orb—the "sudden marriage"?)

GG's parents were well-off, the owners of a plantation in Georgia. Their slaves had been freed before GG's birth, but there were still servants to do the physical work. They lived through the Civil War, and knew of others who were victims of Sherman's "march to the sea" when troops from the North burned the homes in their path. It is not clear whether someone on GG's side of the family, or someone in her husband's family, had their large home burned by one of Sherman's three sets of troops. According to the family traditions, they had treated their slaves well, and the slaves took the pregnant wife of the owner into one of their cabins and cared for her. The plantation owner was away at the time, fighting in the war. GG grew up in relative luxury, as is suggested by her Jupiter. She even attended one semester of what at the time was called a "college," a rare privilege for women in her day. Since she was only fifteen at the time, it would be more like high school today, though tuition was charged. After that one semester of two courses, she eloped at age sixteen, marrying an older, dominating man, and bore six children. But her life in the nineteenth century in the South with limited medical information expressed some of the negative astrological traditions associated with her Mars in Scorpio in the 5th house in a grand cross that included Uranus, Saturn, Juno, and Pluto. She bore four boys and two girls, but all of the boys died in infancy. Her daughters, born five years apart, were made of stronger stuff. Both had their Suns in Leo. This study discusses the older daughter, who is labeled G.

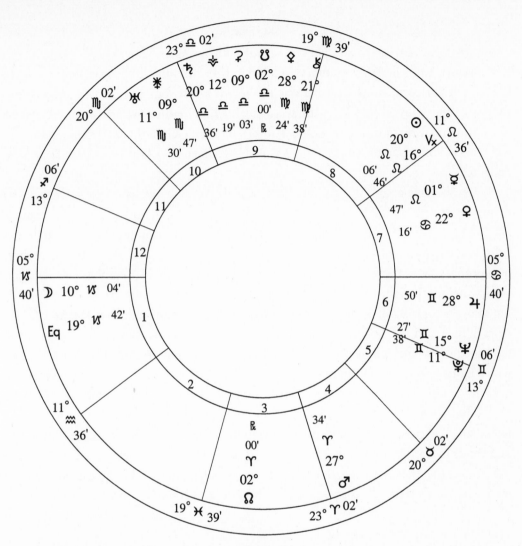

Ms. G
Natal Chart
August 12, 1894
4:00 P.M. LMT
Waycross, Georgia
31N12 82W21
Placidus Houses

Ms. G

Turning to G's chart, we see another strong lady with her Ascendant, East Point, and Moon in Capricorn, Mars in Aries, Mercury and Sun in Leo, and Juno and Uranus in Scorpio in the 10th (Capricorn) house. Saturn was in the 9th house, but conjunct the MC, and it would have progressed into the 10th house during her lifetime. We are fortunate to have the approximate birth times of both G and her mother. GG's father was present when G was born at home, and he told GG that she had been born about the same time as her new daughter.

When we have a family with "all chiefs and no Indians," we have the potential for a major power issue. G saw her parents as holding the power, with both parents as role models. The Moon, for mother, was rising. It was in Capricorn, the sign for father, and the signs ruled and co-ruled by Mars were in the houses of the parents, including Mars there in its own primary sign of Aries. G was obviously intelligent, with a major emphasis on air signs, but like her mother, she did not want to be ruled. She was personally identified with needing to be in control, for security reasons or because she felt responsible. Where GG had Aries in the Capricorn house, G had Capricorn in the Aries house. But parents normally do have the power when children are still young. G looked to marriage to be her salvation, with a Libra stellium in her 9th house and Jupiter close to her Descendant, progressing into her 7th (partnership) house in time. Neptune on Pluto, another key to mate, and Pallas in the 9th house repeat the theme. The preceding combinations show "God" as the role model for a mate, the search for a perfect mate. Juno in the 10th house, Scorpio in the 10th house, and Venus in Cancer in the 7th house point to parents as role models for a mate, and we can suspect that they were negative role models. With her strong air emphasis, G wanted a mate who would treat her as an equal, but also one who could be a protective parent and give her a lot of love to satisfy her Leo in the partnership houses. Amazingly, she found a man who lived up to her dreams.

With her 4th-house Mars and her rising Moon and Capricorn, G was identified with the parent role. She needed to be a nurturing parent with her Cancer Venus ruling the Taurus that is in both the 4th and 5th houses. She also needed to be the strong and responsible parent with her Capricorn. She managed that also, by picking a mate who traveled on business, leaving her at home to handle both roles some of the time. Note that this let her have the power while her husband was away, and that it also fit her Libra in the 9th house of travel to have a traveling husband.

What G did not have was satisfying work outside of her home, and she needed it with her Neptune and Jupiter in the Virgo house, Chiron and Pallas in the sign of Virgo, plus her Capricorn and 10th-house emphasis. Her Virgo side might have been satisfied with caring for her home or with hobbies and crafts. But she rejected the traditional female role, saying that as a child she had wanted to be a boy, equating males with freedom and power. She wanted to do something bigger in the world, but her husband was old-fashioned. He said that his wife was in full control in the home and he lived by that standard, but he believed that men should support their wives. He provided G with a full-time maid, so she did not have to do the menial, female work she rejected, but she did not have a sense of accomplishment to satisfy the earth side of her nature. G's happiest years came after her children were grown when she was able to travel with her husband, sharing his work. It was icing on the cake that her husband was in religious sales work, which satisfied G's desire for a spiritual career with her Neptune and Jupiter in her 6th house and her Chiron in Virgo in her 9th house. It also satisfied her air and Leo talent for sales.

As previously described, G's early life was not happy. She experienced both of her parents as domineering and often rejecting. Like her mother, with her strong Capricorn theme in her chart, G wanted to be the authority, but initially, parents wield the power. G challenged the authority of her parents while her younger sister was more skillful in manipulating them, and G always ended up feeling blocked by her parents. With Saturn on the MC and Uranus in her 10th house, she was a rebel against authority, but she usually lost. Her parents prevented her from fulfilling two very different desires. With her strong 9th house, at one point she wanted to be a missionary in Africa. Later, her Leo was eager be an actress. Instead, her parents sent her to the local women's college, where she earned a bachelor's degree in microbiology. Following that, she left on her own, going to a university in the North where she met her future husband.

G had four children. M, her only daughter, was born first, followed by three sons. Education remained a family value. All four children earned college degrees, and two went on to graduate school. G's husband went into business with two partners, and was able to provide for his family despite the pressures of the Great Depression of the 1930s. G had a deeply loving marriage to a devoted husband who did his best to fulfill all her desires except for one. As already mentioned, with her 10th-house Saturn and her rising Moon and Ascendant in Capricorn, she wanted to do more in the world than simply raise a family. Her husband believed that men should support their wives, that having a wife who worked outside of the home indicated a failure on his part. G's happiest period came after her children were grown and she was able to work with her husband in his business until he retired.

G's Sun in Leo in her 8th house fits this love by her partner, and she expressed her strong Capricorn by handling their finances carefully. She was very frugal, watching for bargains with food and other household needs. GG was less fortunate financially, one of the potentials of GG's grand cross in fixed signs and houses. The orange grove where she and her husband raised their two daughters was at the edge of the area where citrus could be grown. Periodic cold snaps decimated their crops and put them in debt. G's husband bailed them out several times when they would otherwise have lost their property. Note GG's stellium in Taurus in her 11th house. The 11th can signify the partners of one's children in the 5th house. Eventually, when GG's husband died, she deeded the property to G's husband, and came to live with G in the Southwest where G, her husband, and M and her family had relocated.

When G's husband died, she continued to provide financial support for her mother, GG, but she still carried emotional scars from her childhood. Both GG and G made friends in their new area, but GG expressed her strong 11th house by forming a wide circle of new friends until her death shortly before she was ninety years old. She probably experienced those final years as being the most free and pleasurable time since her childhood. In contrast, G was desolate after being widowed, having centered her life around her husband. She shifted her main focus to her grown children and her grandchildren, but she was often depressed and lonely. She once remarked that her life had been hell until she married, that it was heaven while she was married, and that it was hell again after she was widowed. One hazard of idolizing a part of life is that we will eventually lose it, and it can feel like losing "God."

Synastry

The synastry between GG and G includes many of GG's keys to power. Her Neptune and Pallas showed the potential for an idealistic partnership, but they were in her 10th house in Aries in a close conjunction to G's Mars, indicating a potential confrontation of wills.

GG's Mars, her personal identity and power, were conjunct G's Uranus (and Juno more widely), with a similar message. Juno and Scorpio could have invited an adult partnership, but a Uranus conjunction with Mars is often an explosive confrontation of wills if either individual tries to control the other one.

GG's Saturn, a key to her father and later her husband, was on G's Antivertex, an angle equivalent in meaning to Mars. If the mother and daughter had expressed the tolerance

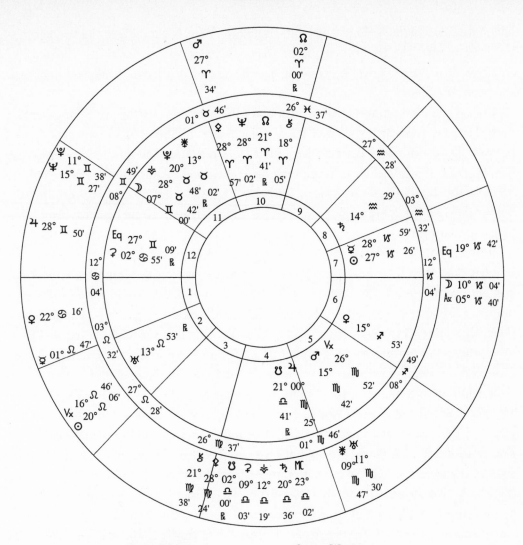

INNER WHEEL
Ms. GG
Natal Chart
January 17, 1875
4:00 P.M. LMT
Columbia County, Georgia
33N28 82W12
Placidus Houses

OUTER WHEEL
Ms. G
Natal Chart
August 12, 1894
4:00 P.M. LMT
Waycross, Georgia
31N12 82W21
Placidus Houses

and mutual acceptance of Aquarius, they could have been friends. Since GG and her husband manifested the traditional parent roles and tried to control their strong-willed daughter, there were frequent times of impasse as the parents tried to break the will of their stubborn daughter.

GG's South Node conjunct G's Saturn and MC really sum up the power impasse and mutual lesson of two strong women. It was not a happy childhood for G, who experienced her parents as domineering, restrictive, critical, and rejecting. She was their job, and they felt obliged to discipline her into conforming to their will. (Although fathers are not the focus of this book, G's father—born February 21, 1863—had his Saturn conjunct G's South Node. All the conjunctions took place in Libra—lessons about equality, justice, fair play, and sharing.)

It might well have been a happier story in the psychological climate of the twentieth century, since there were also many potentially positive aspects between the charts of GG and her mother. G's Moon was on GG's Descendant and they could have produced a mutually supportive partnership. Instead, they produced the negative potential—emotional separation. G's Pallas was on GG's IC, also showing that she might have had a partnership with her mother. And G's Jupiter on GG's East Point in Gemini could have been expressed as shared knowledge and values, with open, equalitarian communication.

In addition to conjunctions, GG's Saturn was trine four of G's factors in air signs: Pluto and Neptune in Gemini and Ceres and Vesta in Libra. GG's Ascendant also was trine G's Juno and Uranus. What a shame that, with that much air, they did not manage to build a peer relationship after G was grown. Both women loved to talk, but never were comfortable talking to each other. We can better understand the tense relationship when we note that G's Antivertex and Uranus-Juno landed on GG's fixed grand cross, intensifying the power-struggle potential. The message was repeated with GG's Ceres, her identification as a mother, completing a cardinal-sign grand cross with G's lunar Nodes and Ascendant. The basic issue with both the cardinal and fixed dilemmas is the ability to protect our own needs while fully respecting the rights and needs of the others with whom we form close relationships.

G left home as soon as she was an adult, moving to the North to attend graduate school where she met her future husband. When cold spells hit the area where GG and her husband had a citrus grove, G's husband made their mortgage payments on more than one occasion. And after the death of G's father, G provided a home and money for necessities for her mother in the western city where she and M were living. But even though G took responsibility for the financial support of her mother, she was not able to overcome the memory of her difficult childhood.

Ms. M

Turning to the chart of M (G's daughter), her major focus is on home and family with a rising Moon, Venus (the Ascendant ruler) in Cancer, Mars as a major key to identity in the 4th house, and Mercury, another ruler of the 1st house, in the 5th house conjunct the Sun and Ceres. The identification with Mother as a role model and with being a mother could hardly be said more emphatically. This does not tell us whether G was perceived as a positive or a negative role model, or some of both. The latter seems very possible, since the Moon is in a T-square to Uranus in Pisces and Ceres, Sun, and Mercury in Virgo while at the same time making sextiles to Neptune, Mars, and Pallas in the 4th house of mother. Venus in Cancer sextile the Ascendant and Vesta are also suggestions that a positive relationship was possible. M's 10th house is ruled by Uranus in Pisces in the 11th house, which suggests an intelligent, idealistic father who might have been distant or might have been like a friend. Saturn, usually a key to father and also a co-ruler of Aquarius, has very harmonious aspects with a conjunction to Jupiter, a sextile to Venus, and trines to M's Ascendant and Vesta. Saturn is also in the natural house of Leo, with the potential of loving and being loved.

The identification with ideals is also very strong in M's chart, with Mars conjunct Neptune and factors in Aries in the Pisces (12th) house. The theme of work is another major one with a stellium in Virgo, and Vesta closely conjunct the Ascendant. Unlike her mother, G, marriage seems less important to M, though she is looking for a perfect mate with Juno in Sagittarius in the 8th house, and she does have the North Node in Libra. However, its placement in the 6th house of work could suggest that a job as a counselor might take care of her partnerships needs, and sometimes the search for an ideal mate is expressed as "Perfect, or I'll skip it." Both parents could be role models for a mate with Venus in Cancer, Pluto ruling the 7th house also in Cancer, Jupiter ruling the 8th house in a conjunction with Saturn, and Saturn ruling part of the 8th house since part of its sign, Capricorn, is there.

M could have seen her mother as somewhat dominating, in light of her Leo in her 4th house and Ceres in the Leo house conjunct the Sun. But unless it is manifested as excessive expectations, Neptune in the 4th house is likely to be empathic and compassionate. Pallas, also in the 4th, represents Libra desires, and along with the Moon in Gemini, they associate M's mother with the element of air, which tends to be equalitarian. Ceres is in Virgo, which is more service-oriented than domineering, especially since it is also conjunct Mercury, a co-ruler of Virgo. So M may have seen G as loving and generous with the Leo, but also able to be practical, intelligent, and idealistic. The very strong Neptune conjunction with Mars

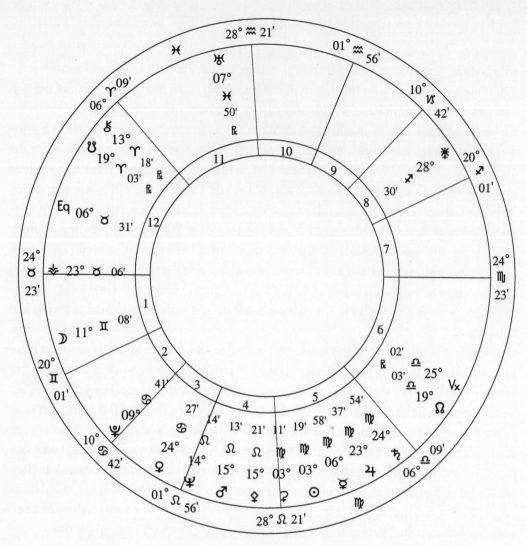

Ms. M
Natal Chart
August 26, 1921
9:48 P.M. CST
Chicago, Illinois
41N51 87W39
Placidus Houses

and Pallas could have described G as an active counselor/savior, or she could have been seen as a dramatic martyr and victim.

Synastry

The synastry between G and M includes an interesting reversal of the Nodes in contrast to GG and G. Where G's Saturn and MC are on her mother's South Node, G's Saturn and MC are on her daughter's North Node. Any combination of Saturn and/or the MC with either lunar Node suggests past-life connections and mutual lessons, but in general, the North Node is more easily handled and the South Node more challenging. Obviously, neither Node should be neglected. With any opposition in astrology, we are dealing with a polarity principle, and they "need" each other. Our goal is to manage a partnership, to do justice to both ends of the opposition.

Another important double conjunction involves G's Chiron and Pallas on M's Jupiter and Saturn in Virgo. Where G hated typical female tasks, M is comfortable with her Virgo. She gets a sense of satisfaction from small accomplishments such as cooking, doing the dishes, and getting the clothes clean, even before the days of automatic washers and dryers. She also has a strong sense of equality and social justice despite only having her Moon and MC in air signs. Also, Uranus in its own house in a long-term progressed aspect to Mercury connects the air planets, and increases their emphasis in her nature. M felt that as long as G was providing financial support, it was fair for M to do the housework in exchange.

G's Pluto is closely conjunct M's Moon, and G's Neptune is more widely connected, showing a potential bond at a deep, subconscious level. The combination manifested in psychic openness, in shared idealism, and in mutual help. As already mentioned, G provided financial support to M and her family while M provided services in their homes, which were next door to each other, especially shopping for food, cooking, and doing the dishes. When M returned to school for graduate work, G was there to care for her grandchildren.

Another conjunction includes M's South Node and Antivertex, an auxiliary Ascendant, on G's IC. The combination repeats the themes of a shared home (Node and IC) and personal action (Antivertex and the sign of Aries).

Finally, one of the most important conjunctions links the Venus in Cancer of both G and M. Though this did not guarantee a positive relationship, it was certainly appropriate for a shared home in Cancer and for a potential partnership of mutual support.

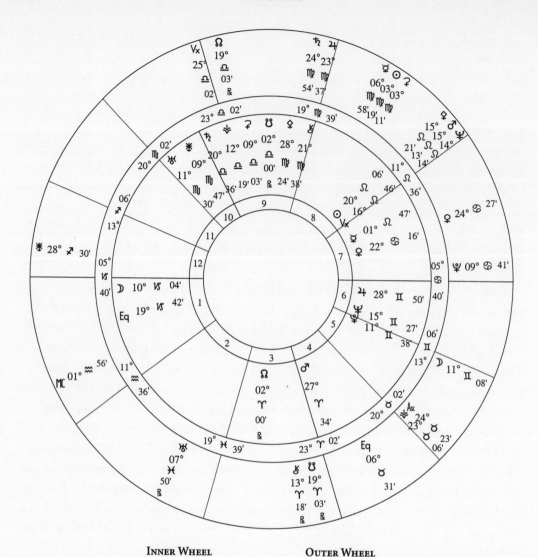

INNER WHEEL
Ms. G
Natal Chart
August 12, 1894
4:00 P.M. LMT
Waycross, Georgia
31N12 82W21
Placidus Houses

OUTER WHEEL
Ms. M
Natal Chart
August 26, 1921
9:48 P.M. CST
Chicago, Illinois
41N51 87W39
Placidus Houses

There are also a good many trines between the two charts. G's lunar Nodes are sextile/trine M's MC. G's Ceres and Vesta are trine M's Moon. G's Mars is trine M's Juno. G's Moon and Ascendant make a grand trine to M's Ceres, Sun, and Mercury in Virgo and her to East Point (an auxiliary Ascendant) in Taurus. G's Juno and Uranus also form a grand trine to M's Pluto and Uranus. G's Chiron and Pallas are trine M's Ascendant and Vesta. Yet, despite such an impressive amount of harmony, and despite the mutual assistance, which continued until G's death, their relationship was not completely comfortable.

Ms. M's Own Words about Her Mother

I saw my mother as an extraordinarily generous person who was continually hurt when others took advantage of her or just did not appreciate her generosity. She and my father adored each other. I never heard them argue over anything. One experience that Mother described is an example of that. She was playing bridge with three women friends, and the others in turn described what was wrong with their husbands. After each of them had contributed their complaint, they turned to the silent fourth and said, "Well, M, you haven't said anything." M said, "'I can't contribute to this conversation. My husband is perfect." Obviously, that was the end of that topic for the day.

Despite the love shared by my mother and dad, she was frequently unhappy, and I used to be puzzled. As a child, I thought I would be perfectly happy to have a loving husband and children. I could not understand why my mother was not happy. Much later, I realized that she carried the emotional scars of her childhood: her experience of being criticized and rejected, of being full of self-doubt and needing the approval of others to feel okay about herself. A career might have at least partially filled that void, but raising children was not enough for her. When she did finally travel and work with my father, she was already suffering from some chronic health problems. When he died not long after that, she was desolate and her health really went downhill, though she survived for nearly twenty more years. So, I did see my mother as both a positive and a negative role model. I admired her generosity and love for her family. I knew and enjoyed my grandmother, who basically was a resilient and friendly person, but I must admit that my mother was a far better parent. However, I rejected Mother's self-doubt and self-criticism, her tendency to feel like a martyr, and her insecurity that made her so vulnerable to the opinions of others. I pitied her lack of ability to feel good about herself, and consciously based my sense of self-esteem on my own work accomplishments so it did not depend on the opinions and actions of others. I also reacted negatively to Mother's tendency to exaggerate. She was well aware when I would look at her skeptically while she recounted some incident. She would say, "Ask your father. He will tell you that is what happened." I always knew that I could count on my father to be straight with me. I never felt that Mother was deliberately lying, but she so needed to be noticed and important.

Since my initial focus was totally on my family of three sons and one daughter, I was grateful that my parents were willing to support me financially when my marriage broke up. I was able to stay home with my kids until the youngest was in school, and then return to graduate school to prepare for a professional career. I was always an avid reader, and my kids were also good students who liked each other and shared family activities with minimal friction. My parents moved next door to me when Dad retired, and Mother actually showed more of her potential for domination with my kids than she had with my brothers and me. That might be because my instinct was to treat my kids as I like to be treated—to give suggestions rather than orders. "It would be nice if you would (fill in the blank)." So maybe Mother was filling in what she felt was a vacuum of authority.

Messages/scripts

Neither my mother nor my father were cuddlers, and they rarely mentioned love, but they showed their love to each other and to their children by doing things for them. Without words or caresses, I knew that my parents loved me. The unspoken script was "We will protect you and see that all of your needs are met." As an example, the first college I attended was near enough for me to live at home and walk to school. My parents paid all the expenses, but for months I did some babysitting to earn spending money. Eventually, Dad asked me what I was earning during the evenings I was away taking care of other people's children. I said it might be about ten dollars a week. He said, "If I give you ten dollars a week, would you be able to stop the work?" I said, "Yes," and after that did not work outside of our home. Ten dollars went a lot farther in those days. Later, when I was away at graduate school, when Dad sent me a letter, there was always a twenty-dollar bill in it.

How was she a positive role model?

I most admired her generosity to everyone, and her love for my father.

How was she a negative role model?

She was her own worst enemy. I rejected her self-criticism and vulnerability to the opinions of other people. I rejected her exaggerations and need to be overly dramatic. I rejected her self-pity and feelings of martyrdom.

Where did she have the greatest impact and how?

I accepted the financial support of my parents, including continued help from my mother even after the death of my father, and I gave to others whenever and whatever I could. Gaining knowledge and sharing it with others was always a primary family value. I choose to be contented with life, rather than frustrated.

Healing Options

If Ms. M felt the need to heal her relationship with her inner mother further, we would suggest Letters 4, 6, and 12 in chapter 8.

Ms. D

Looking at the natal chart of D (M's daughter), we would expect her (like Ms. B) to have a mother who makes a very strong impact on her life, in a number of different areas. D's Moon and Ceres make several conjunctions. The motifs most emphasized in terms of the parental picture are:

1. Mental stimulation: Moon conjunct Mercury; Moon conjunct Jupiter; Moon in the 11th; ruler of the 4th (Mercury) conjunct Jupiter and in the 11th; Ceres conjunct Mercury; Ceres conjunct Jupiter; Ceres in the 11th; Sun (a key to parent) in Gemini; Nodes across 3rd/9th

2. Individuality and independence: Moon in the 11th; Ceres in the 11th; ruler of the 4th (Mercury) in the 11th—this holds the potential for freedom-closeness issues with Mom *or* for Mother as a friend

3. Nurturing/emotional warmth: Moon conjunct Ceres (the Earth Mother asteroid); Ceres conjunct the Moon; ruler of the 10th in the 4th

4. Idealism: Moon conjunct Jupiter; Ceres conjunct Jupiter; Neptune in the 4th; Pisces Midheaven; Sun in the 12th

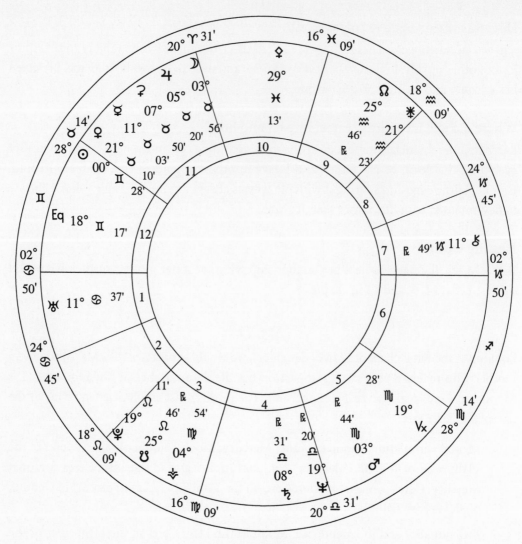

Ms. D
Natal Chart
May 21, 1952
7:36 A.M. MST
Tucson, Arizona
32N13 110W55
Placidus Houses

5. Comfort, sensuality, and stability: Moon in Taurus; Ceres in Taurus; ruler of the 4th (Mercury) in Taurus

6. Partnership: Two planets (Saturn and Neptune) in Libra occupying the 4th; Pallas (a relationship asteroid) in the 10th; ruler of the Midheaven in Libra

7. The mutable dilemma: Moon conjunct Mercury; Moon conjunct Jupiter; Ceres conjunct Mercury; Ceres conjunct Jupiter; Neptune in the 4th; Pisces Midheaven—Mother is dealing with the issue of having multiple talents and the danger of becoming scattered, and working on the balancing act between the real and ideal

What D "meets and greets" upon incarnation is very similar to her parental motifs, since the Moon rules her Ascendant, yet there is one major difference. We find an emphasis on:

1. Freedom, individuality, and independence: Uranus in the 1st; Moon (ruler of the Ascendant) in the 11th

2. Mental stimulation: Uranus in the 1st; Moon (ruler of the Ascendant) conjunct Jupiter and conjunct Mercury and in the 11th; Sun in Gemini

3. The fixed dilemma: Uranus (fixed planet) in the 1st; Moon (the Ascendant ruler) in a fixed sign (Taurus) and fixed house (11th); Mars in Scorpio (fixed sign) and in the 5th house (fixed house)—Daughter has issues about learning to share power, possessions, and pleasures

The major difference between D and her experience of her mother is that Mom is pictured as extremely intellectual, mental, and idealistic, whereas the daughter has a very strong sensual/sexual streak.

The picture we are getting is of a very stubborn and self-willed daughter, who might be rebellious (Uranus in the 1st is square Saturn in the 4th). The combination of the Moon, Ceres, Jupiter, and Mercury is also opposite Mars, which could indicate clashes of will. Or, this could simply indicate ambivalence in the daughter's mind about how much to take Mom as a positive role model and when to take her as a negative role model, or differences about handling anger, sexuality, etc. Saturn in the 4th is also quincunx Ceres, which pulls in Mercury, ruler of the 4th, and the Moon and Jupiter. This points to challenges about balancing conditional and unconditional love (could be too much conditional love *or* too much unconditional love with the child being spoiled or overindulged). Mars is quincunx the Sun (assertion issues connected with the father figure), and Neptune in the 4th is quincunx Venus (beauty emphasis, but idealism and imagination could create challenges in regard to love or material pleasures). Since Dad was out of the picture early on, several of the quincunxes can also refer to separation between the parents.

The Moon is sextile the Ascendant and pulls in Jupiter, Ceres, and Mercury, all of which imply harmony between the mother and daughter. Neptune and Pluto are in a (wide) yod (double quincunx) with the Midheaven. This again suggests possible conflicts with authority figures, or challenges for D to bring her vocational dreams down to earth.

The chart suggests that Mom is very bright, curious (perhaps overextended), and equalitarian, while D is also bright, but very resistant to outside influences and inclined to go her own way. The clashes with authority figures, as it happens, were with a grandparent. The Saturn in the 4th was played out by a grandmother—Capricorn is on the 7th-house cusp, so Saturn rules the 7th, and the 1st and 7th houses traditionally represent grandparents.

Synastry

There are many harmonious contacts between the mother and daughter (M and D), reinforcing the potential for partnership and friendship.

D's early Taurus collection (Moon, Jupiter, Ceres, Mercury) is trine her mom's early Virgo placements (Ceres, Sun, Mercury), which certainly suggests they can get together in terms of earthy accomplishments and pleasures. The Taurus bunch also sextiles the mother's Uranus and Pluto. D's Ascendant sextiles her mother's early Virgo collection and trines her Uranus, although it quincunxes Mom's Midheaven (work took Mother away?) and opposes her Juno (other relationships took Mom away or Mom chose motherhood over wifehood?). D's Mars also sextiles her mother's early Virgo placements.

The toughest aspects are from D's Midheaven, which quincunxes her mother's Neptune, Mars, Pallas, and North Node. Perhaps this is indicative of both people struggling with the tension between the real and ideal, bringing dreams down to earth without succumbing to perfectionism, procrastination, or chronic discontent.

One of the nicest contacts is D's Venus and Sun conjunct (widely) her mother's Ascendant. This is usually a contact implying mutual pleasure and gratification, although with Vesta in the picture as well, work could compete with the relationship, or the work-oriented or critical attitude could be a problem if either party directs it at people rather than at solving problems. D's Venus is also trine her mother's Jupiter-Saturn conjunction. Her Vesta is conjunct her mother's early Virgo Sun, Ceres, and Mercury, so we have strong Vesta both ways. This is excellent if people are working together, but a hazard if the flaw-finding energy is put into the relationship rather than the physical world.

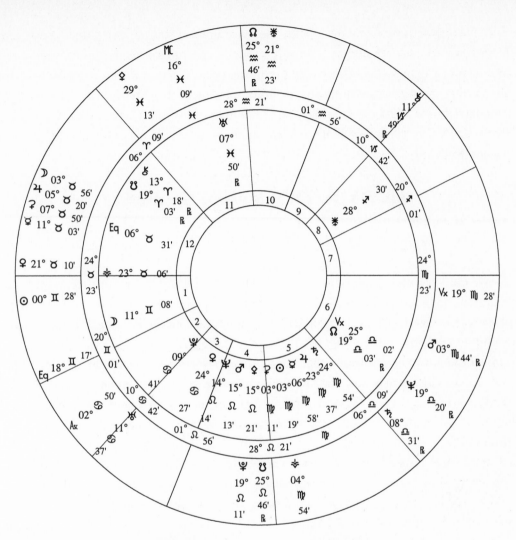

INNER WHEEL
Ms. M
Natal Chart
August 26, 1921
9:48 P.M. CST
Chicago, Illinois
41N51 87W39
Placidus Houses

OUTER WHEEL
Ms. D
Natal Chart
May 21, 1952
7:36 A.M. MST
Tucson, Arizona
32N13 110W55
Placidus Houses

D's Saturn square her mother's Pluto does have a power-struggle potential, but so many of the other contacts are supportive that it is tough to get too worked up about it. Since D's Moon and Mars make a T-square with her mother's Midheaven, we do see possible issues about work, power, status, authority, or accomplishment. If either party is not working productively, the relationship is likely to be much less positive. If both are working effectively—including the potential of working together—we would expect a mutually gratifying connection.

Ms. D's Own Words about Her Mother

Any "relationship" with a parent is complex and multilayered. It evolves and develops over time with many permutations. My relationship with my mother is no exception. There are, however, some motifs that I believe are predominant.

My mother's most important gift to me was her philosophy or worldview. She lives, breathes, and practices the conviction that the Universe is Good—that help is always available when we need it. (This is a spiritual or metaphysical concept; it is not connected to any traditional religion.) My mother used to joke that she did not have to worry because her mother did it for her. I now joke that I don't have to worry because my partner does it for me. (He uses his "melancholy Slav" background as the excuse.) When he is concerned, my usual response is, "It will all work out" or "The Universe will come through for us." My experience—validated for almost fifty years now—is that the Universe always has come through!

My mother has an incredible zest for new experiences. She is always learning, reading, discussing ideas, traveling, or exposing herself to new input and information of one sort or another. I got from her the script that life is exciting and full of vast possibilities. I consider her among the brightest people I know.

My mother was extremely hardworking. Indeed, I would say that we were probably "spoiled" as children. We had few responsibilities and no set duties, unlike many children. (Of course, we also had no set allowance.) My mother was extremely busy all the time (all those interests and activities) and worked very hard at her job, her schooling, her home, etc. Even though I was allowed to be quite lazy, I somehow picked up the work ethic from her and exhibited it in my years in the corporate world. I also worked in various family businesses with a variety of family members. I followed in my mother's footsteps vocationally, and she contributed much time, resources, and material support to furthering my career.

My mother indirectly encouraged my individuality, and I was a natural rebel in many ways. Although I do not recall any specific messages like "It is okay to be different" or "You need to be true to yourself," I do recall a childhood in which my mother was always different from other mothers—and generally more interesting. Indirectly, I got permission to become someone outside of the norm.

I idealized my mother. I considered her "almost perfect" for most of my life. I still consider her the best possible mother I could have had. Obviously, it might not have been such a good fit if I had been a different sort of child. Her independence suited mine, for one thing. It is possible that my idealization of my mother contributed to my decision not to have children (How could I ever do motherhood as well as she did?!), but I think the major factors were my need for independence and my preference for focusing on my own pleasures rather than on raising a family. (Even as a young child, I stated my determination not to be a mother because it was "too much work.") My major power struggles in childhood were with my maternal grandmother, whom I saw as a drama queen (Sun in Leo) who loved the role of martyr. I also found her to be critical, rigid, and too concerned with conventional concerns. Ironically, as a young child, I tried to "protect" my mother from my grandmother. Because I loved my mother so much, I could not imagine that she loved her mother any less, so I felt bad for my mother when my grandmother and I clashed. I would try to avoid letting my mother see it or know about it.

The only arena in which I became aware that my mother had any shortcomings was that of sexuality. As I came of age and became interested in the opposite sex, it became more and more obvious to me that my mother was really not very interested in intimate relationships, at least with men. She seemed to have little sexual drive and found most of her emotional closeness with her children. My mother was never closed to my sexuality. For instance, when I told her I wanted to become sexually active, she supported me going on the pill. However, it was a struggle to sort out how I wanted to be different from my mother in regard to love, sexuality, and relationships, because I considered her to be a role model for just about everything.

My mother has been a positive role model for me in regard to philosophy, education, vocation, work ethic, intellectual curiosity, family ties, compassion, humanitarian instincts, and nurturing. She has been a negative role model in terms of sexuality and intimate, opposite-sex relationships. I thank the Universe often for all the blessings of my life, and I believe my greatest good fortune was having her for a mother.

Healing Options

If Ms. D feels the need for more resolution, we would suggest she focus on Letters 3, 6, 9, and 12 in chapter 8.

Themes over the Generations

M continued her **focus on family** and her **care-taking role** by becoming a professional counselor, and she also helped others in need by letting them live in her home after her children were grown and living in other areas. G and her husband had set an example for her, living in a large house and hosting frequent guests. They called it "Southern hospitality." At one point, they built an apartment in their basement so that the assistant priest in their Episcopalian church could bring his wife from India to live with him. The parish pay was not enough to let him rent an adequate apartment for his family.

As already indicated, another important family value was **education.** It was quite unusual for women to go beyond grade school in GG's time. Even in G's time, her choice of major subject and additional graduate studies was unusual for women. M and D both earned graduate degrees, and two of M's three sons also earned a second degree. We can see the Gemini emphasis in G's chart with three planets in that sign. She lived up to that with a wide-ranging curiosity and a love of talking to friends. Three of G's four children had their Moon in Gemini to describe their view of their mother. M's chart is dominated by mutables with her T-square of Uranus, Moon, and Sun/Ceres/Mercury in mutable signs, plus Jupiter and Saturn also in Virgo. Her Moon in Gemini in her 1st house, her Ascendant ruler in the Gemini house, and her Mars conjunct Neptune also added to the mutable theme. M has continued to read omnivorously, and to write prolifically throughout her life. As a frustrated, would-be actress, G projected her Leo Sun and Mercury into M, so M was given classes on the side in addition to standard schooling. Over the years she had classes in piano, violin, voice, drama, and tap and ballet dancing. However, her strong Virgo emphasis overshadowed her own Leo, and she remained largely an introvert with minimal interest in seeking the limelight. This may also have been partly due to taking her mother as a negative role model since she saw her as overly dramatic. After the age of fifty, M accepted a more public role, lecturing and conducting workshops on counseling, but she learned from her mother to reject the Atlas role. She did not try to make people change or support them except for providing temporary shelter. In her counseling, she offered information to others, but then let them go. It was their responsibility whether they used the information to change their lives for the better.

Another theme running through the generations was **an interest in the psychic side of life.** Psychic receptivity can be defined as receiving information that does not come through the physical senses or through logic built on physical-sense information. Two of GG's experiences that she described to M are illustrative of this ability. While still young, GG was visiting one of the old Southern mansions that had escaped Sherman's march to the sea, during which he had burned many of the elegant homes belonging to the plantation owners. As she entered the front hall of one of these old mansions, she was astonished to see the large hall filled with what looked like coffins. She blinked her eyes, and the coffins were gone. Later, she found that this home had been used to store coffins during the Civil War.

Many years later, soon after GG was widowed but still living in her home in the South, she was driving down a country road, driving somewhat faster than she usually did. She was coming to a bend in the road and heard her "dead" husband's voice from the car seat beside her say, "Slow down GG!" in his standard dictatorial tones. She put her foot on the brakes automatically, came around the bend in the road, and saw the road full of cattle. If she had not slowed down, she would have plowed into them.

G was also psychic, both receiving information and experiencing physical phenomena periodically. On one occasion, she saved her daughter's life, insisting that a doctor perform surgery at midnight after seeing saw a vision of a death's head. The doctor had checked M earlier in the day, and had diagnosed a minor problem. When he surgically opened her abdomen at midnight, he found that she was bleeding internally and would have bled to death by morning. M acknowledged that everyone was psychic, but she believed that her mother's sensitivity was often a problem for her, so M preferred to focus mostly on her conscious mind rather than encourage her potential subconscious openness. M's Mars-Neptune conjunction in the 4th house and her Uranus in Pisces and Pluto and Venus in Cancer do show psychic potential, but she refuses to encourage it. D also feels that psychic ability is a human talent, but does not view herself as psychic. She identifies much more with the earthy pragmatism and airy intellect of her horoscope. G had a conjunction between Neptune and Pluto, two of the water planets that are keys to the subconscious side of the mind. It is through the subconscious that we are connected to the Whole. G also had her Moon, the third water factor, close to her Ascendant, Mars, and the Sun in water houses, and Juno and Uranus in Scorpio. GG's potential for psychic ability is less emphasized. In fact, water may be the least emphasized element in her chart, though she did have some factors in water signs and houses. The two stories recounted to M may have been her only important psychic experiences, while G's life was full of dramatic incidents.

A shift between the generations was that both M and D received degrees in the field of psychology, taking the idealistic/psychic focus in a somewhat different direction. Also, the chain of the Capricorn focus (Letter 10) was broken with M. After a great-great grandmother, a great-grandmother, and a grandmother with the Sun in Capricorn, plus a mother with the Ascendant and Moon in Capricorn, M had no planets in Capricorn or the 10th house, and a very harmoniously aspected Saturn.

CASE STUDY 3

We will look at three generations in our final case study. We will label them Ms. K, Ms. K's Mother, and Ms. L (Ms. K's daughter).

Ms. K

Looking at Ms. K's chart, we notice the conjunction of Ceres (the Earth Mother asteroid) with Saturn (normally a key to the father), so we know we have some sorting out to do. When keys to Mom and Dad are mixed, we have several possibilities, and they are *not* mutually exclusive:

1. Father may have been the more nurturing parent

2. Mother may have wielded more power or authority than was usual within the home, or Mother may have had to work outside the home or exhibited Saturnian qualities

3. Both parents may have played both maternal and paternal roles (a mixture of conditional and unconditional love in the home), which could have been done well or poorly

4. The individual (Ms. K) may have felt that she had to parent her own parent(s), taking on responsibilities from an early age

We notice that the Nodes of the Moon are across Cancer/Capricorn, reiterating the issue of balancing conditional and unconditional love. (If there is too much conditional love, the child is raised in a harsh, restrictive, critical, or punitive environment. With too much unconditional love, the child is spoiled and may have trouble developing her own strength and competence.) Those Nodes also form a T-square with the Moon. The Moon also makes an out-of-sign square to Ms. K's Ascendant, suggesting possible conflicts or differences in regard to either beliefs and values (Moon in the 9th and the Sagittarian Ascendant) and/or in regard to the cardinal dilemma (balancing time and energy for self, family, relationships, and contribution to society). If we include Juno in the package, the Moon and Nodes make a grand cross in cardinal signs and in cardinal and mutable houses. The square between Mars in the 4th (which also rules the 4th) and Venus repeats the issue of assertion versus accommodation, or being alone versus being together. That Letter 1 versus Letter 7 issue is repeated several other times: Nodes across the 1st/7th; Mars (Letter 1) in and ruling the 4th, but Pallas (Letter 7) in the 10th; Moon in Libra (Letter 7); Aries (Letter

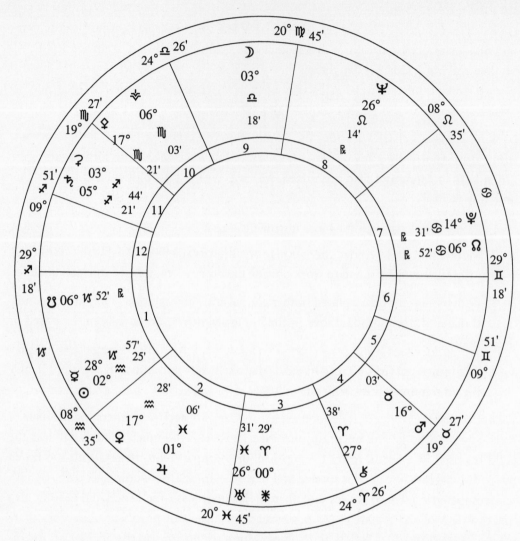

Ms. K
Natal Chart
January 23, 1927
5:08 A.M. EST
Winchester, Massachusetts
42N27 71W08
Placidus Houses

1) and Libra (Letter 7) across the MC/IC axis; Cancer intercepted in the 7th; the planet (Saturn) conjunct Ceres rules the (intercepted) 1st house.

We are getting the picture of a mother who is dealing strongly with cardinal dilemma issues. Mars in and ruling the 4th reiterates that satisfying one's personal desires could be a major issue for at least one parent—probably Mom. We would tentatively assign the mother to the 4th house, although we may later decide that the houses are mixed, just as parental motifs are mixed with the Saturn-Ceres conjunction. Chiron in the 4th suggests that Mother might be very religious, spiritual, or idealistic, reiterating the 9th-house placement of the Moon and the Ceres in Sagittarius. If her expectations are unreasonably high, the "wounding" associations with Chiron could occur for both Ms. K and her mother. Since the Moon is quincunx Jupiter while Ceres and Saturn are square Jupiter, it would appear that there are issues or conflicts to resolve around religion, philosophy, values, and expectations.

The Moon is, however, trine the Sun (and Mercury) in the 1st house, so there is some potential harmony, particularly in regard to creativity and intellectual matters. The Moon trine Sun shows potential harmony between the parents as well, although the Mars (ruling the 4th) square Venus (ruling the 10th) points to potential conflict—particularly in terms of alone versus together, or my way versus your way (the basic nature of Mars and Venus), or in regard to money and possessions (the square involves fixed signs and Venus is in the 2nd house of finances and material matters). The fact that Taurus and Scorpio are occupied (by planets and asteroids) in the 4th and 10th houses reiterates issues around money, possessions, and pleasures for both parents. Any oppositions across the 4th and 10th houses (here we have Mars opposite Pallas) repeat the balancing act between conditional and unconditional love, between home/family and outer work demands and duties, and the possibility of stress, polarization, or separation between the parents.

Father could be a friend or partner. The keys to Dad are mostly connected to the air element, emphasizing equalitarian potentials and communication: Sun conjunct Mercury (Letter 3); Saturn in the 11th; Sun in Aquarius (Letter 11); ruler of the 10th, Venus, in Aquarius (Letter 11); Pallas (Letter 7) in the 10th. Of course, if air is expressed negatively, Father (and Mother, who has her share of air) could have been cool, aloof, or distant.

We get the impression that Ms. K had to face reality at a young age. Although Sagittarius is rising, the South Node and Mercury both occupy Capricorn in the 1st house. Either Capricorn or Virgo in the 1st house can indicate someone who had to work at a younger-than-average age, someone who had to be responsible or "face the facts" when other people got to be children. The South Node in the 1st is also commonly found in people with early insecurity and self-doubts. In Capricorn, those self-doubts tend to be exacerbated by negative messages from authority figure(s). The Saturn conjunct Ceres also suggests that the early nurturing might have been rather limited, or might have demanded work and labor from Ms. K. A child with this combination can feel like she is valued only for what she can do (if she performs well), not for who she is. Occasionally, these individuals have to face literal limits or restrictions (e.g., physical) from a young age. Sometimes grandparents or other authority figures are playing parental roles.

Fortunately, Ms. K also has a strong focus on Letter 11 (and a fair amount of fire and air) in terms of her own identity, so she could have used the struggles of her childhood to strengthen her individuality, originality, and ingenuity. She has her Sun in Aquarius in the 1st; Sun conjunct Mercury, the planet of communication; Sagittarius rising; and Saturn, ruling the intercepted Capricorn in the 1st, is in Sagittarius and in the 11th. The earth emphasis—South Node in Capricorn in the 1st; Mercury in Capricorn in the 1st; Saturn, ruling the 1st, conjunct Ceres; Jupiter, ruling the Ascendant, in the 2nd; Mars in Taurus—reinforces Ms. K's practicality and ability to handle the material world.

Vesta in the 10th also suggests that at least one parent was either ill, into working hard, or critical and judgmental (allowing the work attitude to affect personal relationships). If we assign all of the 10th house to Dad, then Vesta should be his, but that seems at odds with the affable, friendly, and nurturing potentials evident with other placements. Vesta squares the Sun (normally a key to Dad), which could show Dad's inner conflicts, or, if Vesta is Mom, the potential of tensions between Mom and Dad over fixed issues (possessions, power, pleasures, money). On the other hand, Mom does have a lot of Letter 7 connections, which can be partnership, on the positive side. On the negative side, Mother might have seen Ms. K as a competitor (perhaps for Dad's affection?) and been critical for that and other reasons. Much depends on how Mom's idealism (or religion/philosophy) was expressed and whether the Mars in the 4th manifested as a very self-centered mom or as a mom who was confident and independent, and could be seen as a positive role model (that Mars is widely tri-octile or sesquisquare the Moon).

Synastry

The synastry between Ms. K and her mother has two major repeated themes. One relates to conflict with Venus, and the other emphasizes issues around beliefs, values, religion, or idealism/perfectionism. Ms. K's Sun is square her mother's Venus, and—in a double whammy—her mother's Sun is square Ms. K's Venus. Ms. K's Moon and Ceres form a yod (double quincunx) to her mother's Venus, and Ms. K's Saturn is also quincunx her mother's Venus. Vesta is opposite her mother's Venus. The only harmony in regard to Venus is that Ms. K's Nodes are sextile/trine her mother's Venus.

So, we would expect major issues with Ms. K's mother around money, comfort, femininity, grace, and beauty. Ms. K could have experienced her mother as putting personal comfort and pleasure ahead of Ms. K's needs. We suspect that the fixed issues (sharing money, possessions, and power) indicated in the natal chart are confirmed here. The parents probably had major issues in that realm, and we suspect that Ms. K's mother was probably a negative role model regarding finances, personal indulgence, possessions, and (probably) relationships.

There is a double whammy in terms of Jupiter as well. Ms. K's Mercury is quincunx her mother's Jupiter, and her mother's Mercury is square Ms. K's Jupiter. This can indicate intellectual stimulation on the positive side, but also suggests differences in regard to beliefs. The potential clashes around religion, philosophy, idealism, or perfectionistic standards are reinforced with Ms. K's Sun quincunx her mother's Jupiter, Ms. K's Jupiter opposite her mother's Jupiter, Ms. K's Jupiter square her mother's Saturn-Uranus conjunction, Ms. K's Ceres square her mother's Jupiter, and Ms. K's Juno quincunx her mother's Jupiter. The only harmonious aspect is Ms. K's Ascendant trine her mother's Jupiter. Chiron, the "little brother to Jupiter," is also quincunx Ms. K's mom's Uranus and Saturn.

So, high expectations are likely an issue. It might be that Ms. K's mother was very religious, or that spiritual, idealistic, educational, or adventurous pursuits (Letter 9) took her away from the family. It might be that Ms. K's mother held unreasonably high standards for family members, and it was impossible for anyone to measure up. Mother was probably intellectually stimulating (her Mercury is trine Ms. K's Sun and Moon), but the potential danger of expecting "Heaven on Earth" from human beings is certainly present. The idealistic factors in astrology (Letters 9 and 12) can easily get out of hand because they tend to take things to the infinite power! If Ms. K and/or her mother were able to direct this positively, we would expect that the interactions would encourage Ms. K to develop intellectually and to find a firm and deep faith in something greater than herself.

Ms. K's Own Words about Her Mother

This is turning out to be much harder than I had anticipated. Many of the feelings I had toward my mother have been buried very deep.

In many ways she was almost a stranger to me. She was aloof, distant, cold, and emotionally isolated. I never achieved anything like a close, trusting, warm bond with her.

Our home atmosphere was strained. From my earliest memory, she and my father were estranged, although they lived in the same house until she left when I was fifteen and my brother was thirteen. It was a difficult time because I had to assume the role of "mother" to my brother, become housekeeper and cook, work part-time (at sixteen), and maintain an A average in my studies. However, in many ways it was a relief that she left. I had a lot of feelings of shame and embarrassment connected with her leaving—people like to gossip (rumors of another man, etc.). I never asked and she never volunteered any details. I felt bad for my dad, as it was very embarrassing for him. I was always highly protective of him and resented her coldness toward him, which bordered on cruelty. Silence! There was always silence in the house—no conversations allowed at the dinner table, etc. She never ate with us, but would retire to her bedroom and say the rosary. It was a very lonely environment for a child with no positive feminine role model to emulate. There were never any family outings, vacations, laughter, or sharing. My mother spent most of her time in her room with the door closed to the rest of us. Another distant memory was of her pretending to commit suicide. She would close the bathroom door and slump against it—and not answer our pounding for minutes at a time. I was ten, and my brother was eight.

It was a loveless marriage on her part. She had three children, each eleven months apart. I was the oldest. The next youngest was born with severe jaundice, requiring much of her attention. They formed a very strong bond, which lasted until he was struck by an automobile and killed at age seven. A younger brother was born eleven months after the second child, so I was more or less under the care of my dad and our family doctor. My mother never really recovered from the loss of her favorite child. She was uncommunicative for six months, and our family doctor and his wife took me in for that period of time. The doctor and his wife even wanted to take me in as a foster child. An aunt and uncle wanted to adopt my younger brother. These were hard times for all of us. My mother grieved for the rest of her life. I always felt great pity for her.

The marriage was a disappointment for her as well. My dad was a chronic alcoholic, losing his two businesses, a lovely home, and our savings that he carelessly lent to borrowers. The great Wall Street crash destroyed our financial security. My mother had money of her own from property her family owned in St. John's, Newfoundland. She was able to buy a smaller house in a shabby neighborhood in another town—another "nail in the coffin" of their miserable marriage. She never forgave him for reducing her to living in these conditions, and for his total dependency on alcohol.

Through it all, my loyalties remained with him. He was my "mother" (note the Ceres conjunction to my Saturn). I adored him. He loved me unconditionally, pampered and encouraged me, worried about my problems, and was always interested in anything I was involved with. My friends all loved him, too.

On the other hand, my friends were always puzzled by my loyalties to my mother. She came back to the "family home" (because it was in her name) when I was about thirty. I never did ask her why she returned. I then assumed responsibility for her—shopping, chauffeuring, helping out so that she wouldn't burden my dad. I took her on trips to Washington, D.C., Greece, Italy, Switzerland, and to London for three months, and she was complaining all the time. My friends could never comprehend why I felt that I had to cater to her so much. I also took on a lot of responsibility for her three childless sisters and their husbands: trips to doctors, hospitals, nursing homes, shopping, etc.

Messages/scripts

The messages I received were puzzling. There were no words of affection, no hugs and kisses, no inquiries into what I might want for my life, my disappointments, etc. But special foods I liked were there when my mother was around, which made me happy.

How was she a positive role model?

I admired my mother's independent spirit when she was younger, and her honesty about her need to answer to and for herself. She loved animals, flowers, nature, the sea, and poetry, and I relate strongly to that side of her character. I also admired her loyalty to her faith, though that is something we don't share.

How was she a negative role model?

She was never kind, affectionate, or encouraging toward me. She was very critical and demeaning as I was growing up. Consequently, I had a poor self-image. She repeatedly told me how plain I was. She said that I had poor hair, small eyes, bad teeth, bad posture, etc., which are very negative images to carry around as a young person. As a result, I developed a distrust of women that lasted for many years. I felt more comfortable around men, no doubt because of the trust I had in my dad's acceptance of me. I was fifteen years old before I had a female friend; I didn't want one prior to that.

Where did she have the greatest impact and how?

I think she made the greatest impact on my ability to trust, on all levels. I have a deep-rooted fear of abandonment. My mother basically abandoned me as an infant—my two brothers absorbed my "babyhood." My father's catastrophic financial woes followed. She developed severe manic depression. He retreated more into alcoholism, and at nine years old, I had no one to lean on for strength, hope, or guidance—no one to truly trust. My mother wasn't a caring, protective guardian, not did she provide me with a loving foundation. I could not share my fears or worries with her. She was a distant entity in my life. So, I developed a lasting fear of revealing myself to anyone, a fear of rejection, a handicap I still live with.

Still, I loved her, worried about her when she was gone, corresponded with her when she had moved out of state, and was relieved when she finally moved back home. I then played referee during the remaining years that my father lived.

The ironic twist to this saga is that as he lay dying in the hospital, his last spoken word was to her. He called her name and reached out his hand to her. She did not acknowledge his offering. Seconds later, he drew his last breath. Even to the bitter end, she did not forgive him.

Healing Options

We would suggest that Ms. K focus on Letters 6, 9, 10, and 12 to seek further resolution of her internal relationship with her mother.

A Footnote

It is not the topic of this book, but we wish to draw the reader's attention to the 3rd house (of siblings) in Ms. K's chart. Note that it is occupied by Juno, which has Plutonic overtones, and Uranus, which is connected, among many other things, to accidents. Neptune, the ruler of the 3rd, is in the 8th house (elimination, intense emotions, death, taxes, etc.). Neptune is involved in a yod (double quincunx) to Mercury in the 1st and Uranus in the 3rd. Quincunxes are separative aspects and are often involved with death as well as moves (leaving one home for another), operations (losing a part of the body), relationship changes, etc.

By solar arc direction, that Neptune would have been at 4 degrees Virgo when Ms. K was eight and her brother died in the accident—squaring Saturn and Ceres. Uranus would have been at 4 degrees Aries and just leaving the opposition to the Moon. The IC would have been at 2 degrees Taurus and just into the quincunx to the Moon. Mercury (the natural ruler of the 3rd) would have been at almost 7 degrees Aquarius and quincunx the North Node of the Moon, just leaving the square to Vesta.

Ms. L

Looking to the next generation, Ms. K had a daughter (call her Ms. L). We see some common themes. Ms. K had Vesta in the 10th; so does her daughter (barely). Ms. K had Ceres in Sagittarius; so does her daughter. Ms. K had the Nodes across the 1st/7th houses; her daughter has the Nodes across Aries/Libra. There are, however, major differences between the two charts.

Issues of hard work and/or health are highlighted in both cases. With Ms. K's daughter, however, the work/health emphasis is much more connected to parents, whereas much of it was connected to personal identity and action for her mother. Ms. L has Vesta (the workaholic asteroid) in the 10th, Saturn in the 4th, and Virgo occupied twice (by Saturn and Juno) in the 4th. All of these placements emphasize a parent or parents who worked very hard, emphasized practicality, and may have had health problems or been heavily into nutrition, holistic health, etc., or a parent who was critical and judgmental. Of course, more than one of these potentials could exist.

Mars in Virgo indicates that Ms. L is quite capable of working hard and being practical and perhaps self-critical, but most of her personal identification and expression is tied to independence and the intellect. She has Uranus (Letter 11) in the 1st house. Mercury, ruler of her Ascendant, is in Aries (Letter 1) in the 11th house (Letter 11). Her Sun is also in Aries (Letter 1) in the 11th house (Letter 11). (The strong Letter1/11 motifs accentuate freedom. Gemini rising, along with Letter 11 and Mars in Mercury-ruled Virgo, emphasize the mind and communication.) The dominant need for independence could create ambivalence about close relationships, with Mom, Dad, and/or romantic partners. Ms. L does not want to be confined or "trapped" in any way! Yet, activity in her 4th and 5th houses shows a need for home and love.

The 4th and 10th houses in Ms. L's horoscope give us two very different pictures, suggesting strong differences in her experience of her parents. Saturn in the 4th suggests that we should assign the father to that house. Juno, having many Plutonic overtones, gives us a repetition of power issues with the 4th-house parent. Power struggles are possible, particularly

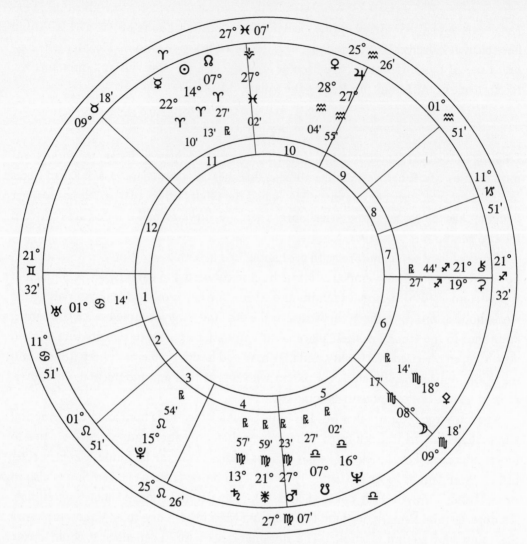

Ms. L
Natal Chart
April 4, 1950
8:46 A.M. EST
Stoneham, Massachusetts
42N28 71W06
Placidus Houses

with Juno exactly square the Ascendant/Descendant axis and quincunx Mercury, the Ascendant ruler. Juno, on the positive side, can indicate partnership (and Sun in the 11th could speak to friendship), but Virgo (particularly with Saturn and Juno) tends to be a parent who is very wrapped up in his work or who is judgmental, restrictive, and critical, and/or the child may feel critical of him. The stress aspects (including Sun quincunx Saturn in 4th) suggest some challenges with the father (figure).

The Vesta in her 10th echoes Ms. L's Mars in Virgo and the Juno and Saturn in Virgo. So, we get the feeling that everyone in the family is willing to work very hard. There may have been criticism from more than one family member, or illness could have been an issue within the home. Venus and Jupiter, however, bring in a very different picture. Usually, when Venus is involved, there is a strong bond of affection with that parent. Occasionally, Venus will indicate a self-indulgent, complacent parent, but generally the relationship is positive and pleasant. Mother might also be very artistic with the Venus emphasis, and the Moon in the 5th emphasizes creative possibilities, as well as a fun-loving, childlike spirit on the positive side, or a childish attitude on the negative side. Jupiter in the 10th can indicate an idealistic, religious, or spiritual parent, and Ceres in Sagittarius and conjunct Chiron strongly reinforces that motif. Often, the parent is idealized. If that is overdone, disappointment can result. In moderation, however, the child places a very high value on that parent. We also see at least one parent as a personal role model: Uranus (ruling the 10th) is in the 1st, and Mars (natural ruler of the 1st) is conjunct Juno in the 4th. (Hmmm . . . perhaps we will have to give part of that Juno in the 4th to Mom after all!) Also, the Sun ruling the 4th is in Aries, another key to a parent as a personal role model, whether positive or negative.

The Moon makes almost no close aspects. A quincunx to the North Node suggests the possibility of a separation or interruption in the nurturing experience. Ceres, the Earth Mother asteroid, is strongly aspected: it is conjunct the Descendant (possibly partnership with Mom; competition on the negative side); conjunct Chiron (a spiritual, religious, or idealistic mother); widely trine the Sun (Mother probably reinforcing Ms. L's self-esteem); trine Mercury (Mother probably being supportive of Ms. L's intellect); trine Pluto (possible ongoing partnership, psychological understanding, intense connection); square Juno (Mother may not approve of marital partner or vice versa); and semisextile Pallas (again, partnership motifs are highlighted between Ms. L and her mother).

So, the picture is of a mother who is highly idealistic (Ceres in Sagittarius; Ceres conjunct Chiron; Jupiter in the 10th and conjunct MC; Vesta occupying Pisces in the 10th),

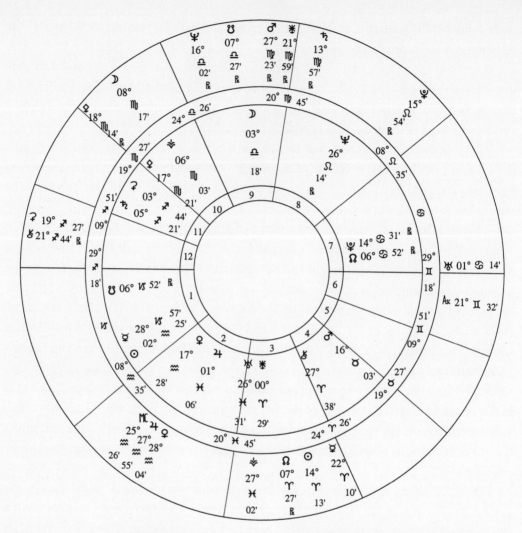

INNER WHEEL
Ms. K
Natal Chart
January 23, 1927
5:08 A.M. EST
Winchester, Massachusetts
42N27 71W08
Placidus Houses

OUTER WHEEL
Ms. L
Natal Chart
April 4, 1950
8:46 A.M. EST
Stoneham, Massachusetts
42N28 71W06
Placidus Houses

hardworking, pragmatic, ill, or critical (Vesta in the 10th; Ceres in the 6th; perhaps Juno in Virgo in the 4th), and independent/original (Aquarian Midheaven; Venus and Jupiter occupying Aquarius in the 10th; ruler of the 10th, Uranus, in the 1st).

Partnership potentials with the mother are strong: Moon in Scorpio (Letter 8); Venus (Letters 2/7) in the 10th; Jupiter, ruler of the 7th, in the 10th; Ceres conjunct the Descendant (Letter 7) and—perhaps—Juno (Letter 8) in the 4th; plus the Ceres connections with Pallas and Pluto. Sometimes parent-partner mixtures call for attention to sharing power and responsibility once the daughter reaches adulthood. A comfortable interdependency lets each one help the other in her own areas of strength.

Despite all the likely affection and possibility of an ongoing partnership (as an adult) with her mother, there are indications of possible separations or pulling apart as well. Mars (a key to Ms. L herself) is quincunx (potential separation) the Midheaven, Jupiter, and Venus in the 10th house (which we believe is Mom in this case). Mars is also opposite (potential separation) Vesta in the 10th house. The Moon is quincunx the North Node, and Ceres is opposite the Ascendant. Mercury, ruler of the Ascendant, is quincunx Juno in the 4th. Perhaps Mom had to work and Ms. L missed her company a lot, or illness within the home curtailed their time together. The main stress aspects involve Mars in Virgo widely square the Ascendant/Descendant axis; Juno square the Ascendant/Descendant; and Vesta widely square the Ascendant/Descendant axis. On the other hand, there is also much harmony. The Midheaven (Mom) is trine the Ascendant (Ms. L) as are Jupiter and Venus in the 10th more widely. Jupiter and Venus, however, are closely (but out-of-sign) trine Uranus in the 1st house. Mercury, the Ascendant ruler (a key to Ms. L), is sextile the Midheaven (Mom). Ceres (Mom) is trine Mercury, the Ascendant ruler.

Synastry

Ms. L's Sun (a key to self-esteem and personal vitality) is square her mother's Pluto (possible power struggles or intense emotional exchanges), but sextile her Venus (reinforcing the potential of an affectionate and pleasurable relationship and an artistic/creative emphasis). Mercury (the Ascendant ruler for Ms. L) is conjunct her mother's IC, an aspect that usually indicates strong nurturing from the mother to Ms. L. Parental support is also implied with Ms. L's Ascendant (a key to herself and her own action) trine her mother's Midheaven (parental responsibilities and pragmatism).

Ms. L's Moon is conjunct her mother's Vesta, so we again wonder if work or health issues interfered with Ms. L's nurturing. That Moon is sextile/trine the mother's Nodes, so much reinforcement and support are also possible. Interdependency would be the best expression of that bond. Ms. L's Vesta is conjunct Ms. K's Uranus and Juno, so work or health concerns would have to be balanced with relationship needs and the urge for independence and individuality. That Vesta is also square the Ascendant/Descendant axis of the mother (love versus work; illness may curtail relationships), and quincunx her Neptune (balancing the real and ideal). A repeated Vesta/Virgo motif is present! The sextile from Ms. L's Vesta to her mother's Mercury adds to the mental focus.

Shared values are possible with the conjunctions of their Jupiters, which also includes Ms. L's Venus—suggesting affectionate exchanges. They may reinforce one another in regard to philosophy, religion, spiritual goals, education, travel, etc. Ms. L's Jupiter, Venus, and, more widely, her Midheaven are sextile her mother's Chiron (accenting idealism) and semisextile her mother's Mercury and Uranus (emphasizing intellectual stimulation and possibly shared interests).

Ms. L's Uranus (in the 1st house) is strongly aspected by her mother's chart, as is Ms. L's Mars (natural ruler of the 1st house). This would back up the placements in the natal chart suggesting Mother as a role model and Mother affecting Ms. L's sense of identity, personal freedom, and self-expression. Uranus is square her mom's Moon and Juno (classic freedom-closeness dilemma); quincunx Ceres and, more widely, Saturn (suggesting a need to compromise between following the rules and breaking them); trine Jupiter (reinforcing a meeting of the minds, particularly in terms of philosophy, spiritual quests, etc.); and quincunx the Sun (both freedom versus closeness and balancing head and heart). Ms. L's Mars is square her mother's Ascendant/Descendant axis, bringing up the issue of whose personal needs get priority. Mars is also opposite Uranus, quincunx Chiron, and trine Mercury, reinforcing intellectual capacities, but adding to pressure for freedom and going one's own way. Ms. L's Mars is also semisextile her mother's Neptune, indicating that they can get together in terms of dreams, imagination, beauty, or compassion.

The Nodes of the mother and daughter are square one another, so they face a full-fledged cardinal dilemma in their interactions: balancing freedom (Letter 1) versus dependency/nurturing (Letter 4) versus equality (Letter 7) versus control (Letter 10). Or, finding time and energy for personal desires and development, maintaining a home and family (which might be pets, a garden, etc.), having significant partnership(s), and making a contribution to the outer world. The daughter's Nodes emphasize the freedom-closeness dilemma in terms of both signs (Aries/Libra) and houses (5th/11th). Ms. L's South Node is widely conjunct her mother's Moon, which emphasizes the potential of each taking care of the other as well as possible past-life ties. Ms. L may have wanted to—or tried to—nurture, protect, and safeguard her own mother, even from an early age. That South Node is sextile Ms. K's Saturn and semisextile her Vesta, suggesting a good integration of competence and compassion.

The tension between freedom and closeness, or being alone versus being together, is repeated with Ms. L's Pallas (a key to partnership) opposite her mother's Mars and square her Venus, yet conjunct Ms. K's Pallas. So, the partnership potential between the mother and daughter is repeated, but with some hot/cold reactions or ambivalence to work through.

Summary of Synastry

Important issues are connected to work and health, particularly for the mother, but could well be for the daughter as well. The daughter's intense need for independence could lead to some separations in relationships (including with Mom), although work or illness may also be factors. This mother can teach the daughter what to do, and what not to do, in regard to balancing her own cardinal dilemma. Yet, overall, the prospects are good for lots of affection and the possibility of an ongoing partnership even after the daughter is an adult. The bonds between the mother and daughter are particularly strong in regard to shared beliefs and values and intellectual stimulation.

Ms. L's Own Words about Her Mother

This is a story about a relationship between two women. Being a mother and daughter is just a coincidence. It is a continuation of many lifetimes and many more to come, so the story is always evolving and growing in many directions. We're just a couple of landscapers working on a perpetual garden. Each time we are together, we cultivate a new area of our project. I think it's quite a colorful environment, with interesting textures, contrasts, energies, and emotions for growth in our landscape design. Challenges abound. There are some full of hope, love, encouragement, and fulfillment. There are challenges that leave one with a sense of loss, disappointment, and a lack of direction. All are approached with some sense of adventure, love, compassion, a sense of the ridiculousness of the situation at hand, and with the ultimate goal of making some growth when faced with life's challenges.

Life has been a tremendous challenge for my mother from the beginning. Her mother was a very peculiar person—totally self-contained and very stingy in every possible way. She never expressed any love or affection toward my mother, and didn't give her any guidance or encouragement. When she did speak to my mother, it was by way of criticism. She was always so negative about everything in life—just a cold, self-absorbed person.

My mother had a very lonely and emotionally barren childhood/young adulthood. Being left on her own at such at a young age (her father was an alcoholic) both physically and emotionally, she pursued things on her own. With a combination of intelligence, creativity, and inquisitiveness, she sought out answers to her questions. She developed into a very independent thinking and acting individual who was also competitive and practical. Always disciplined, she excelled in all areas of her life. She was always her own person, never one to follow the crowd. Another thing she instilled in my brother and me was a "sense of consequence": i.e., think things through before you act. My Saturn and Mars are both in Virgo, and my brother has his Sun and Mercury in Virgo, so analyzing/overanalyzing is a given!

My first memory of my mother was of her illness, rheumatoid arthritis, which she has had since she was a teenager. She was in the hospital off and on when I was very young. When I was four or five, my younger brother and I were separated for about six months and sent to relatives, who took care of us while my mother spent time in the hospital after a flare-up. It was difficult being away from her.

I always felt *so* protective of her, physically and emotionally. When I was around four years old, I used to dream that I was like Superman (this was in the 1950s). I'd scoop her up and fly her away to protect her from illness and especially from my father and his family. We lived with his parents, two sisters, a brother, and their families in two two-family houses that were next door to each other. They were very volatile and verbally abusive, and could be violent. Anything could set off an incident. It was a terrible environment for anyone at any age. From that young age, in my little mind I was here to protect and take care of my mother in any and all situations.

Of course, she hardly ever complained about her physical limitations, or anything else. She is so stoic, independent, and resourceful. She just bided her time, continued her lifetime interests and studies. She always nurtured and encouraged my brother and me in all creative outlets, introducing us to theater, music, and art at a young age. On Sundays, she took us, cousins, and friends to the Boston Museum of Fine Arts. We traveled in packs, roaming the different galleries. She opened the door to many cultural activities for family and friends. As I said, she always encouraged us to develop our creativity and also to be practical. I like to think of her as a "practical idealist." My brother is a successful writer and playwright, and is also very much into music and playing the guitar (but he won't dance!).

During the '60s, "women's lib" was the hot issue, though not in my world. As I've mentioned, independence was as natural as breathing for my mother, her mother, and even my father's mother! Who knew there were so many women who needed liberation? Being self-sufficient was a way of life. If something has to be done, just do it! I had friends who wouldn't leave the house on Saturday night if they didn't have a date.

My mother has always treated me as an equal, and therefore I always felt equal to her and all authority figures. The only person who intimidated me was my father, and that was only until my early thirties (my Mars was retrograde at birth, and between my twenty-ninth and thirtieth birthdays, it went direct by secondary progression). All of that has been resolved and we now get along as well as he possibly could with anyone.

Being married has never been all that important to me. The issues I've had with my father and my parents' marriage left me without a strong desire to be tied down. When I became engaged, the ring felt like it was around my throat instead of my finger . . . a sensation I still have! Yes, the issue of freedom versus closeness has reared its head, and it just isn't that ugly. As with everything in life, there are choices to be made. I made mine, but it doesn't mean I won't change my mind at some point. So far, being single has been the right choice for me.

My mother is, without a doubt, "The Star" in my galaxy, the largest influence on me in this lifetime. She's the best our garden has to offer, with lots of texture and color. She can be part of a rough terrain, uncompromising, like a cactus, all prickly one minute and in bloom with beautiful flowers the next, but always changing, growing, and so fascinating. She's just so damn interesting. Besides loving her, I just really like her and get a kick out of her. Who could ask for more?

Healing Options

Ms. K and Ms. L have had a partnership on many levels—sharing a home for many years and traveling together often. If Ms. L feels the need for any healing in her relationship with her mother, we would suggest focusing on Letters 6, 9, and 11 in chapter 8.

PART FIVE

Where Do We Go From Here?

SEVEN

Significant Astrological Factors and Mother-Daughter Issues

This chapter is designed to organize the information presented earlier in the book in a more compact fashion. A list of the kinds of wounding or damage that can occur when relationships are not constructive is provided for each letter of the astrological alphabet. The astrological factors—in the daughter's (or mother's) natal chart and in the synastry between them—are listed for each letter. Readers are referred to the next chapter, "Healing Options," for solutions to the various problems and dilemmas that can exist.

Items listed in parentheses are "maybes" due to the uncertainty of which parent "owns" the fourth house and which "owns" the tenth house (or both) in a horoscope. As we have mentioned repeatedly in this book, every placement and aspect has an upside and a downside. *It is important to remember that all of these aspects and placements can be expressed positively or negatively!* However, some combinations do seem to be inherently more challenging, and some tend to be easier to express on a constructive level. We've made divisions accordingly for the various astrological combinations.

Letter 1

Developing an Identity and Owning Personal Power

Aspects/Placements in Daughter's Chart (OR in Mother's Chart)

Tend toward Challenging	*Neutral/Both*	*Tend toward Support*
Moon square/quincunx/ octile/tri-octile Mars	Moon conjunct Mars Ceres conjunct Mars	Moon sextile/trine Mars
Ceres square/quincunx/ octile/tri-octile Mars	Moon conjunct Ascendant Ceres conjunct Ascendant	Ceres sextile/trine Mars
Ascendant in conflict aspect to Moon, Ceres	Mars in 4th (Mars in 10th)	Ascendant sextile/trine Moon and/or Ceres
Planet(s) in 4th in conflict with Ascendant	Moon opposite Mars Ceres opposite Mars	Moon, Ceres sextile/trine ruler of 1st
Planets in 4th in conflict with planet(s) in 1st	Moon in 1st Ceres in 1st	Planet(s) in 4th sextile/ trine planets in 1st
(Planet[s] in 10th in conflict with Ascendant)	Ruler of 4th in 1st Ruler of 1st in 4th	Any ruler of 1st in harmony aspect to any ruler of 4th
(Planet[s] in 10th in conflict with planet[s] in 1st)	(Ruler of 10th in 1st) (Ruler of 1st in 10th)	Nodes sextile/trine Mars, Ascendant, or 1st-house ruler
Any ruler of 1st in conflict aspect to any ruler of 4th (or 10th)	Nodes in Aries/Libra	
Nodes in conflict aspect to Mars, Ascendant, ruler of 1st	Nodes across 1st/7th	

Synastry

Tend toward Challenging

Mom's Mars, Ascendant, or 1st-house ruler square/quincunx/opposite/octile/tri-octile the daughter's Moon, Ceres, or any of her other planets, asteroids, Nodes, or angles

Mom's Saturn, Uranus, Neptune, Pluto, Pallas, Juno, Vesta, Chiron, South Node, or Midheaven conjunct/square/quincunx/opposite/octile/tri-octile the daughter's Mars, Ascendant, or 1st-house ruler

Neutral/Both

Mom's Sun, Moon, Ceres, Mercury, Venus, Jupiter, or North Node conjunct the daughter's Mars

Mom's Mars conjunct the daughter's Sun, Moon, Ceres, Mercury, Venus, Jupiter, or North Node

Mom's stellium in the daughter's 1st house

The daughter's stellium in Mom's 1st house

Tend toward Support

Mom's Sun, Moon, Venus, Mercury, Ceres, Jupiter, or North Node conjunct the daughter's Ascendant or 1st-house ruler

Mom's Ascendant or 1st-house ruler conjunct the daughter's Sun, Moon, Venus, Ceres, Mercury, Jupiter, or North Node

Harmony aspects between Mom's Mars, Ascendant, or 1st-house ruler and any of the daughter's planets or points

Harmony aspects between the daughter's Mars, Ascendant, or 1st-house ruler and any of Mom's planets or points

Issues

Becoming one's own person and developing physical, emotional, and mental strength are two of the tasks of becoming an adult. Courage, initiative, and independence are in focus.

Wounding can occur through:

1. A very self-centered mother and/or daughter

2. An angry mother and/or daughter

3. A mother who squelched (through criticism, denial, restriction, etc.) the daughter's assertive acts

4. A mother and/or daughter who was violent

5. A mother who was so submissive/dismissive of herself that the daughter thought that was how women were supposed to be

6. A mother whose own needs for freedom prevented her from fully supporting her daughter's needs to develop strength and independence

7. A mother who was competitive with her own daughter

8. A mother-daughter pair who had very different personal drives and desires

9. A daughter who felt she had to struggle to develop a sense of personal identity and power

Note the importance of each person's horoscope. For example, a daughter with lots of air and water is more at risk for disowning her own power; so is a daughter with several rulers of the 1st house in the 7th house (including Mars). A daughter with lots of fire or strong aspects between Mars, Pluto, and Saturn may have challenges learning to handle her own rage or power drives in a healthy way. A daughter who identifies strongly with Letter 6 or 10 (e.g., Virgo rising, Saturn in the 1st house) tends to be self-deprecating and to judge herself too harshly, but can build confidence through productive work.

Solutions

See chapter 8, "Healing Options."

Letter 2
Learning to Enjoy the Material and Sensual World

Aspects/Placements in Daughter's Chart (OR in Mother's Chart)

Tend toward Challenging	*Neutral/Both*	*Tend toward Support*
Moon in conflict with Venus	Venus in 4th	Moon conjunct Venus
Ceres in conflict with Venus	(Venus in 10th)	Ceres conjunct Venus
Ruler of 2nd in conflict with Moon, Ceres	Moon opposite Venus	Moon sextile/trine Venus
Planet(s) in 4th in conflict with 2nd-house ruler	Ceres opposite Venus	Ceres sextile/trine Venus
Planet(s) in 4th in conflict with planet(s) in 2nd	Moon in 2nd	Ruler of 2nd sextile/trine Moon or Ceres
(Planet[s] in 10th in conflict with 2nd-house ruler)	Ceres in 2nd	Planet(s) in 4th sextile planet(s) in 2nd
(Planet[s] in 10th in conflict with planets in 2nd)	Ruler of 4th in 2nd	Any ruler of 2nd in harmony aspect to any ruler of 4th
Any ruler of 2nd in conflict aspect to any ruler of 4th	Ruler of 2nd in 4th	Nodes in harmony with Venus or any ruler of 2nd
Nodes in conflict with Venus or ruler of 2nd	(Ruler of 10th in 2nd)	
	(Ruler of 2nd in 10th)	
	Nodes in Taurus/Scorpio	
	Nodes across 2nd/8th	

Synastry

Tend toward Challenging

Mom's Venus or 2nd-house ruler square/quincunx/opposite/octile/tri-octile the daughter's Moon, Ceres, or any other planets, asteroids, Nodes, or angles

The daughter's Venus or 2nd-house ruler square/quincunx/opposite/octile/tri-octile any of Mom's planets, asteroids, or angles

Mom's Mars, Saturn, Uranus, Neptune, Pluto, South Node conjunct the daughter's Venus or 2nd-house ruler

Neutral/Both

Mom's Venus or 2nd-house ruler conjunct the daughter's Juno, Vesta, Chiron, or angles

The daughter's Venus or 2nd-house ruler conjunct Mother's Juno, Vesta, Chiron, or angles

Mother's stellium in the daughter's 2nd house

The daughter's stellium in Mother's 2nd house

Tend toward Support

Mom's Sun, Moon, Ascendant, Venus, Mercury, Jupiter, North Node, Ceres, or Pallas conjunct the daughter's Venus or 2nd-house ruler

The daughter's Sun, Moon, Ascendant, Venus, Mercury, Jupiter, North Node, Ceres, or Pallas conjunct Mother's Venus or 2nd-house ruler

Mother's Venus or 2nd-house ruler in harmony aspect to any of the daughter's planets, asteroids, or angles

The daughter's Venus or 2nd-house ruler in harmony aspect to any of Mother's planets, asteroids, or angles

Issues

The daughter's developmental tasks are to become comfortable in her own body, to appreciate and indulge in sensual pleasures in moderation, to achieve ease in handling the material and financial world, and to have a healthy capacity to enjoy life.

Wounding can occur through:

1. A complacent, self-satisfied mother and/or daughter
2. An overly hedonistic mother and/or daughter

3. A mother who gave little or no training—or negative scripting—around money

4. An overly indulgent mother, in terms of providing pleasures and gifts, allowing laziness, etc.

5. A mother and/or daughter who gave too much weight to comfort and having an easy flow in life (avoiding confrontations and possible unpleasantness)

6. An excessively stubborn mother and/or daughter

7. A mother and/or daughter who was too materialistic

8. A mother and daughter who had very different ideas about beauty and/or comfort

9. A mother and daughter who had widely diverse styles in regard to sensuality

Solutions

See chapter 8, "Healing Options."

Letter 3
Developing One's Thinking, Communication Skills, Humor, and a Light Touch

Aspects/Placements in Daughter's Chart (OR in Mother's Chart)

Tend toward Challenging	*Neutral/Both*	*Tend toward Support*
Moon in conflict with Mercury	Mercury in 4th	Moon conjunct Mercury
Ceres in conflict with Mercury	(Mercury in 10th)	Ceres conjunct Mercury
Ruler of 3rd in conflict with Moon, Ceres	Mercury opposite Moon	Moon, Ceres conjunct ruler of 3rd
Planet(s) in 4th in conflict with planet(s) in 3rd	Mercury opposite Ceres	Moon sextile/trine Mercury
Planet(s) in 4th in conflict with ruler of 3rd	Moon in 3rd	Ceres sextile/trine Mercury
(Planet[s] in 10th in conflict with planet[s] in 3rd)	Ceres in 3rd	Moon, Ceres sextile/trine ruler of 3rd
(Planet[s] in 10th in conflict with ruler of 3rd)	Ruler of 4th in 3rd	Planet(s) in 4th sextile planet(s) in 3rd
Any ruler of 3rd in conflict with any ruler of 4th	Ruler of 3rd in 4th	Any ruler of 3rd in harmony aspect to any ruler of 4th
	(Ruler of 10th in 3rd)	Nodes in harmony with Mercury or ruler of 3rd
	(Ruler of 3rd in 10th)	
	Nodes in Gemini/Sag	
	Nodes across 3rd/9th	

Synastry

Tend toward Challenging

Mom's Mercury or 3rd-house ruler square/quincunx/opposite/octile/tri-octile the daughter's Moon, Ceres, or any other planets, asteroids, Nodes, or angles

The daughter's Mercury or 3rd-house ruler square/quincunx/opposite/octile/tri-octile any of Mom's planets, asteroids, or angles

Mom's Mars, Saturn, Neptune, Pluto, or South Node conjunct the daughter's Mercury or 3rd-house ruler

Neutral/Both

Mom's Mercury or 3rd-house ruler conjunct the daughter's Pluto, Neptune, Uranus, Mars, Juno, Vesta, Chiron, or Midheaven

The daughter's Mercury or 3rd-house ruler conjunct Mother's Uranus, Juno, Vesta, Chiron, or Midheaven

Mom's stellium in the daughter's 3rd house

The daughter's stellium in Mom's 3rd house

Tend toward Support

The daughter's Sun, Moon, Ascendant, Mercury, Venus, Ceres, Pallas, Jupiter, IC, or North Node conjunct Mom's Mercury or 3rd-house ruler

Mom's Sun, Moon, Ascendant, Mercury, Venus, Ceres, Pallas, Jupiter, IC, or North Node conjunct the daughter's Mercury or 3rd-house ruler

Mother's Mercury or 3rd-house ruler in harmony aspect to any of the daughter's planets, asteroids, or angles

The daughter's Mercury or 3rd-house ruler in harmony aspect to any of Mother's planets, asteroids, or angles

Issues

Intellectual concerns are in focus. The daughter is working on learning, gathering, and disseminating information, sharpening her communicative abilities, and cultivating a broad perspective and the capacity to be lighthearted and to operate as an observer when appropriate.

Wounding can occur through:

1. A mother who talks too much or is much too reticent (from the daughter's perspective)

2. A mother who does not listen to her daughter or discounts what the daughter says

3. A mother and/or daughter who is gossipy, superficial, flighty, or scattered

4. A mother who is too wrapped up in intellectual concerns at the daughter's expense

5. A mother who obviously and strongly favors a sibling

6. A mother who undercuts, restricts, or inhibits her daughter's mental development, or a daughter who is scornful or dismissive of her mother's intelligence

7. A mother who is a negative role model in terms of humor and lightheartedness

8. A mother and daughter who feel like the other is speaking a "foreign" language

9. A mother and daughter whose intellectual styles and preferences are very different

Solutions

See chapter 8, "Healing Options."

Letter 4

Balancing Dependency with Nurturing, and Establishing a Secure Emotional Foundation

Aspects/Placements in Daughter's Chart (OR in Mother's Chart)

Tend toward Challenging	*Neutral/Both*	*Tend toward Support*
Moon in conflict with Ceres	Moon, Ceres in 4th	Moon sextile/trine Ceres
Moon in conflict with any ruler of 4th	(Moon, Ceres in 10th)	Moon sextile/trine ruler of 4th
Ceres in conflict with any ruler of 4th	Ceres opposite Moon	Ceres sextile/trine ruler of 4th
Planet(s) in 4th in conflict with any ruler of 4th	Ruler of 4th in 4th	Moon conjunct Ceres
(Planet[s] in 10th opposite or quincunx planet[s] in 4th)	(Ruler of 4th in 10th)	Moon conjunct ruler of 4th
(Any ruler of 10th in conflict with any ruler of 4th)	(Ruler of 10th in 4th)	Ceres conjunct ruler of 4th
Nodes in conflict with Moon, Ceres, or any ruler of 4th	Nodes in Cancer/Capricorn	Planet(s) in 4th trine planet(s) in 10th
	Nodes across 4th/10th	Any ruler of 4th in harmony aspect to any planet(s) in 4th
		Any ruler of 4th in harmony aspect to any other ruler of 4th
		Nodes in harmony with Moon, Ceres, ruler of 4th

Synastry

Tend toward Challenging

Mom's Moon, Ceres, or 4th-house ruler square/quincunx/opposite/octile/tri-octile the daughter's Moon, Ceres, or any other planets, asteroids, Nodes, or angles

The daughter's Moon, Ceres, or 4th-house ruler square/quincunx/opposite/octile/tri-octile any of Mom's planets, asteroids, Nodes, or angles

Mom's Saturn, Uranus, Neptune, Pluto, or South Node conjunct the daughter's Moon, Ceres, or 4th-house ruler

The daughter's Saturn, Uranus, Neptune, Pluto, or South Node conjunct Mother's Moon, Ceres, or 4th-house ruler

Neutral/Both

Mom's Moon, Ceres, or 4th-house ruler conjunct the daughter's Mars, Juno, Vesta, Midheaven, or Chiron

The daughter's Moon, Ceres, or 4th–house ruler conjunct Mother's Mars, Juno, Vesta, Midheaven, or Chiron

Mom's stellium in the daughter's 4th house

The daughter's stellium in Mom's 4th house

Tend toward Support

Mother's Moon, Ceres, or 4th-house ruler in harmony aspect to any of the daughter's planets, asteroids, or angles

The daughter's Moon, Ceres, or 4th-house ruler in harmony aspect to any of Mother's planets, asteroids, or angles

The daughter's Moon, Ceres, or 4th-house ruler conjunct Mother's Sun, Moon, Ascendant, Ceres, IC, Mercury, Venus, Pallas, or North Node

Mother's Moon, Ceres, or 4th-house ruler conjunct the daughter's Sun, Moon, Ascendant, Ceres, IC, Mercury, Venus, Pallas, or North Node

Issues

Gaining a sense of safety and establishing a home base are two of the developmental tasks. The daughter is learning to move comfortably between taking care of others and allowing them to assist her. Healthy emotional connections are made, nourished, and maintained.

Wounding can occur through:

1. A needy, whiny mother (the daughter may mother her own mother)

2. An overly protective "smother mother"

3. Abandonment, neglect

4. Dysfunctional patterns in the home around food and eating

5. Too much family (e.g., members, activities, focus) for the independent daughter or too little for the very sensitive daughter

6. A mother who is too involved with her family of origin to give sufficient time and attention to her own family

7. A mother and daughter with widely disparate views of what family life should be; different beliefs and values about what is important for family well-being

8. A mother and daughter with clashing styles in regard to domestic duties, pets, emotional support, etc.

Solutions

See chapter 8, "Healing Options."

Letter 5

Developing Healthy Self-Esteem, Creative Outlets, a Playful Side, and a Place to Shine

Aspects/Placements in Daughter's Chart (OR in Mother's Chart)

Tend toward Challenging	*Neutral/Both*	*Tend toward Support*
Moon in conflict with Sun	Sun in 4th	Moon conjunct Sun
Ceres in conflict with Sun	(Sun in 10th)	Ceres conjunct Sun
Ruler of 4th in conflict with Sun	Sun opposite Moon	Moon sextile/trine Sun
Moon, Ceres in conflict with ruler of 5th	Sun opposite Ceres	Ceres sextile/trine Sun
Planet(s) in 4th octile planet(s) in 5th	Ruler of 5th opposite Moon or Ceres	Moon conjunct ruler of 5th
Planet(s) in 4th in conflict with ruler of 5th	Moon in 5th	Ceres conjunct ruler of 5th
Planets in 5th in conflict with ruler of 4th	Ceres in 5th	Moon, Ceres sextile/trine ruler of 5th
(Planet[s] in 10th in conflict with planet(s) in 5th)	Ruler of 4th in 5th	Planet(s) in 4th sextile planet(s) in 5th
(Planet[s] in 10th in conflict with ruler of 5th)	Ruler of 5th in 4th	Any ruler of 5th in harmony with any ruler of 4th
Nodes in conflict with Sun or ruler of 5th	(Ruler of 10th in 5th)	Nodes in harmony with Sun or any ruler of 5th
	(Ruler of 5th in 10th)	
	Nodes in Leo/Aquarius	
	Nodes across 5th/11th	

Synastry

Tend toward Challenging

Mom's Sun or 5th-house ruler square/quincunx/opposite/octile/tri-octile the daughter's Moon, Ceres, or any other planets, asteroids, Nodes, or angles

The daughter's Sun or 5th-house ruler square/quincunx/opposite/octile/tri-octile any of Mom's planets, asteroids, Nodes, or angles

Mom's Mars, Saturn, Uranus, Neptune, or Pluto conjunct the daughter's Sun or 5th-house ruler

Neutral/Both

Mom's Sun or 5th-house ruler conjunct the daughter's Juno, Vesta, Nodes, or Midheaven

The daughter's Sun or 5th-house ruler conjunct Mother's Juno, Vesta, Nodes, or Midheaven

Mom's stellium in the daughter's 5th house

The daughter's stellium in Mother's 5th house

Tend toward Support

Mom's Sun, Moon, Ascendant, Mercury, Venus, Pallas, Ceres, IC, or Jupiter conjunct the daughter's Sun or 5th-house ruler

The daughter's Sun or 5th-house ruler conjunct Mother's Sun, Moon, Ascendant, Mercury, Venus, Pallas, Ceres, IC, or Jupiter

Mother's Sun or 5th-house ruler in harmony aspect to any of the daughter's planets, asteroids, Nodes, or angles

The daughter's Sun or 5th-house ruler in harmony aspect to any of Mother's planets, asteroids, Nodes, or angles

Issues

Gaining a good opinion of one's self is vital. The daughter is also developing the capacity to take sensible risks (for greater gain), to garner positive attention and applause, to express creatively or through onstage activities, and to cultivate a sense of fun and joy.

Wounding can occur through:

1. A mother who feels she is sovereign of all she surveys; entitled to special privileges and power

2. A mother and/or daughter who exaggerates and overdramatizes life

3. A mother and/or daughter who gambles, speculates, or takes foolish risks

4. A mother who is childish and self-centered, or a daughter who stays that way when it is no longer age-appropriate

5. A mother and/or daughter who is too susceptible to flattery

6. A mother who is too involved with recreational or creative hobbies to give sufficient time and attention to her family

7. A mother and/or daughter who expects life to be all play and no work

8. A mother and daughter who compete for the limelight

9. A mother and daughter whose ideas about children, creativity, risks, or self-expression clash greatly

Solutions

See chapter 8, "Healing Options."

Letter 6
Becoming Competent, Dedicated, Pragmatic, Physically Healthy, and Able to Maintain Good Relationships with Colleagues

Aspects/Placements in Daughter's Chart (OR in Mother's Chart)

Tend toward Challenging	*Neutral/Both*	*Tend toward Support*
Moon conjunct Vesta	Vesta in 4th	Moon sextile/trine Vesta
Moon square/quincunx/octile/tri-octile/Vesta	(Vesta in 10th)	Ceres sextile/trine Vesta
Ceres conjunct Vesta	Vesta opposite Moon	Ruler of 6th sextile/trine Moon, Ceres
Ceres in conflict aspect to Vesta	Vesta opposite Ceres	Planet(s) in 4th in harmony aspect to planet(s) in 6th or any ruler of 6th
Ruler of 6th in conflict aspect to Moon, Ceres	Moon in 6th	Any ruler of 6th in harmony aspect to any ruler of 4th
Planet(s) in 4th in conflict with planet(s) in 6th	Ceres in 6th	Nodes in harmony with planet(s) in 6th or any ruler(s) of 6th
Planet(s) in 4th in conflict with ruler of 6th	Ruler of 4th in 6th	Nodes in conflict with any planet(s) in or ruling 6th
Any ruler of 4th in conflict with any ruler of 6th house	Ruler of 6th in 4th	
(Planet[s] in 10th in conflict with 6th-house ruler)	(Ruler of 10th in 6th)	
(Planet[s] in 10th in conflict with planets in 6th)	(Ruler of 6th in 10th)	
	Nodes in Virgo/Pisces	
	Nodes across 6th/12th	

Synastry

Tend toward Challenging

Mom's Vesta or 6th-house ruler square/quincunx/opposite/octile/tri-octile the daughter's Moon, Ceres, or any other planets, asteroids, Nodes, or angles

The daughter's Vesta or 6th-house ruler square/quincunx/opposite/octile/tri-octile any of Mom's planets, asteroids, or angles

Mom's Mars, Saturn, Uranus, Neptune, Pluto, or South Node conjunct the daughter's Vesta or 6th-house ruler

Neutral/Both

Mom's stellium in the daughter's 6th house

The daughter's stellium in Mother's 6th house

Mom's Vesta or 6th-house ruler conjunct any of the daughter's planets or points

The daughter's Vesta or 6th-house ruler conjunct Mother's Vesta, Moon, Ascendant/Descendant axis, Sun, Ceres, Venus, Mercury, Jupiter, North Node, Chiron, or MC/IC axis

Tend toward Support

Mother's Vesta or 6th-house ruler in harmony aspect to any of the daughter's planets, asteroids, Nodes, or angles

The daughter's Vesta or 6th-house ruler in harmony aspect to any of Mother's planets, asteroids, Nodes, or angles

Issues

The daughter is learning to function efficiently in her own body (maintaining good health) and to be effective in working with the material world. She is also honing her skills in terms of relating with coworkers, being of service, taking care of details, and being organized and productive.

Wounding can occur through:

1. A mother who *has* to work or is so caught up in her work that the daughter feels neglected

2. A mother or daughter who is critical, judgmental, and flaw-finding toward family members

3. A mother who is ill or has to contend with an ill family member

4. A mother or daughter who is perceived as being too practical, and not sufficiently warm emotionally

5. A mother who takes on the role of servant at work and/or at home, doing too much (overworked and underpaid), and who trains her daughter to perceive that as appropriate feminine behavior

6. A mother who is too busy serving others or fixing the outer world to give sufficient attention to the needs of her family

7. A mother and daughter who have strong conflicts about health habits and managing their physical well-being

8. A mother and daughter who have vastly different ideas about what productive work and doing a good job entail

Solutions

See chapter 8, "Healing Options."

Letter 7

Establishing Healthy Peer Relationships, Appreciating Beauty, and Seeking Balance, Harmony, and Fair Play

Aspects/Placements in Daughter's Chart (OR in Mother's Chart)

Tend toward Challenging	*Neutral/Both*	*Tend toward Support*
Moon square/quincunx/octile/ tri-octile Venus or Pallas	Venus or Pallas in 4th	Moon conjunct Venus
Ceres square/quincunx/octile/ tri-octile Venus or Pallas	(Venus, Pallas in 10th)	Ceres conjunct Venus
Ruler of 7th in conflict with Moon or Ceres	Moon in 7th	Moon sextile/trine Venus
Planet(s) in 4th in conflict with planet(s) in or ruling 7th	Ceres in 7th	Ceres sextile/trine Venus
Planet(s) in 7th in conflict with planets ruling 4th	Ruler of 4th in 7th	Moon sextile/trine Pallas
(Planet[s] in 10th in conflict with planet[s] in or ruling 7th)	Ruler of 7th in 4th	Ceres sextile/trine Pallas
Any ruler of 4th in conflict with any ruler of 7th	Venus, Pallas opposite Moon	Moon, Ceres conjunct ruler of 7th or Descendant
Nodes in conflict with any planet(s) in or ruling 7th	Venus, Pallas opposite Ceres	Moon, Ceres sextile/trine ruler of 7th or Descendant
	Moon conjunct Descendant	Planet(s) in 4th in harmony aspect to planet(s) in or ruling 7th
	Ceres conjunct Descendant	Any ruler of 4th in harmony with any ruler of 7th
	(Ruler of 10th in 7th)	Nodes in harmony with planets in or ruling 7th
	(Ruler of 7th in 10th)	
	Nodes in Libra/Aries	
	Nodes across 1st/7th	

Synastry

Tend toward Challenging

Mom's Venus, Descendant, Pallas, or 7th-house ruler square/quincunx/opposite/octile/tri-octile the daughter's Moon, Ceres, or any other planets, asteroids, Nodes, or angles

The daughter's Venus, Pallas, Descendant, or 7th-house ruler square/quincunx/opposite/octile/tri-octile any of Mom's planets, asteroids, Nodes, or angles

Mom's Mars, Saturn, Neptune, or South Node conjunct the daughter's Venus, Pallas, Descendant, or 7th-house ruler

Neutral/Both

Mom's Venus, Pallas, Descendant, or 7th-house ruler conjunct the daughter's Saturn, Uranus, Neptune, Pluto, Vesta, Chiron, Nodes, or Midheaven

The daughter's Venus, Pallas, Descendant, or 7th-house ruler conjunct Mother's Uranus, Pluto, Vesta, Chiron, or Midheaven

Mom's stellium in the daughter's 7th house

The daughter's stellium in Mother's 7th house

Tend toward Support

The daughter's Venus, Pallas, or 7th-house ruler conjunct Mother's Sun, Moon, Mercury, Venus, Jupiter, Ceres, Pallas, Juno, North Node, Ascendant, or IC

Mother's Venus, Pallas, or 7th-house ruler conjunct the daughter's Sun, Moon, Mercury, Venus, Mars, Jupiter, Ceres, Pallas, Juno, North Node, Ascendant, or IC

Mother's Venus, Pallas, or 7th-house ruler in harmony aspect to any of the daughter's planets, asteroids, or angles

The daughter's Venus, Pallas, or 7th-house ruler in harmony aspect to any of Mother's planets, asteroids, or angles

Issues

The daughter's developmental tasks include creating and maintaining a healthy give-and-take with others, building good friendships and (usually) a romantic partnership, enjoying aesthetic activities, and pursuing justice, equality, and fairness within her life.

Wounding can occur through:

1. A mother or daughter who is too caught up in appearances or "looking good" for others

2. A mother or daughter who is too dependent on approval from other people

3. A mother whose artistic activities take away from her time for family

4. A mother who competes with her own daughter (or other family members)

5. A mother or daughter who expects life to be easy, smooth, and effortless

6. A mother or daughter who is unwilling to act unless someone else is with her

7. A mother and daughter who have widely different (and clashing) ideas about art, music, cosmetics, fashion, and politics, and about what justice entails

8. A mother who provides a very negative role model for one-on-one relationships

9. A mother and daughter with conflicting viewpoints on how to create and maintain a relationship

Solutions
See chapter 8, "Healing Options."

Letter 8

Developing Self-Understanding and Self-Mastery, Learning to Share the Sensual, Sexual, and Financial Worlds, and Establishing Psychological Intimacy with at Least One Person

Aspects/Placements in Daughter's Chart (OR in Mother's Chart)

Tend toward Challenging	*Neutral/Both*	*Tend toward Support*
Moon conjunct Pluto	Pluto in 4th	Moon sextile/trine Pluto
Moon conjunct Juno	Juno in 4th	Moon sextile/trine Juno
Ceres conjunct Pluto	Moon in 8th	Ceres sextile/trine Pluto
Ceres conjunct Juno	Ceres in 8th	Ceres sextile/trine Juno
Ruler of 4th conjunct or in conflict aspect to Pluto or Juno	(Pluto in 10th)	Ruler of 8th sextile/trine Moon or Ceres
Moon in conflict aspect to Pluto or Juno	(Juno in 10th)	Ruler of 4th sextile/trine Pluto or Juno
Ceres in conflict aspect to Pluto or Juno	Ruler of 4th in 8th	Planet(s) in 4th in harmony with planet(s) in or ruling 8th
Ruler of 8th in conflict aspect to Moon or Ceres	Ruler of 8th in 4th	Any ruler of 8th in harmony with any ruler of 4th
Planet(s) in 4th in conflict with planet(s) in or ruling 8th	(Ruler of 10th in 8th)	Nodes in harmony with Pluto, Juno, or ruler of 8th
Any ruler of 8th in conflict with any ruler of 4th	(Ruler of 8th in 10th)	
(Planet[s] in 10th in conflict with any planet[s] in or ruling 8th)	Nodes in Scorpio/Taurus	
Nodes in conflict with Pluto, Juno, or 8th-house ruler	Nodes across 2nd/8th	

Synastry
Tend toward Challenging

Mom's Pluto, Juno, or 8th-house ruler square/quincunx/opposite/octile/tri-octile the daughter's Moon, Ceres, or any other planets, asteroids, Nodes, or angles

The daughter's Pluto, Juno, or 8th-house ruler square/quincunx/opposite/octile/tri-octile any of Mom's planets, asteroids, Nodes, or angles

Mom's Pluto, Juno, or 8th-house ruler conjunct the daughter's Sun, Mars, Saturn, Uranus, Neptune, Pluto, South Node, Vesta, Midheaven, or Ascendant

Mom's Sun, Mars, Saturn, Uranus, Neptune, Pluto, South Node, Vesta, Midheaven, or Ascendant conjunct the daughter's Pluto, Juno, or 8th-house ruler

Neutral/Both

Mom's Pluto, Juno, or 8th-house ruler conjunct the daughter's Moon, Mercury, Venus, Jupiter, Ceres, Juno, Pallas, Chiron, North Node, IC, or Descendant

The daughter's Pluto, Juno, or 8th-house ruler conjunct Mother's Sun, Moon, Mercury, Venus, Jupiter, Ceres, Juno, Pallas, Chiron, North Node, IC, or Descendant

Mom's stellium in the daughter's 8th house

The daughter's stellium in Mother's 8th house

Tend toward Support

Mother's Pluto, Juno, or 8th-house ruler in harmony aspect to any of the daughter's planets, asteroids, Nodes, or angles

The daughter's Pluto, Juno, or 8th-house ruler in harmony aspect to any of Mother's planets, asteroids, Nodes, or angles

Issues

Looking beneath the surface of life (and other people) is vital. The daughter is learning to probe the depths of her own psyche—and of those who are intimately connected with her. She is mastering the art of giving, receiving, and sharing the world of the senses, money, and possessions. She is committing herself to loyalty, perseverance, intimacy, and completion as well as forgiving and forgetting when necessary.

Wounding can occur through:

1. A mother who is vengeful, vindictive, power-hungry, abusive, controlling, etc.

2. A mother who sets a negative role model in terms of betrayal or lack of loyalty

3. A mother and/or daughter with major issues around addiction (with food, money, sex, etc.)

4. A mother who fails to respect her daughter's need for privacy and appropriate boundaries and separation

5. A mother and/or daughter who is manipulative or uses emotional blackmail

6. Power struggles between the mother and daughter

7. A mother who discounts her daughter's psychological courage and insight into hidden agendas and motivations

8. A mother and daughter who have problems forgiving one another and moving on

Solutions
See chapter 8, "Healing Options."

Letter 9

Developing Faith in a Higher Power, Confidence in One's Own Efforts, a Love of Adventure, Expanded Horizons, Independence, and Enthusiasm for the Quest

Aspects/Placements in Daughter's Chart (OR in Mother's Chart)

Tend toward Challenging	*Neutral/Both*	*Tend toward Support*
Moon square/quincunx/ octile/tri-octile Jupiter or Chiron	Moon conjunct Jupiter or Chiron	Moon sextile/trine Jupiter
Ceres square/quincunx/ octile/tri-octile Jupiter or Chiron	Ceres conjunct Jupiter or Chiron	Ceres sextile/trine Jupiter
Moon or Ceres square/ quincunx/octile/tri-octile 9th-house ruler	Moon, Ceres opposite Jupiter or Chiron	Moon, Ceres sextile/trine Chiron
Planet(s) in 4th in conflict with planet(s) in or ruling 9th house	Jupiter in 4th	Moon, Ceres sextile/trine ruler of 9th
Any ruler of 9th in conflict with any ruler of 4th	Chiron in 4th	Planet(s) in 4th in harmony with planet(s) in or ruling 9th
(Planet[s] in 10th in conflict with planet[s] in or ruling 9th)	Moon in 9th	Any ruler of 4th in harmony with any ruler of 9th
Nodes in conflict with planet(s) in or ruling 9th	Ceres in 9th	Nodes in harmony with any planet(s) in or ruling 9th
	(Jupiter in 10th)	
	(Chiron in 10th)	
	Ruler of 4th in 9th	
	Ruler of 9th in 4th	
	(Ruler of 10th in 9th)	
	(Ruler of 9th in 10th)	
	Nodes in Sag/Gemini	
	Nodes across 3rd/9th	

Synastry

Tend toward Challenging

Mom's Jupiter, Chiron, or 9th-house ruler square/quincunx/opposite/octile/tri-octile the daughter's Moon, Ceres, or any other planets, asteroids, Nodes, or angles

The daughter's Jupiter, Chiron, or 9th-house ruler square/quincunx/opposite/octile/tri-octile any of Mom's planets, asteroids, Nodes, or angles

Mom's Mars, Saturn, Neptune, Pluto, South Node, Juno, or Vesta conjunct the daughter's Jupiter, Chiron, or 9th-house ruler

The daughter's Mars, Saturn, Neptune, Pluto, South Node, Juno, or Vesta conjunct Mother's Jupiter, Chiron, or 9th-house ruler

Neutral/Both

Mom's Jupiter, Chiron, or 9th-house ruler conjunct the daughter's Moon, Ceres, North Node, or angles

The daughter's Jupiter, Chiron, or 9th-house ruler conjunct Mother's Moon, Ceres, North Node, or angles

Mom's stellium in the daughter's 9th house

The daughter's stellium in Mother's 9th house

Tend toward Support

Mother's Jupiter, Chiron, or 9th-house ruler in harmony aspect to any of the daughter's planets, asteroids, or angles

The daughter's Jupiter, Chiron, or 9th-house ruler in harmony aspect to any of Mother's planets, asteroids, or angles

The daughter's Jupiter, Chiron, or 9th-house ruler conjunct Mother's Sun, Mercury, Venus, Jupiter, Uranus, Pallas, or Chiron

Mother's Jupiter, Chiron, or 9th-house ruler conjunct the daughter's Sun, Mercury, Venus, Jupiter, Uranus, Pallas, or Chiron

Issues

The search is oriented up and away. The daughter is learning to find joy and excitement in exploratory activities such as writing, travel, spiritual quests, etc. Freedom is important.

She may be building her confidence, increasing her willingness to take reasonable risks, and developing or strengthening her faith in something larger than herself.

Wounding may occur through:

1. A mother (or daughter) who is foolhardy and acts rashly

2. Clashes of religious or spiritual beliefs and principles

3. A mother whose desire for freedom or adventure takes her away from her family

4. A mother who is too wrapped up in religious practices, philosophical questions, educational pursuits, or other transpersonal concerns to pay attention to her family

5. Overly idealistic expectations on the part of the mother, daughter, or both—of each other or of family relationships in general

6. A mother who cripples her daughter's self-confidence, perhaps through making unreasonable demands, being a "super" parent, stepping in too quickly before the daughter can learn on her own, etc.

7. Self-righteous attitudes within the home

8. An absent or idealized mother figure resulting in a daughter who struggles with unclear images around nurturing or dreams of a family that might have been (if only the world were perfect)

Solutions

See chapter 8, "Healing Options."

Letter 10

Owning One's Expertise, Becoming Responsible, Patient, and Disciplined, Making a Contribution to Society, Working within the Rules, and Coping Effectively with Powerful People

Aspects/Placements in Daughter's Chart (OR in Mother's Chart)

Tend toward Challenging	*Neutral/Both*	*Tend toward Support*
Moon conjunct Saturn	Saturn in 4th	Moon sextile/trine Saturn
Ceres conjunct Saturn	Moon in 10th	Ceres sextile/trine Saturn
Moon in conflict with Saturn	Ceres in 10th	Ruler of 10th sextile/trine Moon or Ceres
Ceres in conflict with Saturn	(Saturn in 10th)	Any ruler of 10th in harmony with any ruler of 4th
Ruler of 10th in conflict with Moon or Ceres	Ruler of 4th in 10th	Planets in 4th in harmony with planets in or ruling 10th
Planet(s) in 10th in conflict with planet(s) in or ruling 4th	Ruler of 10th in 4th	Nodes in harmony with planet(s) in or ruling 10th
Planet(s) in 10th in conflict with planet(s) ruling 10th	(Ruler of 10th in 10th)	
Any conflict between rulers of 10th and 4th	Nodes in Capricorn/Cancer	
Nodes in conflict with any planet(s) in or ruling 10th	Nodes across 4th/10th	

Synastry

Tend toward Challenging

Any of Mom's planets, asteroids, Nodes, or angles conjunct the daughter's Saturn or 10th-house ruler

Any of the daughter's planets, asteroid, Nodes, or angles conjunct Mother's Saturn or 10th-house ruler

Mom's Saturn or 10th-house ruler square/quincunx/opposite/octile/tri-octile the daughter's Moon, Ceres, or any other planets, asteroids, Nodes, or angles

The daughter's Saturn or 10th-house ruler square/quincunx/opposite/octile/tri-octile any of Mom's planets, asteroids, Nodes, or angles

Neutral/Both

Mom's stellium in the daughter's 10th house

The daughter's stellium in Mother's 10th house

Tend toward Support

Mother's Saturn or 10th-house ruler in harmony aspect to any of the daughter's planets, asteroids, Nodes, or angles

The daughter's Saturn or 10th-house ruler in harmony aspect to any of Mother's planets, asteroids, Nodes, or angles

Issues

The daughter is learning to own her own power, to take on appropriate responsibility (and say "No" to inappropriate burdens), and to understand and work effectively within the Establishment and structures of society. She is selecting an avenue through which to pursue a vocation or gift to the world.

Wounding could occur through:

1. A harsh, punitive, judgmental, constrictive, restrictive, or controlling parent

2. A mother who works so hard (just for survival or for her own ambitions—the workaholic) that the daughter feels neglected or unimportant

3. A home environment that is limited, poor, or oriented toward subsistence only

4. A mother and/or daughter who is pragmatic and disciplined rather than warm and supportive

5. A daughter who has to parent her own parent, carrying heavy responsibilities from a young age

6. A blocked, inadequate, depressive parent who teaches the script of "The world is too powerful; you cannot do anything successfully."

7. A mother who does so much that she unconsciously cripples her daughter's competence, robbing the daughter of opportunities to practice, gain experience, hone skills, and learn from mistakes

8. Vastly different attitudes between the mother and daughter about rules, regulations, and rebellion

9. Clashes between the mother and daughter about status or vocational choices

Solutions

See chapter 8, "Healing Options."

Letter 11

Strengthening Personal Independence, Individuality, Innovation, and the Capacity to Cooperate with Like-Minded Individuals in Humanitarian Pursuits

Aspects/Placements in Daughter's Chart (OR in Mother's Chart)

Tend toward Challenging	*Neutral/Both*	*Tend toward Support*
Moon conjunct Uranus	Uranus in 4th	Moon sextile/trine Uranus
Ceres conjunct Uranus	Moon in 11th	Ceres sextile/trine Uranus
Moon conjunct ruler of 11th	Ceres in 11th	Ruler of 4th sextile/trine Uranus
Moon, Ceres in conflict aspect with Uranus or ruler of 11th	(Uranus in 10th)	Ruler of 11th sextile/trine Moon or Ceres
Planet(s) in 4th in conflict with planet(s) in or ruling 11th	Ruler of 4th in 11th	Planet(s) in 4th in harmony with planet(s) in or ruling 11th
(Planet[s] in 10th in conflict with planet[s] in or ruling 11th)	Ruler of 11th in 4th	Any ruler of 4th in harmony with any ruler of 11th
Any ruler of 11th in conflict with any ruler of 4th	(Ruler of 10th in 11th)	Nodes in harmony with any planet(s) in or ruling 11th
Nodes in conflict with any planets in or ruling 11th	(Ruler of 11th in 10th)	
	Nodes in Aquarius/Leo	
	Nodes across 5th/11th	

Synastry

Tend toward Challenging

Mom's Uranus or 11th-house ruler square/quincunx/opposite/octile/tri-octile the daughter's Moon, Ceres, or any other planets, asteroids, Nodes, or angles

The daughter's Uranus or 11th-house ruler square/quincunx/opposite/octile/tri-octile any of Mom's planets, asteroids, Nodes, or angles

Mom's Moon, Mars, Saturn, Neptune, Pluto, South Node, Juno, Ceres, Vesta, or Midheaven conjunct the daughter's Uranus or 11th-house ruler

The daughter's Moon, Mars, Saturn, Neptune, Pluto, South Node, Juno, Ceres, Vesta, or Midheaven conjunct Mother's Uranus or 11th-house ruler

Neutral/Both

Mom's Uranus or 11th–house ruler conjunct the daughter's Sun, Venus, Uranus, Pallas, North Node, or angles

The daughter's Uranus or 11th–house ruler conjunct Mother's Sun, Venus, Uranus, Pallas, North Node, or angles

Mom's stellium in the daughter's 11th house

The daughter's stellium in Mother's 11th house

Tend toward Support

The daughter's Uranus or 11th-house ruler conjunct Mother's Mercury, Jupiter, or Chiron

Mother's Uranus or 11th-house ruler conjunct the daughter's Mercury, Jupiter, or Chiron

Mother's Uranus or 11th-house ruler in harmony aspect to any of the daughter's planets, asteroids, Nodes, or angles

The daughter's Uranus or 11th-house ruler in harmony aspect to any of Mother's planets, asteroids, Nodes, or angles

Issues

The daughter is learning to exercise and affirm her unique qualities, to seek out friends and other associates with whom to share ideas and explore fresh possibilities, to investigate new technology, to contribute to humanitarian causes, and to strengthen personal independence and inventiveness.

Wounding could occur through:

1. A mother or daughter who is excessively rebellious, freedom-oriented, unusual, eccentric, or offbeat (family is dealing with freedom-closeness dilemma)

2. A mother who seems too cool, aloof, and detached, from the daughter's perspective

3. A home life that is erratic, unpredictable, and unstable

4. A mother who spends too much time with social activities, clubs, friends, or humanitarian pursuits and not enough time and energy with her family

5. A mother who is so unconventional that she scripts her daughter to become the alien or outcast in society

6. A mother and/or daughter who tends to rationalize or intellectualize matters

7. A mother and daughter who have widely divergent views on friends, lifestyle choices, democracy, and humanity

8. A mother and daughter whose concepts of progress (technological, social, societal, etc.) clash with one another

Solutions
See chapter 8, "Healing Options."

Letter 12

Making Mystical Connections, Strengthening Aesthetic and Imaginative Abilities, Exercising Empathy and Compassion, and Making the World Better or More Beautiful

Aspects/Placements in Daughter's Chart (OR in Mother's Chart)

Tend toward Challenging	*Neutral/Both*	*Tend toward Support*
Moon conjunct Neptune	Moon in 12th	Moon sextile/trine Neptune
Moon conjunct Chiron	Ceres in 12th	Ceres sextile/trine Neptune
Ceres conjunct Neptune	Neptune in 4th	Moon or Ceres sextile/trine Chiron
Ceres conjunct Chiron	Chiron in 4th	Moon or Ceres sextile/trine ruler of 12th
Moon or Ceres conjunct ruler of 12th	(Neptune in 10th)	Planet(s) in 12th in harmony with planets in or ruling 4th
Moon or Ceres in conflict with Neptune, Chiron, or ruler of 12th	(Chiron in 10th)	Any ruler of 4th in harmony with any ruler of 12th
Planet(s) in 12th in conflict with planet(s) in or ruling 4th	Ruler of 4th in 12th	Nodes in harmony with Neptune, Chiron, or any planet(s) in or ruling 12th
Any ruler of 4th in conflict with any ruler of 12th	Ruler of 12th in 4th	
(Planet[s] in or ruling 10th in conflict with planet[s] in or ruling 12th)	(Ruler of 10th in 12th)	
Nodes in conflict with planet(s) in or ruling 12th	(Ruler of 12th in 10th)	
	Nodes in Pisces/Virgo	
	Nodes across 6th/12th	

Synastry

Tend toward Challenging

Mom's Neptune, Chiron, or 12th-house ruler square/quincunx/opposite/octile/tri-octile the daughter's Moon, Ceres, or any other planets, asteroids, Nodes, or angles

The daughter's Neptune, Chiron, or 12th-house ruler square/quincunx/opposite/octile/tri-octile any of Mom's planets, asteroids, Nodes, or angles

Mom's planets, asteroids, Nodes, or angles conjunct the daughter's Neptune, Chiron, or 12th-house ruler

The daughter's planets, asteroid, Nodes, or angles conjunct Mother's Neptune, Chiron, or 12th-house ruler

Neutral/Both

Mom's stellium in the daughter's 12th house

The daughter's stellium in Mother's 12th house

Tend toward Support

Mother's Neptune or Chiron in harmony aspect to any of the daughter's planets, asteroids, or angles

The daughter's Neptune or Chiron in harmony aspect to any of Mother's planets, asteroids, or angles

Issues

The daughter is seeking infinite love and beauty. She may explore aesthetic realms, other-worldly images, imaginative pursuits, mystical quests, charitable activities, or anything that uplifts and inspires herself and others. She is learning to set appropriate boundaries, to aid and assist others without falling into martyrdom, and to ask for help without succumbing to a victim mentality. Transcendent urges are highlighted.

Wounding could occur through:

1. An absent, missing, or idealized mother figure where the daughter creates a dream image of what could (or "should") have been

2. An ill, alcoholic, drug-addicted, escapist, (or other victim role) mother and/or daughter

3. A martyr mother who teaches the daughter that this is appropriate feminine behavior

4. A mother who is too caught up in her spiritual, religious, charitable, or other transpersonal pursuits to spend time with her family

5. A family that expects "Heaven on Earth" with loved ones (and experiences disappointment and disillusionment). The mother may expect herself or her daughter to be perfect, and the daughter may expect the mother to provide "happily ever after" endings

6. Beauty could be overvalued in the home, with too much focus on appearances or deception to hide potential unpleasantness

7. The mother and daughter may have widely divergent tastes in terms of art, music, and aesthetic judgments (what they view as beautiful)

8. The mother and daughter may differ considerably in their approach to transcendent realms and mystical urges

9. The mother or daughter may look for "God" (the Absolute Ideal) in areas of life that are limited, e.g., human beings, a bank account, a job, etc.

Solutions

See chapter 8, "Healing Options."

EIGHT

Healing Options (Especially for Daughters)

The family crucible has a profound and long-lasting impact on each of our lives. What we experienced as infants and young children established a set of reactions and assumptions. One vital function of the brain is as a filtering mechanism—telling us which input from the world is worth noting and which can be ignored, and interpreting the data that we are constantly absorbing from the physical world. Our early upbringing "sets" certain filters in place. We are conditioned to believe, feel, and act in particular ways. Much of this conditioning is unconscious. We are not fully aware of the many ways in which we recapitulate the feelings we had as youngsters. Reams have been written in psychological texts and self-help books about how our parents influence our vocational choices, the mate(s) we select, our health, and much more.

Since Mother provides the very first image a daughter receives of what being female means, her impact is incredible. The goal of this chapter is to identify the more salient issues associated with each letter of the astrological alphabet, and offer healing options for the daughter to pursue: tips and techniques for increasing awareness and tools and suggestions for transforming negative patterns into more positive ones. Naturally these ideas are available to the mother as well. The major focus of this book, however, is on the experiences and viewpoints of daughters. Every daughter has or had a mother, but many women have not had daughters.

When using the astrological viewpoint, we must remember that each side of life can be overdone, underdone, or expressed at a time and place that is not constructive for us. As has been apparent throughout this book, there are inherent conflicts between the twelve sides of life. To some extent, they are competitive with each other. A full, healthy life requires us to do some juggling. The squares, oppositions, and quincunxes in astrology show us sides of life that tend to compete more with one another. (The three dilemmas that we discussed early on—the cardinal, fixed, and mutable dilemmas—apply to the grand crosses of astrology.)

When a daughter is blocked or having trouble expressing one side of life, it is usually the case that she has overdeveloped another side (or sides)—usually one that forms a square, opposition, or quincunx to the underdeveloped drives. Thus, part of the solution is working on ways to strengthen the less robust qualities. Another part of the solution is to tone down those drives that have been used more often than is appropriate or healthy. As an example, if a daughter is having trouble asserting herself or if she has inner scripts that deny her right to exist, to be, to do her thing in the world, she has underdeveloped Letter 1. It is likely that she has too much of any of the following:

- Letter 10 (a square)—rules, regulation, obligations, duties, sensitivity to authority figures

- Letter 4 (a square)—the need to protect others, or feelings of dependency

- Letter 7 (the opposition)—awareness of the needs of others; desire to accommodate them or anxiety in regard to their power

- Letter 6 (a quincunx)—self-critical or judgmental messages; emphasis on doing rather than being

- Letter 8 (a quincunx)—awareness of the power of others; need for their support, so she is vulnerable to emotional manipulation

The road to health and balance will involve the daughter strengthening Letter 1 drives in her nature and toning down any of the five competing sets of drives that are interfering with her Letter 1 need to be herself.

Ironically, these natural conflicts also show us the road to health when any one of the twelve sides of life has been *overdeveloped*. Look to the squares, oppositions, and quincunxes for a "way out" when one set of life drives is being carried to an extreme. As an example, if someone is too assertive, too forceful, too intent on getting what she wants, when she wants it (overdoing Letter 1), the solutions lie in developing more of Letter 7's empathy and understanding of other people's viewpoints (the opposition); Letter 4's compassion and desire to protect and care for others (a square); Letter 10's recognition that the world is bigger than us and we have to accept some limits to live in society (another square); Letter 6's competence and focus on humble service (a quincunx); and Letter 8's emphasis on sharing power and pleasures with others (the other quincunx).

Letter 1

Mars, Aries, 1st House

The major personal issues for daughters revolve around identity, physical existence, dealing with anger, and developing healthy assertive skills.

Personal Identity/Existence

In cases of severe abuse, the daughter may develop very self-destructive habits. If that is the case, psychotherapy is advisable. If suicidal thoughts or actions are in the picture, outside intervention is also imperative. If violence was a problem in the home, the daughter may have to work long and hard to build her inner and outer strength. Therapy and a safe haven are essential. Counseling can be of assistance in many other circumstances, but is not such a life-and-death matter. Where the daughter is physically self-destructive or involved in abusive relationships, outside assistance is usually necessary.

In more mild forms of conditioning, the daughter may have felt "invisible" or insignificant in the family. Perhaps she got (or interpreted) messages that she did not matter, or that a parent saw her as a burden, or that her personal needs were not worthy of attention. (With a very self-centered parent, the parents' desires are regularly given priority over the daughter's needs.) Perhaps the script in the home was "You are not okay" or that her individual qualities were somehow unacceptable. Perhaps the family seemed to value only doing (particularly any work or chores the daughter could contribute) over being (providing love and acceptance for each person simply for being themselves). That is often connected to an overdevelopment of Letter 6 or 10 at the expense of Letter 1 or 5.

Here are the steps the daughter can take:

1. Reading psychological, spiritual, or inspirational literature that affirms the worth and importance of each individual human being, e.g., Desiderata poem.

2. Spending time with friends who notice and respond positively to her needs.

3. Cutting off "toxic" relationships (with people who take advantage of her, criticize her unnecessarily, ignore or belittle her, etc.).

4. Developing and repeating affirmations of personal worth and significance.

5. Learning physical skills that help her stay centered and "present" in her body.

6. Keeping a journal to recognize patterns in her thinking and feelings, and to give more weight to the importance of her own inner life.

7. Identifying small challenges to tackle one by one, to build her sense of self. (For example, holding her own with someone who tends to monologue might be one task.) Each success helps her build to the next. If there is a setback, she can start with a smaller, less demanding task next time, gradually building her courage and personal will.

Dealing with Anger

We know now that anger can be a very destructive emotion. People who register high on hostility scales are more likely to have cardiovascular problems and may die younger than their peers. Anger triggers "flight or fight" responses and pumps stress hormones into the body. With time and repetition, these can affect the heart, the arteries, etc.

If a daughter has been *conditioned to be angry often*, she can train herself to do the following:

1. Breathe. Taking deep breaths and concentrating on your breathing can lower the body's level of arousal and take your focus off your anger, allowing you to cool down.

2. Talk a walk or exercise. Physical exercise can work off much of the stress and help you think about other things.

3. Cry. Many women find that tears can be a release for anger or frustration, helping them move on after the crying jag.

4. Focus on perspective. Asking yourself questions may help you realize that the matter is not that significant. Consider whether what angers you is worth the time and attention you are devoting to it. Ask yourself if it will really matter in another day, or

a year. Look for a pattern. If your anger is connected to a recurring problem, you need to analyze the problem and figure out how to fix it.

5. Remember the Serenity Prayer: "God grant me the serenity to accept those things that I cannot change . . ." Some things are beyond our control. Being able to forgive and move on is vital.

6. Humor. Laughter can be incredibly healing. If you can find something funny in the situation, you can defuse your anger. Small children laugh hundreds of times a day. Many adults forget to laugh. Recapture the lightheartedness of a young child.

If the daughter has been *conditioned to repress anger*, she will need to develop skills at identifying anger and probably other emotions as well. One technique is to make a habit of doing a "self-check" several times a day. During a self-check, you ask yourself what you are feeling, starting with any physical symptoms, and seeking an emotional label that seems to fit best. The daughter may learn that a tight chest, a hurting stomach, an itchy ear, or other signs are signals that she is angry. The daughter can also ask other people what makes them angry, and see if what she hears triggers any insights. She might try keeping a diary or journal to help elicit feelings. She could pound pillows (or punch a punching bag, etc.) and see if feelings emerge. She could also complete sentences about anger, saying what first comes into her head without censorship; e.g., "I am angry at _____." Or, "I am upset about _____." Or, "What ticks me off the most is _____."

Once the daughter becomes more skilled at identifying anger, then she can decide whether to take action or use these techniques to get her anger out of her system.

Asserting Oneself

If a daughter feels that she has overdeveloped her assertive side, then checking some of the skills of accommodation and empathy (Letter 7), nurturing and protection (Letter 4), understanding limits (Letter 10), being practical and of service (Letter 6), or self-awareness and self-mastery (Letter 8) would be helpful.

In most cases, daughters will be dealing with underdeveloped assertiveness. This is because many parents put their own needs ahead of their children's and unconsciously encourage the children to put their own needs last. Also, sex-role conditioning pressures women to be sweet and nice rather than strong and assertive. A mother who is constantly submissive and undervalues herself and other females teaches her daughter that her own needs and desires are unimportant.

There are a number of self-help books and classes designed to help people develop more assertiveness. Practicing saying "No" is one technique. The "broken record" technique (useful with salespeople), where you simply say the same refusal over and over again and refuse to respond to "hooks" or questions from the other person, is also helpful. I often recommend to clients that they ask themselves, every day, "What have I done just for myself today?" Checking inside to see what one really wants is advisable as well. Physical exercise, sports, or any kind of working out can be helpful. Building one's muscles often builds confidence and assertion as well. Since resources are abundant in this arena, any reader can easily get further tools from the local library or self-help bookstore.

General Strengthening

Exercise, physical movement, working out, activities that build courage such as Outward Bound, exploring concepts of the Spiritual Warrior, building fires, being around iron or steel, wearing the color red. (Some people find that the literal physical associations of colors, metals, etc., can help them strengthen the drives associated with that planet, sign, and house.)

Reminder

If Letter 1 is overdeveloped, compensation can include more focus on Letter(s) 4, 6, 7, 8, and/or 10. Letter 4 reminds us of family ties ("No one is an island"), and Letter 7 represents the pleasures of partnership. While Letter 1 can rush in impulsively, Letters 6 and 10 (the earth element) bring in pragmatism, planning, and an awareness of consequences. With Letter 8, we find gratification in intimacy and sharing power, pleasures, and possessions.

Letter 2

Venus, Taurus, 2nd House

The major personal issues for daughters revolve around being comfortable in one's body, finding stability (without stolidity), and gaining a positive relationship with money and possessions.

Being Comfortable in One's Body/Sensuality

Early deprivation can have an impact on the daughter's ability to enjoy the physical and sensual world. A "denial consciousness" could evolve that tends to hold back from perfectly reasonable pleasures. Or, eating disorders could evolve due to a combination of unhealthy messages from society (anorexia is a serious, life-threatening disorder in the United States, particularly among teenagers and young women) and disturbances in the nurturing that the daughter experienced. If eating disorders are in the picture, outside intervention (medical and psychotherapeutic) is essential!

In other forms, the daughter may be dealing with an unhealthy body image, or may "anesthetize" herself from emotional pain through the use of drugs, physically painful acts, overeating, etc. The more severe the reaction, the more important it is that the daughter get assistance. Some things are too tough to handle on our own. Seminars and literature on body image are also readily available to the reader.

With mild forms of self-denial, the daughter may need to learn to pamper herself a bit, to indulge in bubble baths, massages, hot tubs, comfort foods, or other ways of helping herself feel good. If food (or sugar) has been used as a substitute for love, the daughter will have to practice diversification—bringing other sources of pleasure into her life. We are less likely to overeat if we can also indulge our appetites (moderately) through spending money, creating and enjoying beauty, getting massages or other gratifying physical contact, making love, collecting possessions, etc.

Finding Stability without Stolidity

In an increasingly frenetic world, having calm spots within the storms is essential. One of the gifts of Letter 2 is feeling comfortable with one's self, one's body, and in the world. If that has been underdeveloped, the daughter can take several steps:

1. Learn what physical experiences help you feel good—and do them more often. This might range from getting a weekly massage, to taking an art class, to having a particular food for breakfast, etc.

2. Meditate on images that convey solid support, such as being connected to the center of the earth.

3. Seek out comfortable furniture, especially chairs and beds so that your body can relax.

4. Establish routines that you find reassuring.

5. Gather collectibles (in moderation) or a few key possessions that have great emotional attachment as resources for grounding.

6. Periodically review your material/financial circumstances and look for ways to improve them.

7. Spend time with people who are easygoing and even-tempered.

Gaining a Positive Relationship with Money and Possessions

An amazing number of people have not had any real training in terms of managing money. When the daughter has had many negative examples and conditioning from the mother in the financial realm, taking classes or getting informal instruction from a knowledgeable friend is highly advisable. One woman whose mother had a gambling addiction had to learn to budget in her forties. She did not understand the principles of interest payments (why having a credit card with a high rate of interest was not a good idea), how "instant refunds" take much of your money, and other financial facts of life. Here are some basic skills and concepts that would be helpful to learn:

1. How to open and use a checking account.

2. What interest means and how compound interest works.

3. How to find a credit card with low interest and/or no annual fee.

4. How you are losing money by using check-cashing services or companies that get you an "instant refund" on your income tax.

5. What installment plans really cost you.

6. How vital early investment in retirement is (the power of compounding).

7. How to set up and follow a budget.

8. Why savings and "reserves" are important.

9. The purpose and value of insurance (health, auto, home, disability, life, etc.).

10. How to comparison shop.

11. What items you can (and should) bargain for.

12. How to find discounts and sales.

American society is very consumer-oriented. Many of us get an emotional "high" by buying things. If this is a problem, we need to train ourselves to enjoy other pleasures, so we can cut back on our consumption. In astrological terms, the pleasure related to purchasing something can be transferred to gratification from food, drink, sex, creating beauty, enjoying lovely things, or other sensually satisfying activities.

A rule of thumb that one client uses for her purchases is that she has to think about a possible purchase for as long as it would take her to earn the money for that purchase. Since she makes about $30 an hour, she (theoretically) considers a $6 purchase for about five minutes. She would need a "cooling off" period of almost a day (ten hours) to contemplate a $300 purchase. This "rule" is probably too rigid for most of us, but it does help to counter the materialistic orientation of American life.

If a daughter feels she is too self-indulgent (excessive Letter 2), she can pay more attention to her creative side or the needs of children and lovers (Letter 5), to appropriate self-mastery and self-control (Letter 8), to humanitarian desires (Letter 11), to empathy and consideration for partners (Letter 7), and/or to higher values or spiritual aspirations (Letter 9). Also, if she has a wide range of pleasures, such as eating, drinking, making love, creating beauty, or buying pretty things, she is less likely to go to extremes with any one particular channel of material gratification.

General Strengthening

Sensually satisfying activities, relaxation techniques, buying and enjoying lovely things, developing prosperity consciousness, wearing copper jewelry, wearing green or earthy colors, and just taking time to savor pleasures in the here and now.

Reminder

If Letter 2 is overdeveloped, compensation can occur through more focus on Letter(s) 5, 8, 11, 7, and/or 9. When Letter 2 is solid and stuck, Letter 5 creates joy and zest, and Letter 9 sees great, exciting potentials. Letter 8 reminds us to consider other people's needs and pleasures (as well as our own). Letters 7 and 11 (the air element) represent the importance of logic and detachment.

Letter 3

Mercury, Gemini, 3rd House

The major personal issues for daughters revolve around owning one's own intellect, overcoming communication blocks, learning to take life lightly, and dealing with multiple interests.

Owning One's Own Intellect

A daughter may come to doubt her mental abilities through a variety of avenues, such as having a superbright parent, being constantly compared to a "smarter" (usually older) sibling, receiving too many disparaging comments from parent(s), experiencing traumas in early schooling, etc. As an adult, there are a number of steps the daughter can take to improve the situation:

1. Associate with people who listen to and acknowledge the worth of your ideas.

2. Avoid people who criticize you, call you "stupid," or otherwise put you down intellectually.

3. Remind yourself that experience is learning, and take inventory of all that you have absorbed throughout your lifetime.

4. Starting very small, set yourself an intellectual challenge to master, and then build up to bigger successes.

5. Look for "fun" ways to learn, e.g., crossword puzzles, trivia games, card games, and similar pursuits that can build vocabulary, memory, verbal skills, etc.

6. Take classes, read, or get special training in areas where you feel you have "missed out" or need extra information.

7. Take advantage of libraries, the Internet, and other sources of free information.

8. Remember that intelligence has many different aspects and is relative, and that the more we exercise our minds, the better they get.

Overcoming Communication Blocks

In severe cases (suffering from extreme phobias, stuttering, etc.), professional assistance is again advisable. In more mild cases, the individual can usually practice, a little at a time. It is important to start with very, very small challenges—building on successful experiences—and eventually working up to mastering major blocks. With fears and anxieties, the initial step is usually to imagine that you are in a situation that provokes anxiety, and then do physical relaxation techniques and visualization to help yourself feel confident and comfortable. As you "up the ante" in your imagination, you become more and more capable and assured. Eventually, you start with actual situations (again, beginning with something very, very small).

If the examples the daughter received were not helpful—e.g., a mother who talked much too much; a mother who clammed up and hardly said anything; a mother who was gossipy or used words to hurt people; a mother who ignored or criticized what her daughter had to say—the daughter will do best to seek out supportive people with whom to practice conversations. Building new, constructive experiences, bit by bit, will help her feel better about how she expresses herself. The daughter can also consciously and deliberately seek out positive role models for communication skills among friends, teachers, community leaders, coworkers, etc.

If the issue is actual ignorance or lack of training, the daughter can take classes or get special assistance to enlarge her vocabulary, master negotiating skills, become more adept in social situations, learn correct protocol, etc.

Learning to Take Life Lightly
One of the greatest gifts of the air element is the ability to take life lightly, to be more detached, to keep perspective. Letter 3, particularly, includes the childlike sense of play and fun, so humor is a very valuable leavener—allowing us to "lighten up" in several senses! If this is lacking, we can:

1. Read more humor, watch comedies, or listen to funny people to help stimulate our own sense of humor.

2. Seek out opportunities to laugh at life (and ourselves).

3. Practice perspective. If we are feeling overwrought, we can ask ourselves if this will really matter in a hundred years. If not, let it go.

4. Meditate on air, floating, not having to be directly involved in what is going on.

5. Remember that it is okay to sometimes be just a spectator and commentator. We do not always have to do more than that.

Dealing with Multiple Interests

Being scattered or having our fingers in too many pies is one form of too much Letter 3. We can deal with having multiple interests constructively by identifying a few things that are worth doing and doing well (Letter 6—the square), by keeping clear priorities of what is important and what is not (Letter 9—the opposition), and by trusting that the Universe will take over after we do our part (Letter 12—the other square). With a healthy expression of Letter 3, we know how to take things lightly, where Letters 8 and 10, the quincunxes, tend to be overly serious and intense. We can pick up and drop our multiple interests as the mood takes us, rather than being compulsive about finishing everything perfectly (Letters 6, 8, 9, 10, and 12).

General Strengthening

Mind games, puzzles, riddles, jokes, wearing the color yellow, meditating on images of quicksilver or butterflies, exploring comedy and humor, studying Hermes Trismegistus, or exploring Science of Mind, Silva Mind Control, Rational-Emotive Therapy, or other philosophies or approaches that emphasize the intellect.

Reminder

If Letter 3 is overdeveloped, compensation can occur through more focus on Letter(s) 6, 9, 12, 8, and/or 10. If we are too flippant and frivolous, Letter 6 will focus on the job, and Letter 10 will seek responsibility and achievement. Letter 9 broadens our perspectives, and Letter 12 reminds us that the spiritual dimension is a valuable resource. Letter 8 is serious and intense, where Letter 3 is lighthearted and casual.

Letter 4

Moon, (Ceres), North and South Nodes, Cancer, 4th House

The major personal issues for daughters revolve around creating a secure emotional foundation, achieving healthy interdependency, and mastering food issues.

Creating a Secure Emotional Foundation

When the early nurturing has been particularly lacking or destructive, the daughter may be incredibly damaged and very fragile emotionally. Feelings of abandonment and neglect could be pervasive. Such severe circumstances require extensive counseling to help repair the damage.

In more mild forms, the daughter may ask herself such questions as, "Am I safe in the world?" "Will others respond when I need them?" "Does love inevitably mean loss or hurt?" Psychologist Erik Erikson defined the first stage of development (in infancy) as Basic Trust versus Mistrust. When a daughter has been "taught" (usually unconsciously) that the world is not a safe place, that people are not dependable, that is a tough script to overcome. Some steps she can take include:

1. Find at least one person (a therapist, teacher, relative, friend, etc.) who is very nurturing and supportive. Build a positive relationship with that person, gradually learning to trust a little at a time. Start very small.

2. A physical "security blanket" (an object that helps engender a sense of reassurance) can be a useful tool.

3. Certain comfort foods, if associated with safety and feeling good, can be used in moderation.

4. Arranging one's physical surroundings and environments to add to a sense of safety will help. For example, one client prefers to sit where he can see the door in any room he occupies. He ascribes this to paranoia remaining from a past life as a mercenary soldier.

5. Pets can be a wonderful source of unconditional love and acceptance, adding to our emotional security.

6. For many people, owning their own home adds to their security.

7. If blood relatives have been destructive, some people create a "family of choice" with friends. They consciously and deliberately re-create a family atmosphere with more loving interactions, e.g., having dinner together, having picnics and other family get-togethers, celebrating holidays with one another, etc.

Achieving Healthy Interdependency

A daughter's development could be negatively affected by a mother who is too needy and dependent or by a mother who is smothering and overly protective. There are two sides to dealing with this issue. On the one hand, the daughter must understand when it is appropriate to be vulnerable, how to ask for assistance, and how to gracefully accept help from others. On the other hand, the daughter must master the art of compassionate caretaking—learning how to give to others with tact and sensitivity—without playing the "smother mother" (forcing things on them that they don't want or need) or the "grand dame" (glorying in the role of helper and unconsciously attacking the pride or worth of those getting help), and without giving more than is necessary (and unconsciously weakening the other person or fostering excessive dependency).

Keeping the following questions in mind can help the daughter stay balanced:

1. Am I feeling overburdened? Is it time to ask for help?

2. Is there someone who could do what I am struggling with much better than I, and who would be willing to do it—or to teach me how to do it more effectively?

3. Is the assistance I am providing all my idea, or has the other party openly and clearly asked for it?

4. Do I respect the person I am helping, or do I consider myself better than that person?

5. Is the help I am giving making this person weaker or stronger?

6. Can I teach this person what to do rather than do it for him or her?

Food Issues

Nurturing and nourishment are closely related, so mother issues often manifest as food issues. As indicated earlier, when severe disorders such as anorexia are present, outside intervention is imperative. This is a life-and-death issue. Do not avoid getting help!

Where the circumstances are more mild, the individual may have to weaken the association between food and security. (People who had suffered in concentration camps often hoarded and hid food afterward even though it was plentiful and readily available.) Perhaps the "comfort foods" of early childhood are overused. Perhaps "stuffing" one's self is a way to avoid uncomfortable feelings. Perhaps excess weight is seen as an unconscious bulwark against a threatening world. If we provide ourselves with other sources of security, we don't have to rely so much on food. The best source of security, of course, is faith in a Higher Power. We can also look to loving relationships, a home, pets, practical skills, and other resources to help us feel safe.

Many of us eat when we are nervous, scared, upset, bored, etc., rather than when we are hungry. Learning to listen to our bodies is the first step to mastering food issues. If we train ourselves to distinguish real hunger from other emotional states, we will have a much healthier relationship with food. If we learned unhealthy eating habits as a child, there is plenty of information available to teach us the best balance of foods to consume for good health, e.g., lots of fresh fruits and vegetables, whole grains, unprocessed meat or other protein, etc.

General Strengthening

Creating warm, cuddly environments, having a pet, creating and following family traditions and rituals, wearing silver jewelry, being in the moonlight, taking a bath or shower, or being by or in the water in any form, relating to Goddess images and religion, studying Gaia philosophy and concepts, cooking and eating (in moderation).

Reminder

If Letter 4 is overdeveloped (too much nurturing or excessive dependency), we can compensate with a greater focus on Letter(s) 1 (independence), 7 (equal sharing), 10 (practical limits), 9 (faith in a Higher Power), and/or 11 (freedom and equality for all).

Letter 5

Sun, Leo, 5th House

The major personal issues for daughters revolve around self-esteem, creativity, and giving and receiving love.

Attaining Positive Self-Esteem

Although building the self-esteem of children has become a big focus in recent years, it is all too easy for parents to overlook it in the heat of the moment and the press of everyday living. Mothers, as human beings, may succumb to the temptation to use ridicule, contempt, shaming, guilt, criticism or other means that negatively impact the daughter's self-esteem.

This is another arena where lots of seminars, therapy, and self-help books exist to address the subject. There are many affirmations to reinforce positive self-esteem. The reader is encouraged to explore all of these avenues.

One important note: A recent study in *Scientific American* suggests that it is vital to build positive self-esteem in realistic ways.[1] When studying bullies and gang members, the researchers found that people who had high *unrealistic* self-esteem were actually more violent, destructive, and cruel than people who had moderate or low self-esteem were. The first type of individuals became enraged when other people or life circumstances seemed to attack or question their unrealistically high image of themselves. (The underlying principle of the fire element is the feeling that we know what we want and should be able to do it.)

So, we do ourselves and our children no favors by building self-esteem in unrealistic ways. For positive results, we need to base praise on real accomplishments or genuine effort and attention.

Expressing Creatively

One of the basic urges of the Sun (and Leo and the 5th house) is to do something more (new or better) than we have done before, to put it out into the world, and to receive a positive response from the world. Creative self-expression is an inner drive. For some, that will be done through artistic creativity. Others may excel at advertising, sales, or promotion. One daughter may be a skilled actress, while another is a natural entertainer, and another is a beloved, admired teacher. All need an arena in which to shine, a place where they can receive positive attention and applause from other people.

---

1. Roy F. Baumeister, "Violent Pride," *Scientific American* 284, no. 4 (April 2001): 96–101.

The creative zest of Letter 5 is connected to personal vitality. We feel more excited, alive, vibrant, and happy when we are doing what we love. Finding that "bliss" is an important goal in life. People may explore many different avenues, but the search is worthwhile, because the energizing, revitalizing feeling of pouring out from your own center is quite powerful! The definition of an amateur (as opposed to a professional) is someone who does something "for the love of" it. That is the essence of Letter 5. In our games, hobbies, recreation, and creative pursuits, we do it "for the love of" it. Of course, daughters with a strong focus on Letter 5 may literally have many loves!

If a daughter is somewhat blocked in this area, her first task is to quiet her "inner critic," to focus on trying things out "just for fun." Being open to experimentation and exploring a number of different venues (potential hobbies or interests) is essential. If you are inclined to disparage your own efforts, share your creative self-expression with friends who are likely to be positive and affirming. Judgment does not really have a place in these activities. Cultivate a fun-loving, playful attitude.

Study children for role models of people who are spontaneous, eager, wanting positive attention ("Look at me, Mommy!"), playful, and full of laughter. Seminars, books, and therapeutic techniques also abound for freeing your "inner child" and encouraging creativity (such as brainstorming exercises). Explore them if you need to feed Letter 5 in your life.

Giving and Receiving Love

Letter 5 is fire by element, so it is eager to pour out and express itself in the world. If a daughter has been psychologically damaged in her childhood, she may feel blocked from giving or receiving love. If she feels unworthy, self-esteem issues have to be addressed. It may be helpful to read biographies of very loving individuals, or to read inspirational literature about the love of God. The daughter can seek out people who are extremely generous, and absorb what that feels like. She may enjoy reading romantic tales or watching romantic movies that encourage people to let love into their lives.

When building any skill, it is helpful to start with whatever foundation we have, no matter how small. If the daughter identifies the most positive relationship in her life, she can gradually transfer those positive feelings to other relationships, and then increase them. Being on the lookout for role models will help. It is much easier to learn from a positive example, whether that example is a real person, a figure from literature, a spiritual concept, an animal, etc. She can make a study of "lovability" and consciously focus on and develop those qualities that help her love and admire others as well as those qualities that are likely to make her more attractive to others.

General Strengthening

Being active creatively, loving and being loved, seeking positive attention for your talents, wearing gold jewelry, being in the sunshine (with appropriate sunblock as needed), going to the theater, playing charades, and taking opportunities to teach, lead, persuade, or share excitement with others.

Reminder

If Letter 5 is overdeveloped (e.g., the desire to be queen gets out of hand, expecting life to be all play and no work, overdramatizing life and exaggerating, or taking foolish risks), compensation can occur through focusing on Letter(s) 2, 8, 11, 10, and/or 12. For example, the arrogance and "royal" attitude of too much Letter 5 can be curtailed by a bit of compassion and sensitivity (Letter 12), discipline and limits (Letter 10), humanitarianism (Letter 11), self-mastery and self-control partly based on respect for the needs of others (Letter 8), or relaxed comfort that does not need attention or approval from others (Letter 2).

Letter 6

Mercury, Vesta, (Ceres), Virgo, 6th House

The personal issues for daughters revolve around developing practical skills, maintaining a healthy body, and using analytical and flaw-finding abilities constructively.

Developing Practical Skills

For a satisfying expression of Letter 6, we need to do something worth doing (usually a job), and do it well. A daughter can aid that process through classes or special training that will increase her skills. Apprenticeship—learning by doing—is particularly a Virgo process. Making lists or learning in a step-by-step process is apt to be effective. Mastering one part of the task at a time allows us to hone our abilities. If a daughter feels she is weak in Letter 6 drives, it might be helpful to take a class in handicrafts, plumbing, carpentry, sewing, crocheting, knitting, model-making, or other tangible, result-oriented activities. Seeing the fruits of her labors is very important, and being able to measure results matters much.

If a daughter's confidence in her competence has been extremely damaged, she needs to start with very small projects. Beginning with the smallest of challenges ensures success. Each success makes the next one a bit easier to achieve.

Individuals with an emphasis on Letter 6 "need" to be productive. They feel guilty if they are not doing something. Such individuals are apt to never completely "retire." They will continue to make a contribution, to be of service, to do something useful, no matter what their chronological age.

Maintaining a Healthy Body

In today's world, there is plenty of information available on maintaining radiant good health. We know the importance of eating a healthy diet, that regular exercise is the best antidote to aging, and that sufficient rest, relaxation, play, and loving human relationships are all factors in good health and a long life. We are somewhat at the mercy of polluted air, water, and other toxins in our environment, but we do have a large measure of control over many other factors that contribute to excellent health. Yet, most of us continue to do things we know are not good for us!

To a large extent, this is because we allow short-term gratification to take over, ignoring the long-term consequences of our behavior, particularly of damaging lifestyle choices such as smoking or excessive drinking. Large numbers of people could benefit from strengthening the Letter 6 drives in their nature.

We may choose to start taking vitamins. We may elect to design an exercise regimen and/or an improved diet—and follow it faithfully. (Like all cases of the earth element, Letter 6 does best if you establish a regular routine.) We might join a gym, start working with a personal trainer, or just make it a habit to make our physical well-being a priority. Often this means we have to overcome self-critical messages or feelings of unworthiness, which are indicative of the flaw-finding skills being misdirected.

Using Analytical and Flaw-Finding Abilities Constructively

Letter 6 "belongs" in the 6th house. Letter 6 represents efficient functioning both in our work and in maintaining a healthy body. In most horoscopes, however, Letter 6 is "mixed" with something else. If mixed with Letter 1, the flaw-finding can be directed (perhaps too harshly) at the self. If mixed with Letters 7 and/or 8, nitpicking and critical judgments can be a problem in peer relationships, etc. If mixed with Letters 9 and/or 12, the individual may yearn for the beautiful dream and feel judgmental of every way in which the world falls short or is imperfect. These are the two sides of perfectionism: the desire for the ideal, and the focus on the failure to attain it.

If a daughter has been conditioned to use her Letter 6 analytical skills in a nonconstructive manner, the first step toward improvement is to recognize that these abilities can be positive if directed into the right arenas in life. Simply identifying flaws may not be helpful. We need to analyze ways to correct the flaws. Also, critical judgments are best directed at projects or problems, not at people's personalities.

If the self-criticism—or criticism directed at the daughter from others—has been pervasive and intense, she may need to develop some of the other sides of life to help balance and compensate. Letter 12 can offer needed compassion and forgiveness, and, along with Letter 9, reminds us to let the Infinite do part of the job. Letter 1 can offer the capacity to focus on personal drives and desires, and Letter 11 repeats the need for personal freedom. Letter 3 can teach us how to "lighten up" and not take life so seriously.

The "transfer" concept is very valuable in making improvements to our lives. When we recognize that we have a talent or have done something well in one area of life, we can learn how to "transfer" those skills to another area. So, a daughter who has strong analytical skills, organizing abilities, flaw-finding faculties, and the mind of an efficiency expert can transfer those abilities to her job and become the superemployee. Or, she can transfer those abilities to her physical functioning and become radiantly healthy. The trine from Letter 2 can also help her enjoy the process and not wait until the work is finished to be happy.

General Strengthening

Honing a practical skill, doing handicrafts, working humbly behind the scenes, taking classes for mental discipline, making lists, learning how to take things apart and put them back together, doing time/motion studies or other means to increase efficiency, eating a healthy diet, practicing deductive reasoning, organizing and ordering files and other areas of your life, gardening, wearing earthy colors.

Reminder

If Letter 6 is overdeveloped, we can compensate through an emphasis on Letter(s) 3, 9, 12, 11, and/or 1. The workaholic of Letter 6 can take things more lightly with Letter 3, gain needed detachment with Letter 11, or pay more attention to personal needs with Letter 1. The nitpicking, detail focus of Letter 6 is balanced by the broad perspectives of Letter 9 and the mystical empathy of Letter 12.

Letter 7

Venus, Pallas, Libra, 7th House

The major personal issues for the daughter are establishing healthy partnerships, making a place for competition, and expressing grace, beauty, and elegance.

Establishing Healthy Partnerships

Letter 7 needs an "other" with whom to relate. For many of us, the most significant other is a marital or romantic partner. Some people, however, find their truest partnership with a close friend, or with a child who becomes a friend. For daughters with a strong focus on Libra, Venus, Pallas, or the 7th house, it is vital to develop and maintain a healthy partnership with one or more people.

If the daughter received very negative role models for relationships, she can consciously seek out positive ones to emulate, e.g., teachers, spiritual advisors, inspirational examples in literature or biographies, suggestions and aid from psychological texts and self-help books, seminars, etc. The daughter can take classes or read about what constitutes a healthy relationship. For example, John Gottman and others in Washington State have been studying what makes for a successful, happy marriage. The most important factors are discussed in their book *Why Marriages Succeed or Fail.*[2] This book is based on quantifiable research, including measuring stress reactions between couples while they are interacting. The researchers have a 94 percent accuracy level in predicting divorce.

Role-playing increases empathy and insight into the other person's point of view. Like any skill, building and enhancing relationships is aided by practice. The more the daughter works on it, the better she can become at creating and maintaining healthy relationships.

If the daughter has been conditioned to be too accommodating, constantly trying to please and appease others, she is likely to be overdoing Letter 7. She can compensate by concentrating particularly on Letter 1 (what she wants as a solitary individual and asserting herself) and Letter 10 (strong, responsible, authoritative).

A Place for Competition

Letter 7 emphasizes face-to-face interactions, but these can be competitive as well as cooperative. Assuming that everything will always be "sweetness and light" will only lead to disappointment. (There are plenty of lawyers and generals with a focus on Libra or the 7th

---

2. John M. Gottman (with Nan Silver contributor), *Why Marriages Succeed or Fail* (New York: Simon & Schuster, 1995).

house.) For the best results, daughters are advised to adopt at least one competitive out-let—for the "fighting side" of Libra. This could be through a sport of any kind, or it might be a game such as chess, card games, board games, etc. The daughter might choose to com-pete in the business world or to test her strength against an opponent in the political or legal world. Along the way, she could develop considerable skills as a negotiator.

It is vital for the daughter to learn to identify who is on her "team" and who is not. With team members (such as children, loved ones, good friends), we are supposed to cooperate and aid one another's efforts. With opponents (in the courtroom, on the tennis court, in courting material success in the business world), we can be competitive. If the daughter masters both areas, she can win (and be gracious to her opponents) or lose (and not be emotionally or otherwise destroyed), and remember that it is just a game (practice that air detachment).

If the mother gave the daughter unclear messages about this distinction, there could have been competition between the mother and daughter. In extreme cases, this is the mother who tries to "steal" her daughter's boyfriends or who is constantly "showing up" the daughter because the mother knows more and has more experience. To recover, the daugh-ter has to recognize that the mother had an unfair advantage—being older and wiser—and seek out level playing fields for future competition. The daughter will also have to find other positive role models to teach her how to have mutually supportive partnerships.

Such a daughter may grow up to expect loved ones to compete with her, which con-tributes to a scarcity mentality (believing in limited resources and willing to take away from others) rather than an abundance mentality. The daughter could end up having power struggles with loved ones, rather than seeking win-win solutions.

The way out is for the daughter to recognize who is on her team, and to treat them with empathy, consideration, and kindness. She also needs to maintain some kind of competi-tive outlet for the more feisty one-on-one interactions. That way, the daughter can have the best of both worlds!

Expressing Grace, Beauty, and Elegance

People with a strong focus on Letter 7 in their horoscope "need" beauty in their lives. They may find it by creating a lovely home and/or working environment, by becoming an artist, by being close to nature's grandeur, by collecting lovely things, by dancing or engaging in other forms of "grace in motion," etc. How things (and people) look matters to them.

Although it is important not to overvalue appearances, these individuals must recognize that having harmony and elegance in their lives is a physical need. Fortunately, they have a wide array of choices as to how to fill their lives with beauty, and lots of talent to call upon.

If a daughter's aesthetic urges were constrained by her mother's conditioning, it is essential for the daughter to recognize that she craves beauty, and that she will feel better and be happier if she has regular, ongoing contact with something lovely in her life. Again, she can choose from many different venues or forms of expression. It is interesting that Letters 2 and 12 (the quincunxes to Letter 7) also seek to enjoy beauty, but do not require human peer relationships for their pleasure. The other keys to a balanced life include Letter 1 (which keeps some space in the life for personal independence), Letter 4 (which can be dependent or nurturing when appropriate), and Letter 10 (which copes with power in the world, power people, and personal responsibility).

General Strengthening

Walking on a balance beam, polarity therapy, training as a mediator, classes in fine art, cultivating good taste, graphic arts, interior design, photography, fashion, painting, wearing pastel colors, beautifying your own appearance or environment, practicing relating to a wide array of people on a one-on-one basis.

Reminder

If Letter 7 is overdeveloped (vacillating, too other-directed, style over substance), we can compensate with a focus on Letter(s) 1 (personal needs), 4 (family orientation), 10 (responsibility and career), 12 (a mystical connection to all of life), and/or 2 (pleasure from the material world—rather than people).

Letter 8
Pluto, Juno, Scorpio, 8th House

The major personal issues for daughters revolve around gaining self-understanding and self-mastery; learning to give, receive, and share power, possessions, and pleasures; and overcoming obsessions, addictions, and depression.

Gaining Self-Understanding and Self-Mastery

The easiest way for a daughter to gain self-understanding and self-mastery is through a positive therapeutic relationship. Karen Horney (a therapist) once said that she takes her clients' neuroses, which are like a mask or blinders in front of their faces, and turns them into outboard motors—a source of strength and power. The goal of a healthy therapeutic relationship is transforming negative emotions into positive ones. If the relationship between the mother and daughter was particularly destructive (e.g., an abusive, cruel, vindictive, power-hungry, invasive mother), some therapy is advisable. The wounds are likely to be rather deep.

If the daughter chooses to work on herself without a therapist, she can take psychology classes or read widely in self-help books or inspirational tomes. She can talk to people, asking questions and paying attention to how they act. She can seek out positive role models to emulate. She can make lists of how she wants to transform herself, and keep track of her progress. She may use occult tools of all kinds (such as meditation, rituals, Tarot, etc.), or keep a journal to gain additional insight into her psyche. Her strength of will, ability to focus and concentrate, and perseverance will be her most valuable resources in this process.

Learning to Give, Receive, and Share Power, Possessions, and Pleasures

The "urge to merge" is strong in Letter 8. Pluto, Juno, Scorpio, and the 8th house yearn for a mate—for someone with whom they can share the secrets of their soul, someone who can deal with their intensity, someone who is capable of the tremendous depth of commitment that they seek. The stakes are high, and many people with a focus on Letter 8 have retreated into a hermit lifestyle when they felt let down, abused, abandoned, betrayed, or otherwise wounded by an intimate other. Part of the reward for dealing with heavy Letter 8 issues is building a deep, intimate relationship with at least one other person. Generally, this includes a sexual bond—but not always. The most important element is psychological intimacy—opening up and being totally vulnerable and honest with the other person, and creating a safe environment for that person to do the same with you.

If the mother's example for the ability to give, receive, and share sex, money, and power is negative, the daughter has a tougher job. (It is always easier to learn from a positive example). The daughter is best off getting a wide range of experience by examining lots of intimate relationships. She can talk to people about how they share with others, or read books on the topic. She can contemplate the issue of fairness, or design dilemmas or questions and then try to answer them. For example, if one partner makes a lot more money than the other, but the other is working in a highly creative, but low-paying, field, is what they are both giving and getting from one another fair?

If the daughter got exceedingly destructive messages about money from her mother (e.g.,compulsive gambler, shopaholic, extremely withholding), it may be helpful to get therapeutic intervention. It may also be helpful for the daughter to take classes in managing money and to educate herself about financial realities.

If the daughter got extremely negative messages about sexuality (or her own sexuality) from her mother, she may have to get amelioration through counseling or sex therapy. Or, she can read up on the topic and design her own regimen of slow, careful steps to reestablish a pleasurable relationship with her body, and to learn to enjoy foreplay and eventually lovemaking.

Often, in the mother-daughter relationship, there is an imbalance in terms of giving and receiving. Some of this is due to age differences. If it is chronic and overdone, the daughter may be conditioned to be a perpetual "giver" or she may be conditioned to be a chronic "taker." With the former, the daughter will unconsciously attract individuals who use and abuse her sexually, who take advantage of her financially, or who are generally withholding and "stingy," emotionally and otherwise. With the latter, the daughter will feel "entitled" to certain things in a relationship, may get angry if her lover does not give her what she feels she deserves, or will unconsciously expect to be pampered.

To overcome these patterns, the daughter must first recognize that there is a pattern. Then, she can change it—with time, effort, and patience. It is best done through repetition and practice, and she must give herself permission and forgiveness for occasional backsliding. She can find positive examples in her environment to emulate, and read books or take classes or therapy to get additional support, suggestions, and helpful techniques. Feedback from others—particularly those who she trusts to be objective—can help her decide what an equitable arrangement might look like. Acting "as if" (even before the new behavior is established as a habit) will help solidify the new behavior. In other words, do what you know is right or healthy for you, even if it does not yet feel "natural."

Facing and Overcoming Obsessions, Addictions, and Depression

Letter 8 is an "all or nothing" side of life, and is associated—on the negative side—with addictions, obsessions, compulsive behavior, and depression. There are a number of excellent self-help books and 12-Step programs to deal with just about any addiction: Alcoholics Anonymous, Gamblers Anonymous, Overeaters Anonymous, Narcotics Anonymous, etc. The issues of Letter 8, because they are so deep-rooted and emotionally intense, are harder to handle alone. So, having a therapist or a support group is a good idea.

Depression can occur because Letter 8 is inclined to look on the dark side of life. An excess of Letter 8 can be ameliorated with more joie de vivre (Letter 5), the ability take life lightly (Letter 3), a focus on comfortable pleasure and acceptance (Letter 2), or intellectual understanding and detachment (Letter 11). In some cases, medication is useful. In others, therapy alone may do the trick. Or, the person (in mild cases) may train herself to get out of depression by using the air element (broad perspective and detachment), the fire element (action that carries out personal desires), or the earth element (productive work).

An essential step of the healing process is for the daughter to forgive and let go emotionally. (Letter 8 has a tendency to hang on too long emotionally.) Studies have demonstrated the physical (as well as mental and emotional) dangers of excessive anger, resentment, etc. Where deep hurts are present, it is vital for the daughter to forgive her mother—not the behavior if it was destructive, but to forgive the mother as a fallible human being. It is equally essential for the daughter to forgive herself—for not being able to protect herself when young, for not being able to "fix" everything, for not being perfect and in total control and mastery of herself. This releasing of emotion will allow full healing to take place. (See also the rituals for letting go that are in the Appendix.)

General Strengthening

Going through closets, files, etc., and cleaning up, clearing out, throwing out, or giving away; reading detective stories; psychotherapy; keeping a journal; any investigative work, occult studies; building physical stamina and endurance, exploring Kundalini concepts, wearing purples, reds, or dark colors, making a will, doing hospice work, raising money for a political candidate; forgiving and letting go.

Reminder

If Letter 8 is overdeveloped, we can compensate by emphasizing Letter(s) 2 (comfort, pleasure), 5 (joy, elan), 11 (intellectual detachment), 1 (direct, open, spontaneous action), and/or 3 (the light touch).

Letter 9

Jupiter, (Chiron), Sagittarius, 9th House

The major personal issues for daughters revolve around developing faith in a Higher Power, creating self-confidence, and establishing a constructive moral and ethical system.

Developing Faith in a Higher Power

In most people's lives, there are times when everything just seems overwhelming. It is at such moments that faith in a Higher Power provides the saving grace. As long as we believe we are alone in the universe, or that everything rests upon our own shoulders, burdens can seem unbearable. If we can trust in something greater than ourselves, if we believe in a loving Supreme Being, or that justice wins out in the end, we can usually move forward. Having the faith that we will receive aid if needed can give us the impetus to take action.

If a daughter had a mother who lacked faith—or a mother whose actions damaged the daughter's faith—she can seek to rebuild it in several ways:

1. Hang around people with faith. Trust in something Higher is contagious. It is more likely to "rub off" if you associate with other people who believe.

2. Read inspirational literature, particularly religious, spiritual, or metaphysical books that feed your sense of purpose, trust, and confidence. Reading biographies of people who have overcome tremendous barriers or challenges is another possibility.

3. Meditate and explore spiritual practices or avenues that might lead to mystical experiences.

4. Work with affirmations that accentuate faith and the goodness of life.

5. Look for connections and links that suggest an underlying meaning and purpose to life.

6. Read "my proof of survival" or "life after life" experiences.

Creating Self-Confidence

Everyone needs some faith in a Higher Power, but also some faith in herself since God won't do it all. We have to do our share. A mother can damage her child's self-confidence in all too many ways: making disparaging remarks (destructive expression of Letter 6), being a Supermom so that the child feels inadequate in comparison, ignoring the child as if she does not matter, sabotaging the child's attempts at gaining power, handicapping the daughter's attempts to gain skills or competence, etc.

Building self-confidence is best done slowly and gradually. It is particularly important for the daughter to ensure that her earliest experiences are successful. Doing well will reinforce her confidence for the next step, while doing poorly may make further action even tougher. You can select something that you can do and want to do, and then do it. Then, select something slightly more challenging. Build toward doing more and more. The more you do, the more you will feel confident that you can do even more.

Seeking out friends and associates who reinforce your self-confidence can also be helpful. Hanging out with positive people will encourage you to look on the bright side of life. Consider making a list of your assets and abilities, and then read them over and over as a reminder. Ask yourself regularly, "What is positive about this situation?" "What can I do to improve these circumstances?" "Can it help me grow?"

Recognizing that people have different kinds of skills and abilities is important. Sometimes our confidence suffers because we compare ourselves to others, particularly to others who are older and wiser, who have more experience, or who have special skills or training that we lack. The daughter can strengthen her confidence by remembering that each of us is different. Sometimes, exposure to a wider array of people, including some from other lands and cultures, will aid this process.

As the daughter reinforces her faith and trust in herself, she will establish a healthy sense of adventure and exploration. She will become more willing to venture into the unknown, to explore new territory physically, mentally, emotionally, and spiritually.

Establishing a Constructive Moral and Ethical System

Each of us grows up thinking that the way we were raised is normal and "right." If the mother was particularly destructive, the daughter may have to do extra work to formulate a healthier moral and ethical system. The first step is recognizing that our family of origin is not necessarily the healthiest environment. The second step is to read widely, discuss ideas with other people, observe behavior, and explore options. By combining common sense, empathy, and compassion, the daughter can design a reasonable system of morality and ethical behavior, or she can adopt one from a religion or philosophy that appeals to her.

While the daughter is formulating her worldview and belief system (a process that we continue to refine over a lifetime), she would do well to ensure that her approach allows her to establish a hierarchy of values ("This is more important than that") and to establish clear priorities for her to follow.

Sometimes the issue is that Mom's moral and ethical framework was excessively rigid or demanding. Some parents think that children should be little adults or little angels, and are unnecessarily harsh, judgmental, or punitive when children act like children. It might be helpful for the daughter to read up on child development, particularly if she plans on having children of her own, so that she has some idea of the range of behavior that is considered "normal."

It will be easier to live in a pluralistic society if the daughter also makes sure that the moral and ethical system and worldview she adopts leaves room for tolerating other beliefs and viewpoints. Letter 3 sees and accepts a broad perspective with room for many different ideas. Letter 6 reminds us to be practical in our expectations. Letter 12 offers compassion and empathy to forgive failure to reach goals. Letter 4 also offers emotional support, and Letter 2 says it is okay to be human and enjoy the world, even when it is not perfect.

General Strengthening

Reading inspirational literature, travel, studying metaphysics or philosophy, associating with people from other cultures, finding rainbows, developing more humor, wearing royal blue, writing down long-term goals, getting further education, writing.

Reminder

If Letter 9 is overdeveloped, we can compensate with an emphasis on Letter(s) 3, 6, 12, 2, and/or 4. Letter 3 reminds us of everyday ideas and communication (not everything is a major philosophical breakthrough). Letter 12's compassion balances the intellectual focus of Letter 9. Letters 2 and 6 keep us grounded in the material world with a sense of achievement, and Letter 4 brings the focus from faraway to family.

Letter 10

Saturn, Capricorn, 10th House

The major personal issues for the daughter revolve around owning one's own expertise, establishing an appropriate status, making a contribution to society, and learning what one can, cannot, and must do.

Owning One's Own Expertise

One of the basic tasks of Letter 10 is that each of us develop our own expertise—identify and strengthen those talents and abilities that allow us to make a contribution to society. In that process, we may overcome blocks and barriers and learn to deal with authority figures appropriately.

If Mother has been an overly dictatorial, controlling parent, we need to break the unconscious script that power is bad, and realize that power itself is neutral. How we wield it is what matters. If the daughter has been criticized, controlled, and constricted, she will have to learn—mostly by experience—that she can do more than she has been given credit for. Since earth is the element involved, the best way for Letter 10 to master skills is to actually do something. Apprenticeship types of training work very well.

The downward spiral of failure breeding more doubts and failure is a danger with Letter 10. If depression and self-blocking kick in, the daughter may feel stuck. The best approach is to choose very small tasks initially. By selecting a challenge that is doable, the daughter achieves success and makes the next success more likely. Planning ahead carefully also increases the likelihood that she will succeed. The motto of one strong Capricorn client is "Proper planning prevents poor performance."

When Letter 10 is emphasized, people may give too much weight to traditional measures of success such as money, degrees in education, high status, etc. Part of the daughter's challenge is to realize that she has her own strengths and abilities, even if she initially lacks some of these traditional measures of success. She learns—usually through direct experience—that degrees do not automatically confer wisdom and that riches and high status do not automatically confer happiness. She might speed up that process by examining the people in her life and noting how often traditional measures of success correlate with personal excellence—and how often they do not. She could read stories or talk to people who have achieved much without getting all the degrees or other tools traditionally considered to be essential. She could learn that age may bring wisdom—but it is not a guarantee. By observing what others do well and what they do poorly, she can improve her own chances for success.

Because tangible, measurable results matter much, the daughter would do well to make lists, to learn in a step-by-step fashion, to plan carefully, and to formulate a clear plan of action. Special or technical training can add to her expertise.

Establishing an Appropriate Status and Making a Contribution to Society

Letter 10 needs to work and to take appropriate responsibility and power. The daughter's challenge is to identify her gift(s) to the world. This might be in terms of a career (or several careers). Or, it might be through community work, neighborhood action, strengthening her own family and others, etc. The key is taking responsibility to create a particular outcome, and then devoting the effort necessary to make it happen.

If the mother's actions have crippled the daughter's sense of competence, the daughter will need to rebuild slowly and carefully. Small initial successes will make it possible for much larger ones later. The daughter may wish to undergo vocational testing, to talk to people in different jobs, to make lists of the qualities she would like to find in her career, and to observe how other people work. If her upbringing has neglected some of the basic "facts of life" about the working world, she may have to learn how to dress and talk appropriately, the importance of being on time, the proper protocol within an office or working environment, or how to be reliable and responsible. The more she practices, the better she will get.

If the daughter has been overburdened (used as a workhorse from a young age), she may need to learn the limits of her responsibility. She may be inclined to take on too much, to unconsciously assume that she is supposed to do it all. It is better for her to get clearly defined job descriptions and measurements of accountability. (Otherwise, she might go to the extreme of having to get sick to get a break.) It would be a good idea to ask herself regularly, "Is this really my job?" "Can someone else do this?" "Does this really have to be done by me (or done at all)?"

If the daughter has been treated in a low-status fashion, she will need time, patience, and practice to get more comfortable taking on authority and working from a higher-status position. She may have to relate to some good managers to help break the unconscious connection she feels between power and its abuse. She may want to read or get extra training to develop her skills for taking charge.

Identifying What One Can, Cannot, and Must Do

A key issue with Letter 10 is dealing constructively with the limits of the world. People who ignore the limits may break the law, damage their own health, or keep on hitting barriers and blocks because they are attempting the impossible. People who see or feel that there are more limits than actually exist end up blocking themselves because they are afraid to try, are sure of failure, or are accustomed to a world where authority figures constantly constrain them. Such daughters may be prone to depression and negative thinking.

More than any other side of life, with Letter 10, in order to prove our strength or to demonstrate our abilities (to ourselves and others), we must *do* something. The Nike motto "Just do it!" is all too appropriate. People dealing with Letter 10 issues must force themselves to take action, even when they fear failure. Often, they discover that the task was not as fearsome nor as difficult as they had anticipated.

Because the downward cycle of failure is a very real risk, it is vital for the daughter to start small, to choose initially a small task that she feels she is highly likely to achieve. With each successful accomplishment, she builds her confidence and her competence to achieve the next one.

It is helpful for the daughter to get a clear understanding of the "rules of the game" in which she is working. This includes reading about corporate culture (or about whatever culture she is working in), talking to colleagues to get a clear sense of what is expected, and having as much as possible in writing—clearly defined. Accountability is important, and clear expectations are vital. If she is not sure exactly what a boss or coworker wants, she should ask for clarification.

If the daughter has a habit of undervaluing her abilities (Mom might have been punitive, or kept her very dependent, or crippled her attempts to achieve), the daughter would do well to seek out people who can realistically remind her of her strengths. Making a list of her abilities (and reading them over and over) can be helpful. Reminding herself of what she has already achieved is a good idea. She can also use the transfer principle of applying skills that have been valuable in one arena to other arenas.

General Strengthening

Working hard, taking responsibility, training to be an executive, making lists, collecting rocks or minerals, fixing or improving your teeth, knees, or hearing, wearing black or dark colors, putting your experience and the wisdom of older people to use.

Reminder

If Letter 10 is overdeveloped, we can compensate by emphasizing Letter(s) 4, 7, 1, 3, and/or 5. Letter 4 reminds us that dependency is a part of life: no one can be in control of everything all the time. Letter 7 can allow peers to have part of the power. Letters 1 and 5 make a place for personal power that needs to be used wisely within the "rules of the game." Letter 3 offers humor, a broad perspective, and flexibility to balance the Letter 10 dangers of being overly serious, narrowly focused, and rigid.

Letter 11

Uranus, Aquarius, 11th House

The major personal issues for daughters revolve around knowing when to break the rules, enjoying individuality, and establishing a good network of like-minded people.

Knowing When to Break the Rules—and Which Ones to Break

There are times when our life pattern (or society) becomes too calcified or rigid. At those moments, we need to be able to break through the barriers and boundaries, to go against the "standard operating procedures." Part of the essence of Letter 11 is to be able to break the rules, but this is only healthy if we have good discrimination in regard to which rules ought to be broken.

A daughter's capacity for rebellion may have been initially crippled by a mother who was extremely rigid, controlling, and rule-bound. The daughter may unconsciously fear change. Once she recognizes the pattern, she can begin to make very small (and less threatening) changes, like getting out of bed from the other side, fixing her hair differently, taking another route to work, trying a new flavor of ice cream, etc. As the daughter experiments more and alters more of the routines in her life, she can become more comfortable with trying out the new and letting go of what has been established.

There are also exercises one can learn for brainstorming and creativity. (For example, take five minutes to write down as many different uses as possible for a brick.) The daughter can hang out with highly original, inventive people and read about trailblazers and groundbreakers in the world. She can adopt people who are open to change as her role models. She can make a point of doing something different every day, every hour—just for the practice.

If the mother overdid Letter 11 motifs to such an extent that the daughter felt her mom was cold, aloof, or unpredictable, the daughter can compensate with the warmth and nurturing of Letter 4 (one of the quincunxes), the love and passion of Letter 5 (the opposition), or the intimacy and psychological understanding of Letter 8 (one of the squares). The daughter may have to seek her emotional connections and support from good friends or from the family that she creates if her mother is simply unavailable.

A daughter whose mother was extremely unconventional, such as the "hippie" mom, may feel that her only path of rebellion lies in becoming very conventional. (One such mother lamented that she had married late, traveled to India and all over the world, raised her daughter in a very open, almost communal style, and the daughter rebelled by marrying at age eighteen the first man with whom she had a serious, sexual commitment.) Over time, such daughters may learn that there is a happy medium between conventionality and unconventionality.

It may be helpful for the daughter to ask herself such questions as, "Is there another way to look at this situation?" "Are there other options that I haven't thought about?" "Would someone from a different race/gender/cultural background/country view this differently or have other ideas?" "If I were a visiting space alien and not a part of this culture, what would I think of this behavior or practice?"

Naturally, some daughters will carry the rebellion too far, perhaps to the point of taking serious risks physically, emotionally, or mentally. Tough consequences may cause them to rethink their behavior. Or, as they get older (particularly past the rashness of the teenage years), they may begin to examine themselves and life a bit more objectively.

In order to weigh and balance rebellious acts, the daughter must clarify her intentions and values. Does efficiency matter most to her? On the job, she might ask herself whether established procedures are the most effective or if perhaps a new approach would get the job done better or faster. Is protecting people's feelings very important to her? In some cases, following protocol or taking indirect approaches will do that better. Does she yearn for a sense of inner creativity? In such cases, she needs to seek fresh answers and new possibilities actively and often. Projecting ahead to determine the logical consequences of different lines of behavior will also help her choose wisely. And, sometimes, the daughter will be extremely rebellious and unconventional in her thinking and beliefs, even though she chooses to keep her outer behavior conventional and circumspect. The key lies in really understanding herself, so she can identify her own best interests.

Enjoying Individuality

A major motif with Letter 11 is individuality. Each of us is a special, unique human being. Some mothers, however, are uncomfortable with daughters who are different. They may have been harsh, punitive, and unaccepting of their daughters, trying to turn them into carbon copies of themselves. Such daughters may fare better by reading about highly unusual people, particularly geniuses and "outcasts" who contributed significantly to society. The daughters may find their own group of friends who encourage them to be true to their inner nature. They may find solace in spiritual paths or religions that cherish individuality. They will be most effective if they rebel first in one minor area. Once they are comfortable with their first act of being different, they can move on to more significant acts of rebellion.

At times, the daughter may take her rebellious behavior to the extreme. In trying to prove how different she is from her mother, the daughter may go in the opposite direction—perhaps too far. Striving for true objectivity (an air talent) will help. The daughter can get feedback, get to know (or read about) a wide range of people, study the vast differences between cultures and personalities, and observe what behaviors are apt to bring more satisfaction in our society. The outer accoutrements are the most visible way to rebel (clothes, hair, makeup, body piercing, etc.), but the inner decisions are ultimately the most important.

One of the developmental tasks of adulthood is to clearly differentiate ourselves from our family of origin. Daughters, particularly, have to work on that with their mothers, because they are both female, so there tends to be a strong unconscious connection. It may be helpful for the daughter to literally make a list of how she sees herself as similar to her mother (from physical appearance and characteristics to mental, emotional, and spiritual ones) and how she sees herself as different. If she wants to change or add to either side of the list, she then has more information.

If the daughter has established clear moral and ethical principles and a hierarchy of values (Letter 9), it will be easier for her to identify the ways in which she wants to be different from her mother—and perhaps much of society as well. She can be a rebel in effective ways.

If the daughter was conditioned to feel totally unacceptable and strange, she may continue as an adult to feel like an alien, outcast, or stranger in a strange land. Adopting the viewpoint of an outsider can be helpful, at times. We more clearly see the biases and assumptions of a society if we take on the persona of an anthropologist, visiting space alien, or other nonmember of the orthodoxy. If this outsider role is too painful, however, the daughter will need to consciously seek out friends who can be supportive, who share some of her unconventional beliefs or behaviors. Literature is full of outrageous characters who can serve as partial role models. A therapy group could offer additional support. Studying and reminding herself of the close connection between originality, genius, and being a "misfit" can also be helpful.

Establishing a Good Network of Like-Minded People

Letter 11 belongs to the air element, and thus includes affiliative tendencies. With these drives, the daughter wants to make a difference in the wider world—to aid humanity or social progress, to join forces with like-minded people. The purpose might be curiosity, mental stimulation, studying or advancing new technology, or any number of humanitarian or future-oriented activities, such as working to support democracy and promote tolerance.

If the daughter has faced rejection from her mother or ostracism when younger, finding a group into which she can "fit" becomes more important. Human beings are social animals. We need some support from others. With Letter 11, this can be somewhat distant and casual, but still valuable as she shares ideas and contacts with other people. The daughter may have to do a lot of searching to find a group that fits her needs, or discover her special friends one by one, but it is worth the effort. Nowadays, there are groups and magazines that cater to just about any special interest, and you can find many of them through the Internet (with the usual cautions applying).

If the mother carried Letter 11 group activities too far (e.g., spending more time at the country club or socializing with friends more than with her family), then the daughter will have to do more "homework" in terms of figuring out what an appropriate balance is for her. She needs to have a network of buddies, but in balance with other priorities in life! Sometimes it helps to make a bar graph or pie chart of how we spend our time over one week. Seeing a black-and-white representation may lead the daughter to make some different choices in how she allocates her time.

General Strengthening

Breaking outmoded rules, strengthening your ankles or enhancing your circulation, studying avant-garde art or concepts, learning about new technology, developing a wide network of very different friends, wearing electric blue or unusual outfits, brainstorming or encouraging inventive thinking.

Reminder

If Letter 11 is overdeveloped, we can compensate through an emphasis on Letter(s) 2, 5, 8, 4, and/or 6. Letters 2 and 6 remind us that living in the physical world requires some practicality. Letters 4, 5, and 8 remind us that a few close emotional relationships are an important part of life.

Letter 12

Neptune, (Chiron), Pisces, 12th House

The major personal issues for the daughter revolve around creating and enjoying grace and beauty, tuning in to an Infinite Source, and helping and healing.

Creating/Enjoying Beauty and Grace

There is an intense need for beauty in the life when Letter 12 is strong in the horoscope. The daughter may pursue that through appreciating the beauty of nature, through artistic expression or appreciation, making lovely things, moving with grace and elegance, or other aesthetic avenues. She will be happier—and feel better physically—if she has consistent and regular contact with beauty in her life.

In some cases, the mother will have overemphasized keeping things "nice" and "pretty," and the daughter will need to learn that appearance is not everything. Perhaps the mother treated the daughter like a cute little doll to dress up and got upset if the daughter got dirty playing or stepped out of her "little angel" role. Perhaps the mother was willing to "play pretend" and lie to herself and others rather than recognize the less pleasant or imperfect aspects of life.

In such circumstances, the daughter will have to balance the quest for infinite beauty with a recognition of reality. The facts of life (Letter 6's pragmatic approach) can complement our aesthetic and idealistic yearnings if we integrate them. Otherwise, they will often clash and bring disillusionment and disappointment. The daughter may have to learn through experience when and where to give beauty priority, and how to balance that need with other sides of life.

If the daughter's aesthetic inclinations have been blocked and stifled, she will have the chance as an adult to explore different venues. She may try a wide variety of artistic avenues before choosing one (or more) that is personally satisfying. She may take classes, experiment on her own, join a group, etc. Through experience, she will learn to appreciate the process, without demanding a particular, precise goal. That is, the picture she sees in her mind's eye (or the music she hears, the garden she envisions, etc.) may not exactly match what she creates in the material world. The process of creating and appreciating beauty is what feeds her psyche. If she insists on perfect results every time, she will be frustrated and chronically discontented.

Other aspects of this talent are visualization skills and a strong imagination, which can be useful in a wide variety of fields and different life circumstances. With practice, the daughter will get better and better at finding a balance between what her imagination and intuition suggest, and what the actual facts and circumstances imply.

Tuning into an Infinite Source

One of the greatest gifts of Letter 12 is the capacity to reconnect with All That Is—the mystical Union with the Whole. A daughter who develops this ability at a young age (perhaps encouraged by her mother or seeing her mother's example) will have a tremendous reservoir of faith and inner strength to see her through just about any trial or tribulation.

If the daughter was raised in a very materialistic household, or one that did not consider or emphasize such mystical concepts, she is likely to keep searching throughout her life for that cosmic connection. Some people indulge in drugs, alcohol, or other addictive substances in the quest for that sense of merging, of losing the self. Some people put their partner up on pedestal and look to that person to be God—to provide "Heaven on Earth." Some people idealize a home, a parent, a child, etc.

If the daughter puts anything or anyone up on a pedestal, she is likely to lose that thing or person in order to find a larger faith. We can find infinite power and potential in a Higher Power, in nature, but are doomed to experience disappointment if we look for Ultimate answers and satisfaction through another human being, a bank account, or any limited material thing. Sometimes, the parent is literally missing with Letter 12, and the child creates a dream image of what she would have/could have been like. In adulthood, we have to balance those wishes and fantasies with what is possible in the real world (the opposition between Pisces and Virgo).

The daughter needs an emotional experience of merging with something greater than herself. Mystical and meditative practices may help. Yoga, tai chi, and other practices that blend the physical and spiritual are options. Reading about the lives of saints and mystics is another possibility. Associating with people who have experienced cosmic consciousness may aid the daughter in her quest. Being in nature may provide that "swept away" feeling. There are many paths to Higher Consciousness that are worthy of exploration.

Helping and Healing (While Avoiding Martyrdom)

Charity comes easily to Letter 12. People with a strong focus on Neptune, Pisces, or the 12th house can find much satisfaction is assisting the less fortunate, aiding the downtrodden, or helping to make a better world. Many of the healing professions are good choices, including medicine, physical therapy, social work, psychology, massage, nutritional counseling, etc. Because Letter 12 is extremely empathic, individuals with a focus here can feel the pain of others, and will put much effort into alleviating that suffering.

Sometimes the urge to "rescue" can be overdone. In some families, the assisting instincts are carried to an extreme. Mother could have been a martyr, or might have expected her daughter to become a martyr. Ideals of femininity may encourage self-sacrifice. The urge to "make it all better" can lead to some women giving way too much in relationships. A daughter dealing with such a background needs to look to the oppositions (Letter 6's pragmatism) and other conflict aspects to be able to set clear boundaries and keep a balance between idealism and realism. The "Rescue Triangle" from Transactional Analysis (a form of therapy) warns us that if our help is making someone weaker instead of stronger, we are in danger of martyrdom or of being put down by the very people we are trying to help.

If the mother (and/or other family members) starved the daughter's yearning to help others, she is likely to intuitively seek out healing paths in her adulthood. She may try several different ways of improving the world. Her challenge is to provide clear contracts and office hours. Marrying someone to "save" that person will just lead to heartbreak. Being available at all times to all people is a recipe for burnout. Whether the daughter volunteers only so many hours a week, helps out at an animal shelter, works with addicts within a structured program, or makes other contributions, she will fare best if her healing work is limited in terms of the time spent and the circumstances and settings involved.

In order to avoid feeling overwhelmed—we cannot save the whole world—it is helpful if the daughter has also developed a firm sense of faith in a Higher Power, so she knows when to "Let go and let God." With a healthy, balanced outlet for her need to aid the less fortunate, the daughter will feel energized and fulfilled.

General Strengthening

Being in, around, or by the water (especially the ocean); meditation, rituals, mystical studies and experiences, training as a healer, practicing charity, using your imagination, doing guided imagery, developing psychic skills, appreciating fantasy and otherworldly motifs.

Reminder

If Letter 12 is overdeveloped, we can compensate through emphasizing Letter(s) 3, 6, 9, 5, and/or 7. Letter 6 is a natural partner of Letter 12, providing the small, daily gifts of practical service to bring the beautiful dream into the world in tangible ways. Letters 3 and 9 help bring the often subconscious ideals and feelings of Letter 12 into consciousness, by verbalizing them and sharing them (in words) with others. Letters 5 and 7 remind us that love and human companionship are also important parts of life. We are more than minds and spirits.

Epilogue

Our case studies suggest that parenting skills in our society are improving with time and greater psychological understanding. The information, insights, and suggestions offered within these pages are designed to assist the process of healing and bridging the generation gaps. Astrology is a unique tool for aiding personal understanding and transformation.

We hope that you have found opportunities to do some healing in your own life and family, and that you can further strengthen the ties of love and your own inner talents and abilities in the years ahead.

Appendix: Other Tools for Forgiving and Moving On

Coming to terms with our feelings about our mothers can take years. Here are a few additional techniques that people have used to help resolve issues that relate to how they were mothered.

Fill in the Blanks

Some women (and men) have indicated that they feel confused about the messages they received in their childhood. For them, a "free association" test can be a helpful preliminary step. Write or say into a tape recorder the very first thing that comes to your mind when reading these sentences. Your responses can help you identify matters that currently are central in your psyche. You can also try these sentences in six months to see if further issues come up.

My mother was a _____ person.

I wish that my mother had _____ .

What I wanted most from my mother was _____ .

My mother was really good at _____ .

When I think of my mother, I feel _____ .

My mother encouraged me to ————————————————————— .

What I heard most often from my mother was ———————————————— .

My mother just didn't understand ———————————————————— .

My mother felt that men were ————————————————————— .

My mother felt that women were ———————————————————— .

My mother felt that money is ————————————————————— .

My mother felt that sex ——————————————————————— .

In regard to my mother, I feel guilty about —————————————————— .

My mother did not believe that I ———————————————————— .

My mother believed that the most important thing in life was ———————— .

The person my mother loved most was ———————————————————— .

I was ———————————————————— important to my mother.

Check Any of the Following that Apply:

My mother's influence affected my own ...

	Positively	*Negatively*	*Both*
Ability to assert myself/define myself			
Ambition, ability to succeed in a career			
Attitudes toward alcohol, drinking habits			
Body image			
Choice of romantic partner			
Creativity			
Decisions about having/raising a family			
Definitions of work and productivity			
Eating habits, weight			
Educational goals			
Feelings about service/altruism			
Financial skills/challenges			
Friendships			
Intellectual development			
Marriage/Decision to remain single			
Relationship/problems with my Father			
Relationships/problems with my siblings			
Religious and/or spiritual choices			
Self-esteem			
Sexual behavior and pleasure			
Social skills			
Spending/saving habits			

Write a Letter

Many people find it helpful to write a letter to a parent, particularly if their mother is no longer living, or simply unavailable or unwilling to face issues. In the letter, you can address feelings that matter. Being able to put ideas and emotions down on paper can be very helpful and may clarify things for you. You do not have to mail the letter. The simple act of expressing yourself can be quite cathartic. Some people choose to mail their letters, and some people choose to use the letters they have written in some of the rituals mentioned in the next section. Some people have written more than one letter—a whole series, even— and found the process very healing.

Rituals for Letting Go

The unconscious mind is very sensitive to symbolism and may respond better to rituals and symbolic acts than pure logic and words. Performing a ritual may allow you to heal yourself on a very deep level by changing some ingrained habit patterns.

For many people, rituals that involve letting go of old, negative, ingrained emotions or habit patterns are worthwhile. Depending on personal preferences, you could:

1. Write down on a piece of paper a habit pattern or negative emotional response that you want to eliminate from your life. Then burn the paper in a fire while listening to inspiring music and meditating on forgiveness and release. Or, chant something appropriate while burning the paper. Perhaps you would prefer to bury the biodegradable paper in the earth, knowing that it will be dissolved into its component molecules in the womb of Mother Earth. Another preference could be inscribing what you wish to let go of on water-soluble paper and watching it dissolve in the liquid.

2. Transfer your negative thoughts, feelings, or associations to an object that you select to be the sacrifice. This might be a wood carving, a stone, a small stuffed animal, a marble, or anything that works symbolically for you. Then, you can bury, drown, or otherwise destroy that selected sacrifice as the representative of the negativity you are eliminating from your life.

3. Have an artist create a picture of your mother in which she expresses unconditional love and affection. You could also add statements at the bottom of the "improved" portrait that are loving remarks your mother could have said, or that you wish she had said.

4. Select objects that are literally associated with your mother (e.g., things she gave to you or that you inherited from her). Designate one object to be the recipient of all the negative imprinting you got from your mother, and another object to be the recipient of all the positive imprinting you got from your mother. (If needed, a third object can represent ambivalent messages or matters about which you are currently unclear.) The "negative" object can be buried, burned, destroyed, or otherwise eliminated, as appropriate. The positive object can be given a place of honor in your house, e.g., featured on an altar, surrounded with flowers, etc. (If you designate an ambivalent object, bring it out periodically in order to examine and further clarify your feelings.) A process such as this allows some people to realize that they are "hanging on" to certain physical objects that still bring them pain. They have the option, then, of giving these things away to charity, throwing them away, destroying them, storing them elsewhere, etc.

Solidifying Your Support System

We all need other people. If your family of origin was very lacking, you can create a "new" family—either by blood or personal choice and friendship. You can build healthy relationships of mutual support, affection, and interdependency. Some people choose a literal "second mother." They may even enjoy calling each other "Mom" and "Daughter," or other terms of endearment.

Be Creative

Human beings are inventive creatures. You may come up with other ideas and insights to help you cope with your feelings about how you were (and were not) nurtured. Be open-minded and willing to try whatever helps you cope more appropriately.

Best wishes!